PRAISE FOR *GETTING RICH IN AMERICA*

"This comprehensive, pragmatic primer on personal finance rivals *The Millionaire Next Door* in its ability to show anyone how to get rich in America. Whether you're rich, poor, or somewhere in between, you'll discover the secrets you need to take risks, get rich, and live a satisfying life."

—Stephen Pollan, author of *Die Broke* and *Live Rich*

"In the land where money talks, *Getting Rich in America* reads like a financial cue-card for the new millennium. Practical and pragmatic, Lee and McKenzie present a surprisingly painless path down the road to riches."

—Jonathan Hoenig, host of "Capitalist Pig"
and author of *Greed Is Good*

"I wish I had read *Getting Rich in America* when I was younger. I could use the extra money, better health, and more balanced life that would now be my reward. Dwight Lee and Richard McKenzie have laid out a life plan that, if followed, will bring better order and better results to what is too often a haphazard approach to living and accumulating. Their eight rules point the way not only to a life of financial success, but also to one of personal growth and service."

—Bob McTeer, president and CEO,
Federal Reserve Bank of Dallas

"Critics of good economic policy often argue that it leads to harsh social policy. *Getting Rich in America* starts with good 'individual social policy' and shows that it makes excellent 'individual economic policy.'"

—Richard J. Mahoney,
Distinguished Executive in Residence
and former chairman, Monsanto Co.,
Center for the Study of American Business

GETTING
RICH
in America

GETTING RICH
in America

8 Simple Rules
for Building a Fortune
and a Satisfying Life

by Dwight R. Lee and
Richard B. McKenzie

A HarperBusiness Book
from HarperPerennial

A hardcover edition of this book was published in 1999 by HarperBusiness, a division of HarperCollins Publishers.

GETTING RICH IN AMERICA. Copyright © 1999 by Dwight R. Lee and Richard B. McKenzie. All rights reserved. Printed in the United States of America. No part of this book may be used or reproduced in any manner whatsoever without written permission except in the case of brief quotations embodied in critical articles and reviews. For information address HarperCollins Publishers Inc., 10 East 53rd Street, New York, NY 10022.

HarperCollins books may be purchased for educational, business, or sales promotional use. For information please write: Special Markets Department, HarperCollins Publishers Inc., 10 East 53rd Street, New York, NY 10022.

First HarperPerennial edition published 2000.

Designed by Kris Tobiassen

The Library of Congress has catalogued the hardcover edition as follows:
Lee, Dwight R.
        Getting rich in America : eight simple rules for building a fortune and a satisfying life / Dwight R. Lee, Richard B. McKenzie. — 1st ed.
            p.   cm.
        Includes bibliographical references and index.
        ISBN 0-06-661982-3
            1. Finance, personal—United States. 2. Wealth—United States.
        3. Investments—United States. I. McKenzie, Richard B. II. Title
        HG179.L417   1999
        332.024—dc21   98-46232

ISBN 0-06-661983-1 (pbk.)

00 01 02 03 04 ❖ /RRD 10 9 8 7 6 5 4 3 2 1

For Walter B. Gerken and the late Bernard B. Ramsey

The way to wealth is as plain as the way to market. It depends chiefly on two words, industry and frugality; that is, waste neither time nor money, but make the best use of both. Without industry and frugality, nothing will do; and with them, everything.

—BEN FRANKLIN

Contents

Acknowledgments

This book has been a professional pleasure. It has given us the opportunity to draw on our academic backgrounds, and, at the same time, it has given us a chance to pass on advice that we wished we had understood with greater clarity of purpose when we were much younger.

But as is true on all book projects, we must credit others for their help over the years and for their kind guidance on how this book developed. We both are indebted to the Smith Center for Free Enterprise at California State University at Hayward and the Center for the Study of American Business at Washington University in St. Louis for distributing publications that carried brief summaries of themes developed here at length. Richard McKenzie is very appreciative of the Lynde and Harry Bradley Foundation for its continuing support on research projects related to the development of this book.

We wrote this book because of the media response to those earlier works, which gave rise to a tide of letters from people who wanted to know more about the rules for getting rich without giving up on a satisfying life. Specifically, we are indebted to Charles Baird, Kenneth Chilton, and Robert Batterson for their work in sharpening our thinking on those earlier publications and to Erma and Owen Smith whose encouragement was responsible for our initial interest in this project.

Special thanks go to Karen McKenzie who edited the early versions of this book and to Laureen Rowland at HarperBusiness who challenged us to better organize and clarify the arguments we make. We are also indebted to Denise Marcil, our agent, for her guidance in developing the project for publication. Anita Rowhani helped with the research. Candace Allen, Aaron Ransome, Triston Byrne, William Gardner, and Charles Baird were kind enough to read early versions of the book and offer valuable suggestions for improvement. Gary Byrne planted the seed for writing this book with one of the authors and then offered a multitude of insights.

Preface

A core theme of this book is that the accumulation of substantial personal wealth by retirement time will be a matter of choice open to almost all Americans at the start of the new millennium. And as Americans build their fortunes, they will also be able—as a matter of choice—to achieve satisfying lives.

Indeed, we argue that the twin goals of building a fortune and a satisfying life go hand in hand. Money wealth is not—and cannot—be everything in life. But when acquired the right way, wealth and the process of building it can work together to make life more satisfying. Money is no guarantee of a satisfying life, but the chances of achieving great wealth are greatly improved by attitudes and actions that are the source of satisfactions which depend little on money. The problem we all face is one of striking a reasonable balance between seeking wealth and a multitude of other things that go into the development of a satisfying life, one full of meaning and personal contentment.

Our perspective breaks dramatically with pronouncements repeated ad nauseam in the morning newspapers and on the nightly news by critics and pessimists of all political persuasions, that Americans have it tough or that wealth is a matter of birth and luck and is only incidentally affected by what we choose to do with our lives. To authorities who continue to parrot such claims, we assert loud and clear, "Bunk, pure bunk!" Americans have never had it better—and while we Americans may not all be wealthy at this moment, we have something far more important: a superabundance of opportunities to radically improve our lot in life. Our task is to make those choices that convert the opportunities that America provides into the reality of more prosperous and fulfilling lives.

The most critical choices we face are not those involving the details of life, such as which job to take, what school to attend, and where to live. These are important choices, but the critical choices we have in mind are those involving the basic *rules* we follow as we go through our lives. In this book, we seek to show how following eight transparently simple rules will affect your ability to achieve the twin goals of building a fortune and a satisfying life. Get all eight rules right, and the good life is assured. Get them all wrong, and your chances of ending your career with either a fortune or satisfying life are slim to none. Strike a reasonable balance in living by the eight rules and your chances of building a fortune and a satisfying life are considerable. By taking seriously the rules we spell out, you will be taking maximum advantage of one of your most valuable assets: being an American.

We start with the proposition that America remains unparalleled as the world's greatest reservoir of wealth and, more importantly, opportunities. We proceed and end with the development of a whole-life approach to seeking the good life, one that stresses the value of building substantial net worth, but also one that gives equal, if not more, attention to the manner in which we conduct our lives. Make no mistake about it: this book is about a way of life that works.

Getting Rich Is a Matter of Choice

When in the winter of 1998 we published a short pamphlet that briefly developed the themes of this book, we were both asked to be on radio talk shows that had open lines to callers. We couldn't help noticing wide differences in the responses of the radio hosts and callers to our arguments. The critical hosts and callers invariably said something to the effect of, "You must be nuts. This can't be. Few can earn enough and save enough at a sufficiently high rate of return to give rise to the wealth you imagine."

Our reaction remains now as it was then: *What do you mean it can't be done?*

We know it can be done—because we've done it. Neither of us grew up financially affluent, and one was raised in an orphanage under conditions that most people would consider seriously deprived. The way we grew out of our initial circumstances is actually not all that unusual in this country. Myriad Americans have overcome backgrounds that were worse than anything we experienced. That is both a fact and a seedbed for much hope.

Indeed, we both consider ourselves fortunate in our upbringing in that we were taught from an early age that we could succeed by our own efforts—that, in fact, it was the *only* way to succeed. That lesson was more valuable to us than more money could ever have been.

Truth is, Americans have been getting rich for more than two hundred years, and they will continue to do so into the twenty-first century.

And most who do get rich do it in the good old-fashioned way—they earn it! If getting rich can't be done today, how was it done decades, and indeed centuries, ago when the incomes of Americans were far lower than they are today, and saving was far more difficult?

Those who start in poverty today might not always rise to the upper rungs of the economic ladder, though some will. But the vast majority do rise several rungs up that ladder, and even more could rise if they followed our rules. Where you start on the economic ladder matters, but not nearly as much as your desire and determination to improve your circumstances.

Indeed, some may argue that what people achieve in life is based in large part on their circumstances, from color and sex to social status and socioeconomic background. And we would be the first to agree that none of us has any choice in defining where we start off in life. However, it is important to acknowledge that while our initial circumstances *can* limit what we do in life, they do not *determine* what we do, or what we can do.

Each time we make a choice, we invariably change our circumstances—and hopefully, improve them. So we can, to a meaningful degree, have a tremendous impact on what our circumstances will eventually be. The further in the future we look, the more our circumstances are of our own making, simply because with time our own actions (or inactions) determine our fate.

In a real sense, we can choose our futures.

This book is concerned with the array of alternative futures. Our most critical choices involve the selection of the path we will follow into the future. We all have a future of some sort; the core concern of this book is whether we will make our way into our future by default or by design.

Hope Breeds Improvement

We are, to a meaningful extent, the "captains of our fates." As you read this book you must assess what you can do with what you have, envision where you want to go, and then set sail with a deliberately defined course in mind.

With choice comes freedom and with freedom, the hope for a better life. If we didn't have choices, there would be no point in worrying about wealth or income or rates of return on investments or any other matter relating to succeeding in this country. If there were no consequential choices in life, we would simply take things as they come. We would be victims of our circumstances (as many Americans think they are), and even then, our "victimhood" would be of no consequence. Without meaningful choices in life, there would be no room for meaningful "improvement," or any reason for hope or despair.

We don't believe that our conditions in this country are ideal—far from it—but we *do* take seriously the power of *hope* and the power of *action.* If you hope for improvement, you can make meaningful choices that affect your future. As an American you can, as we always have, dream of a better day for yourself, your family, friends, and countrymen, and you can work to make that dream a reality.

We know that there are those Americans who have lost hope for a brighter future. Anyone who lives under the constant threat of being harmed by gangs or drugs is not likely to plot a course for the distant future. He or she will likely live for today.

As a country, we must work to provide all people with the necessary foundation for improvement—and hope. But this means extending, and calling attention to, opportunities, while letting people know that their best hope lies within themselves and their own choices, rather than convincing them that they are victims whose only hope lies in the compassion of others. The widely purveyed claims that so many Americans are hobbled by, or at the mercy of, their circumstances are not only untrue, they are self-perpetuating. They throttle improvement because they constrict people's vision of the length and quality of the futures that are theirs for the taking.

This book is about those improved futures, providing the vision of the possible. It is your task to turn these possibilities into your reality.

Eight Rules to Building a Fortune—and a Satisfying Life

There are a host of rules in life that can and should be followed. In this book, we focus on just eight, with a chapter devoted to each. These rules may seem obvious to you, on some level. However, taken together in the context of a plan of action, you will see how taking them seriously can help you build a life of financial success and personal satisfaction:

1. *Think of America as the Land of Choices.* Understand the good fortune you start with by the accident of your birth in this country. Think optimistically about the opportunities you have and of how opportunities amount to unexploited wealth. Pessimism can breed its own conclusions.

2. *Take the Power of Compound Interest Seriously—and Then Save.* Don't expect to make it in this country by brawn, or even brains, alone. The power of "compound interest" is an essential ingredient in building a substantial fortune by saving early and consistently.

3. *Resist Temptation.* Our concern here is not the problem of temptations central to religions (although there are religious/moral ele-
ments in all that we write). Our concern is more practical. Be
prepared to ignore the temptation of the moment by taking control of your life and achieving your long-run goals through saving
and investment.

4. *Get a Good Education.* Be prepared to study hard and long, mainly
because to really make it in the next century, your good fortune will
depend on what you know and can contribute to the welfare of others.

5. *Get Married and Stay Married.* Take marriage seriously because of
the wonderful fulfillment it can provide and because of its economic advantages. There are good reasons married people usually
have more wealth than people who've never married, and for why
divorce can be devastating in three critical ways: emotionally, physically, and financially.

6. *Take Care of Yourself.* Don't forget to take care of your health. People
who don't take care of themselves—who abuse their bodies and
minds—reduce their opportunities to build wealth and to have a
satisfying life.

7. *Take Prudent Risks.* Taking risks is a part of life, which means risks
cannot be avoided altogether. There are some risks—for example,
where the market will head in the short term—that we can't do
anything about. Then there are risks that we can minimize—for
example, through the types and breadth of our investments. As a
dominant investment strategy, we suggest that for most people the
best investment strategy is to "buy the market" by investing in
mutual funds that buy a broad range of stocks (those included in,
say, the Standard & Poor's Composite Index of 500 firms). Beating
the market is tough for the best of investment strategists. Most
importantly, don't procrastinate long for fears that the market will
fall. The time to start investing is now, and then invest regularly.

8. *Strive for Balance.* Recognize the importance of old-fashioned
virtues like honesty, commitment, and integrity for what they are,
as personal constraints that, paradoxically, expand our range of
opportunities for building a fortune and satisfying life if we stick
with them. Most importantly, strike a reasonable balance in the
perspective you take toward the rules you adopt.

There should be nothing particularly surprising about these rules. What we do in this book is show you exactly how following the rules can help you build a fortune (of, say, $1 million or more in net worth) at retirement time—and develop a satisfying life in the process. We provide practical tips to implement the rules in your daily life, along with easy-to-execute exercises and calculations for tabulating your progress. We also show the extent to which choices over whether to follow this or that rule affect your potential fortune at retirement. You will be astounded to see how seemingly *small* choices that you make can have *monumental* consequences years into your future.

We have written this book with one overriding point of view: You can do it! How do we know you can do it? Legions of other Americans have. So have we. If you choose not to build a fortune, that is your choice. People can, and do, have lives rich in personal satisfaction and accomplishment without becoming financially rich. You may not choose to follow the path to riches. If you don't, we will rest comfortably in the thought that after reading this book, you will make your choices with more complete knowledge of the tremendous opportunities that are possible in this great land of ours.

We are pleased to be able to dedicate this book to two individuals— Walter B. Gerken and the late Bernard B. Ramsey—whose lives and accomplishments epitomize the book's core themes. They came from families of modest means, worked hard and smart, rose to great heights in their respective industries, all the while building the respect of their families, colleagues, and friends for the principled lives they led.

DWIGHT R. LEE
Athens, Georgia

RICHARD B. MCKENZIE
Irvine, California

January 1999

Think of America as the Land of Choices

Microsoft CEO Bill Gates, renowned for being the country's most successful nerd, has really made it in America. In the process of creating the world's most widely used operating system for personal computers, plus a growing array of other programs, he has amassed a fortune exceeding $50 billion. At the same time, he has created an unprecedented amount of wealth for other Americans (plus hundreds of millions of citizens of other countries around the world) who either work for Microsoft or have benefited from its products at work and at home.

By making it in this country, Gates has all the trappings of business power and personal fortune that even his well-to-do parents could never have imagined. When he speaks, everyone listens—the business public, the media, and (because of his presumed computer industry market power) the antitrust lawyers in the U.S. Department of Justice. He lives in a modern-age electronic castle on a hillside outside Seattle. Few Americans would not want a portion of his good fortune, which he continues to build. Neither should they want him to stop building his fortune. There are gains for everyone in his efforts to improve his products and best the competition.

Chicago Bulls basketball star Michael Jordan has also definitely made it in America. And while he has nowhere near Gates's vast fortune, he isn't worried about his financial future. He has bankrolled his considerable basketball prowess into a sizable empire of business projects and endorsements, including soft drinks, cologne, a chain of restaurants, and, of course, his signature footwear and apparel line, making him worth hundreds of millions of dollars. Like Gates and just about every-one else who makes it big, he has surely given more value to his consum-ing—and adoring—public than he has taken in accumulated wealth.

Ordinary Americans, Extraordinary Accomplishments

When we think of people who have made it in America, the names of Gates and Jordan—and maybe other less widely known Americans on *Fortune* magazine's list of the country's four hundred richest—come quickly to mind. We've heard and read a great deal about the usual cadre of truly wealthy business and entertainment celebrities, such as Warren Buffett, Michael Dell, Barbra Streisand, Ted Turner, Linda Wachner, Garth Brooks, Donald Trump, Sharon Stone, and Tom Cruise.

This book, however, is not about how the financial elite made it in this country—nor is it about how you can live like them, or be as rich as they are. Wish on!

The focus of this book is on ordinary people of far more modest means and talents and how they have "made it" and will continue to do so. Rather than the rich and famous, the people you will meet in this book are people like Ron and Pam Jones, owners of Handy Andy Janitorial Services in Plano, Texas, who have done well with their busi-ness mainly because of the principles they were taught as children. Ron Jones notes that he grew up in a family where hard work was an ethic: "I guess it goes back to what my uncle used to tell me all the time when I was growing up: If you want your prayers answered, get off your knees and hustle."[1]

The book is also about the Huynhs, Le Thi and Hai Minh, immigrants from Vietnam, who started from scratch and developed Fulton Seafood business in Houston. They believed in the American Dream, that hard work pays off, as it has for them.

It's about what Patrick Kelly has accomplished. He grew up in a Virginia orphanage to go on to build one of the country's largest med-ical supply companies and then to start peeling off the resulting fortune for the benefit of his orphanage home and other charities. And it's about how it was possible for Donald and Mildred Othmer to lead fairly ordi-nary and unassuming lives, only to leave their extraordinary estate, val-ued in 1998 at close to $750 million, to a host of charities (see the nearby box for details on how they did it).[2]

But this book is also about and for many other Americans, like Alex Grumsky, a young man from Irvine, California, who has for three years worked the early morning shift (starting at 4:30 A.M.) at one of the city's Starbucks Coffee houses and the late evening shift (starting at 4 P.M.) at

Ordinary Americans, Extraordinary Wealth

The late Donald and Mildred Othmer were, in one regard, ordinary Americans. He was a long-time chemical engineering professor at Polytechnic University in Brooklyn who died in 1994. She was a teacher and buyer for her mother's dress shop who died in 1998. Both were in their nineties when they died. However, they were extraordinary in one important respect: Shortly after Ms. Othmer's death, their combined estate was valued at more than $750 million, most of which went to charity.

How did the Othmers amass such a fortune? They surely didn't inherit their wealth, and they didn't win a lottery at some early point in their lives. Dr. Othmer was a widely recognized engineering professor and inventor who received forty or so patents over the course of his life, but that success doesn't tell the full story by any means. Basically, they amassed their good fortune by not living ostentatiously and by investing wisely. They did buy a five-story townhouse in Brooklyn Heights, New York, but they lived only in the lower two stories, and rented out the top three floors. One of the Othmers' tenants mused after the Othmers' fortune became front-page news, "It was also clear that they knew the value of a dollar in a way that our softer generation does not. . . . Although crippled by a stroke, Dr. Othmer insisted on personally examining every household problem [in the apartment the tenant rented from him and his wife] before permitting a repair service to be called. He would put his handyman's baseball cap on his handsome, tall head, gather his toolbox, painfully haul himself up the stairs, reminisce for a while about his wartime work distilling gasoline out of banana skins in Central America, gaze at the problem, tinker with it and then gaze at us reproachfully."

The rest of the story is that they invested in the stock market and left their investment in the market for a long time. In the early 1960s, they handed over $50,000 to Warren Buffett, who is today widely viewed as one of the country's smartest and most successful money managers, but who, to the Othmers, was then just a family friend from their hometown of Omaha, Nebraska. When in 1970 they received shares in Buffett's company Berkshire Hathaway, Inc. (which buys stock in other companies), their shares were selling for $42 a share. In mid-1998, their shares were selling for the equivalent of $77,250 per share, making the total market value of their shares more than three-quarters of a billion dollars.

You may think they were plain lucky, and no doubt, they did have the good fortune of knowing Warren Buffett. However, if they had invested all of their funds (those placed with Buffett and in other ventures) widely in the market, they would still have been worth between $50 million and $100 million. James Glassman, a researcher with the American Enterprise Institute in Washington, D.C., was right to point out that the lesson to be drawn from what the Othmers accomplished is not that they were smart or lucky, but it is "to live modestly, invest sensibly, and don't touch the money and grow rich."

another Irvine restaurant. He puts in a total of sixty-five hours a week to pay off educational expenses and to help his father out of bankruptcy. After he has helped to settle his father's and his own debts, he plans to return to school. Alex has yet to make it in America, but along the way he has learned several very important lessons, not the least of which are the dangers of easy credit and the value of hard work and saving for those rainy days. With those lessons in mind, no one should doubt that he will do well.

More importantly, the book is really about you, and what *you* can do to get rich in America, making the world a better place for *others* as well as *yourself.*

If we were concerned solely with how the truly wealthy elite in the country have made it, this book would be much shorter than it already is—and we have kept its length to a minimum, mainly because we know you want to get on with the business of building a fortune, rather than spending all your time reading about it. If this were a book only for the super-rich-to-be, most readers would likely figure it was not for them. And we would be the first to acknowledge that few readers of average income will actually rival the likes of Gates, Jordan, and Buffett. Their substantial talents are exceedingly rare, and each played their talent cards with unique effectiveness, if not with a considerable measure of luck. This book is for you, to whom much has been given and for whom much is possible.

America, Land of Opportunities

Any one of us living in America is blessed with myriad opportunities, which enable ordinary people to pile up fortunes that run into the millions. Moreover, contrary to all the Chicken Littles of the world who continue to cry that the economic skies are falling, we see the opportunities expanding, not contracting. This book is about how you can make it with relative ease in this land of growing opportunities.

When we say you can make it with "relative ease," we don't mean to imply that the road to riches will be an easy one to follow. We mean only that the job of building a fortune, while maintaining a satisfying life, is easier than most people realize. And it's easier for you, an American at the turn of the millennium, to pile up riches than it was for your parents and grandparents. The task ahead is also far easier for you than for just about any other ordinary citizen of any other country.

The challenge that most Americans will face is not finding opportunities to exploit, but figuring out which of the many opportunities available to them they will pursue. No doubt, some Americans will be stymied in their quest to make it by confusion and indecision over what to do, given the complexity and sophistication of the many opportunities out there to exploit. Some Americans will be like the proverbial horse standing an equal distance between two bales of hay, starving—unable to decide which bale of hay to eat first.

We mention the starving horse in passing to fortify our goal: In this book, we won't tell you exactly how to make it by offering you a recipe of daily actions, or by telling you which stocks and bonds or properties to buy (although we will talk in general terms about how you should *think* about investing in stocks for the future).[3] And if you seek only instant success with no dedication on your part, go to Las Vegas. Better yet, save the airfare and buy your state's lottery tickets—which, we might add, for reasons given in another box close by, we don't do. We offer no quick fixes, no methods for instant wealth, and no magic formulas for getting the best of Lady Luck.

Rather, in this book we intend to offer guidance in the form of *rules of behavior* for the long haul. Of the several rules we will cover in this book, none is more important than the one that is most self-evident in the

---

Getting Rich the Easy Way—Slim Chance!

Some people think their only hope of getting rich in America is winning their state lottery. It is, of course possible to win a several-million-dollar jackpot playing the state lotto, in which (depending on the state) you pick from five to seven numbers between 1 and about 45 and hope that the chosen numbers correspond to the numbers randomly drawn by the state.

But what are your chances of picking the right numbers? The chance of winning the New York lotto (as it was formatted in 1986—picking six numbers between 1 and 48) is one out of 12.3 million tickets bought. The chance of winning in Oklahoma (as its lotto was formatted in 1993) is about the same, one out of 12.4 million. The average person who played one of these lotteries every day, beginning at birth, would have to live almost 33,000 years to win one time.

Or to put your chances of winning one of these state lotteries in a different perspective, consider the following: A person has a much greater chance of being struck by lightning, one chance in 1.9 million, than of winning the state lottery. A pregnant woman has a greater chance of giving birth to quadruplets, which is one in 705,000 births. Moreover, someone eating an oyster has a greater chance of finding a pearl, which is one out of 12,000 oysters opened.[4]

Is there any wonder we insist, "Don't count on (lotto) luck!" to get rich.

image of the starving horse: *You must look at this country as a land of opportunities and then you must do something!* While we won't pay much attention to the likes of Gates and Jordan from here on, there is a good reason for mentioning them at the start: They serve as the quintessential example of the fact that making it requires *taking* a positive attitude and *doing* something. But not just anything. In Gates and Jordan's accomplishments, there is admonition that should never be forgotten: You must do something that will be seen to be of value for others. The most effective way of improving your own lot in life is through actions that improve the lots of others, whether you're creating software that allows people to be more productive, or you're providing top-notch entertainment.

What works is to take a whole-life approach to building a fortune, one that requires a lifestyle that is guided by adherence to a few simple rules of behavior that guide your actions from day to day over a long stretch of time. Without the rules in place—and the accompanying lifestyle—that make getting rich possible for ordinary Americans, it is not at all clear that getting "lucky" with the lottery can be a fortunate turn of events in one's life. We've all read stories of people who suddenly become rich, through the lottery or by signing lucrative acting or sports contracts, only to lead miserable, self-destructive lives thereafter because they were unprepared to deal with their good "fortune."

You must also understand that to build a personal fortune most people must first contribute to the betterment of other people. Gates built a business founded on a computer program that is highly productive for computer users. Jordan developed basketball skills that astound fans everywhere. The Joneses created a maid service. The Huynhs built a fish market, while Kelly developed a sales network. They've all worked at what they have done, which has been adding value *for others*, and they did not rest on their laurels. On the contrary, they were energized by their accomplishments.

Some might describe what Gates and Jordan have done as "no mean accomplishment." We intend to assert the opposite, developing something from practically nothing is an important accomplishment in the sense that it is the *means* by which so many Americans have and will continue to make it. At the heart of the process, getting rich in America—or anywhere else, for that matter—requires the redeployment of resources from low-valued uses to high-valued uses. Wealth is the accumulation of the gain for others that is generated in the redeployment process. In no small way, people who make it are *developers*, not *users* or *abusers* of resources. They may never be able to create something out of nothing, but they are always alert to opportunities to get as much value as they can for as close to nothing as possible.

The Americans we had in mind as we wrote this book are not those who are wealthy by virtue of their inheritance. We have no complaint with Americans who have inherited their wealth and have worked to use it productively for the benefit of others and who add to their fortune in the process. We can't fault the wealthy for inheriting their good fortune any more than we can fault the poor for inheriting their impoverished circumstances. But we are not interested in defending the behavior of those Americans who might be tagged the "arrogant and worthless wealthy," those who are often pictured in the movies, using their wealth for strictly self-serving purposes—for example, in conspicuous consumption and in currying political favors and positions—with no intent of producing new wealth. There are no lessons to be learned from them since, while they may appear to have it made, they haven't made it themselves. Indeed, those who inherited great wealth are not to be envied if their inheritance reduces their motivation to produce more wealth. You will, at some point in your life, come to realize that much of the satisfaction from wealth comes from making it, not just having it.

Getting Rich by the Rules

What exactly do we mean by "getting rich"? That's not an easy question to answer, mainly because there are so many answers. "Getting rich" has a lot in common with beauty; the beholder defines it. We don't believe that money is everything in life—far from it—or else this book would not have the subtitle that it carries, which stresses the rules that must be followed for "Building a Fortune—*and* a Satisfying Life." Nor do we believe that the accumulation of financial wealth should be a single-minded goal for anyone.

Certainly, money has never been *the* goal for us. We have separately pursued the "life of the mind" in academia, meaning we suspect that along the way we traded a good deal of income for doing what we wanted with our careers. High up on our list of priorities of things for us to do in life has always been to create new and intriguing thoughts for our students and colleagues to ponder. Any eulogies given on our passing are unlikely to contain estimates of our net worth. However, we can't help but believe (or hope) that others will acknowledge not only *what* we did in life but *how* we did what we did. And much of *how* we played the game of life is bound up in the rules of this book. In limited ways, this book is autobiographical.

Life is made up of opportunities, and, as a consequence, ever-present tradeoffs and choices. People can make it in America in any number of ways. Indeed, the rules of behavior that we lay out for building a fortune in America can, if followed, lead to success in a multitude of financial and nonfinancial ways. The rules we present are hard to fault, if success in any dimension is desired. Those who follow the rules consistently will find success, as they define it, relatively easy to achieve; those who flaunt the rules consistently will find success hard to come by. Fortunately, from an array of studies, it is reasonably clear that building a satisfying life can go hand in hand with building a fortune—if the process of building the fortune is also grounded in the rules covered in this book.[5]

Living requires that we obey a multitude of rules of reasonable behavior, and we do not intend for this book to be all-inclusive. We acknowledge that some of the rules not covered in depth—especially those with religious foundations (for example, the Ten Commandments)—are very important to successful living, and should not be forgotten. However, we leave the development of those rules to others. Here in this small volume we seek to remind you of the importance of certain value-based rules that have an economic foundation and are not widely appreciated for their importance. And mercifully, there are only eight rules to keep in mind, with one chapter reserved for each.

The importance of these eight rules is self-evident to us because of our long years of researching an array of economic and policy issues and trying to convey our findings to our students and the general public. Their importance to successful living can nevertheless be overlooked because they are not the subject of weekly sermons. Other writers stress the negative—what people *don't have*—in explaining why many people aren't wealthier than they are. We stress the positive—what people *can do* to improve their positions in life.

Toward the end of each chapter, we also offer a number of practical tips we have collected from interviewing those who have "made it" on how they believe you can make the rules work day by day, year by year, in your life. In one respect, our suggestions represent common sense. The advice given, however, is worth presenting because "common sense" is clearly not as common as the phrase supposes, or else many more Americans would be richer than they are and would at the same time be leading more satisfying lives. Reiteration of the obvious is often necessary to persuade reluctant minds of the value of the wisdom of the ages. At the end of each chapter, we also provide you with an exercise that will guide you through the development of practical goals and ways of achieving your goals, all of which is designed to reduce the complex task of following our rules for building a fortune and a satisfying life to a step-by-step process.

We start this book with the proposition that the choice of whether to follow the rules, as in so many other things in life, is yours. If you fret that you are a victim of bad circumstances, which will hold you back, then you need not read on. This book is for readers who believe that they are the "captains of their fate," to at least a substantial degree. We assume that people—like you—can make things happen. Otherwise, "Getting Rich in America" is a vacuous expression, devoid of real meaning and value.

Still, we will write our way through this book with reference to one very important measuring rod—one's net worth (assets minus debts) as measured in money terms. We focus on net worth not because it is the *only* legitimate goal, but because it is an *important* goal for most Americans. It is also a goal that is easily measured, and progress toward achieving it can be tracked from the day you begin reading this book. Moreover, achieving a significant net worth is also an important goal, given most people's need for a retirement income, and it is a goal that can be reached by way of a variety of careers. Whether people are plumbers or doctors, they need to worry about their net worth at retirement time. A money measure of net worth helps to determine when a person—you or anyone else—has reached a retirement income goal.

The selection of the money standard for having made it in America is obviously arbitrary. We have selected $1 million in net worth at retirement age (measured in today's dollars) as our standard for several reasons.

- It is a round figure that looks and sounds good, given there are lots of zeros after the $1.
- A net worth of $1 million is a seemingly tough standard, given that fewer than 4 percent of all Americans have a net worth of $1 million or more. In 1995, the *mean* (or *average*) net worth of all American families was $206,000, but the "mean" is greatly distorted by the considerable wealth, running into the tens of billions, of the financial elite (Gates, Jordan, and company). The *median* net worth of American families (which is that net worth in the middle of the distribution, with 50 percent of families having less and 50 percent having more) was far more meager in 1995, $56,000. Even families headed by individuals sixty-five years of age and older only had a median net worth of about $106,000, one-tenth of our established standard.
- $1 million in net worth is not a standard that will allow a luxury lifestyle during retirement, given that it will provide (if the funds are invested in safe federal government bonds) an interest income measured in today's dollars that is close to the income of an American family halfway up the country's income ladder.

- The standard is more easily achievable than most Americans believe from a review of how much net worth families actually have. Indeed, when you finish the book you will probably wonder why so few Americans have achieved our standard.
- We have met our standard. Accordingly, we can talk both from theory and ordinary experience, and we would be the first to attest to the fact that getting rich it is not as hard as you might think. Just read on and see if you don't agree.[6]

In having set our monetary standard for getting rich, we hasten to insist that building a financial fortune is not all this book is about. It is also about living a satisfying life. From our perspective, the two goals go together—each building on the other. Amassing wealth for the sheer sake of doing so, without enjoying one's hard-won fortune, makes little sense to us. In fact, if forced to choose between being wealthy or being happy, we would certainly choose the satisfying life. But such a choice is a false one. The achievement of one goal does not necessarily preclude the other. No doubt, you *will* have to make some tough choices as you build toward your goal—no one can have everything he or she wants—but, as we will demonstrate, you can enjoy life as you build your fortune.

Opportunities as Wealth

We are confident of the ability of most Americans to make our standard simply because they are Americans. We would not be so confident if we were writing for people in most other countries around the world. People around the world who have a subsistence income can hardly expect to ever be wealthy. They have no way to build assets, given that they must use all their time and energy simply to survive. The poverty threshold income for an American family of four (below which the four members of the family would be considered "impoverished") that was about $16,500 in 1997 would be considered a king's ransom by a substantial majority of the world's population.[7]

By world standards the overwhelming majority of Americans not only earn a lot of money, they are wealthy, maybe not so much in terms of their current dollar net worth, but certainly in terms of the *opportunities* they have to generate a considerable net worth by retirement time. Indeed, you should view the opportunities that are available to you and the ones you can create as a form of "wealth" that you start with. Your task is to convert those "opportunities" into outcomes that have financial value.

To see how the income opportunities available to Americans (but not

Important Distinctions: Money and Income, Wealth and Net Worth

Throughout the book, we will frequently refer to terms such as "money," "income," "wealth," and "net worth" as if you understand the differences. The discussion may get confusing if you don't know what we mean. Here are several brief definitions that you need to keep in mind.

MONEY AND INCOME

Money is nothing more than a medium of exchange (or means of making payments) and, at the same time, a method by which we measure the market value of goods and services and the time we spend at work. In the United States money is denominated in dollars; in Britain, money is denominated in pounds; in Japan, in yen. Money is how people pay for the things they want. Americans pay for the things they want with the "greenbacks" they have in their wallets or with the dollar balances they have in their bank checking accounts or with their credit cards.

In the United States, income is *measured* in dollars. For example, you might have an annual income of $30,000. However, your income is not the same as money, or vice versa. At any point in time, you may only have a few dollars in your pocket and several hundred dollars in your checking account. Obviously, the money you have at any point in time is not equal to your income. Income is how much you earn from your work and what you have invested.

WEALTH AND NET WORTH

Wealth and net worth are often used to mean the same thing. In this book, we use the two terms interchangeably, although we favor net worth in most of our discussions because it is the more precise concept. Net worth is the market value (potential selling price) of your assets minus your debts. If you own a house, car, and household furniture worth $150,000 but you have debt outstanding totaling $110,000, then your net worth is $40,000. When we use the term "wealth," we mean "net worth." In this example, your wealth is $40,000. However, some financial commentators might carelessly use "wealth" to refer solely to the value of your assets—the $150,000 figure. You can be assured that we will never use wealth in that way. "Wealth" to us always connotes "net worth."

to others around the world) can be converted into wealth, consider a comparison between the income of a couple in Poland and a couple in the United States. The Polish couple we have in mind is a real couple living in Wroclaw. They are middle-aged and well-educated. The husband has a Ph.D. and teaches at a major Polish university; the wife is a medical doctor. Their combined before-tax income measured at the best available exchange rates is around $20,000 a year. They have been able to do okay in supporting their three daughters. They live well by Polish standards, given that they have a much above-average family income, but they don't live well by American standards. Because of what the communists did to the country for fifty years, life in Poland remains tough ten years after the 1989 downfall of the communist regime. The bright spot in Poland is that life is improving as reforms in the country's economic policies and system take hold.

Consider the couple in the United States. Both the husband and wife chose at age twenty-eight to get MBA degrees from graduate schools that are ranked among the top fifty in the country. On graduation, they took jobs that give them annual salaries of $70,000 each, a figure that is, in fact, on the low side for newly minted MBAs from major graduate management programs. The couple's combined income is a handsome $140,000 a year, or $120,000 a year higher than that of the Polish couple we described.

Beyond their high income, you can bet that the American couple has an array of opportunities that the Polish couple could not imagine in their wildest dreams. But to get an idea of just how much better off the American couple *can be* at retirement because of the fact of their birth, suppose the American couple lived on not the same before-tax income as the Polish couple, but on 75 percent more, or $35,000 a year (after taxes and payments for misfortunes), and then saved the rest (after taxes and other deductions). What would their net worth at retirement be? To make the required calculations, we have to make several simplifying assumptions. We:

- Assume that a third of the American couple's income will go to the various types of state and federal income taxes.
- Assume that the couple will get raises over the courses of their careers that will beat inflation by an annual average of 1 percent, which means that the couple together would be earning $212,631 a year (in today's dollars) at age seventy.
- Assume that over the course of their careers, they meet with misfortunes (for example, accidents, floods, and medical problems) that on average drain away 10 percent of their before-tax incomes each year.
- Assume that they invest their savings in a stock mutual fund, the earnings of which are tied to Standard & Poor's Composite Index of five hundred companies, and that their average *real* (or *inflation-adjusted*) *yield* on their investments (the return from appreciation and dividends after inflation) over their careers is no better or

worse than the average real increase for the S&P Index for the past seventy years. This means that their real rate of return (or annual "yield," including stock price increases and dividends) on their investments is about 8 percent.[8]

How much would the American couple be worth if they decide to retire at age seventy (and we anticipate that seventy, and not sixty-five, will become a more common retirement age as life expectancy continues to rise)? Would you believe that their net worth at retirement would exceed $17.8 million! That means that the couple could at retirement put their nest egg into very safe federal government bonds and draw interest income at about 4 percent (which allows them to hold the real value of their net worth constant over time[9]), they could have a very comfortable retirement income of $712,000 a year. If you think seventy is too old for the couple to retire and they should be expected to retire at sixty-five, then you simply are reducing their retirement net worth to $11.8 million and their annual retirement income to a little more than $472,000.

Do you find those results astounding? You might think them rigged. You can run the numbers. They are right on the money. Moreover, we see the calculations as understating the possible net worth of the American couple, given the conservative rate of income growth we used.

And perhaps you think that we are asking the couple to live on too low an income and that, realistically, no couple making that much money would live on so little. No matter; the calculations in this case were devised to demonstrate our central point: *Americans are very wealthy in terms of their opportunities to build a fortune.* Even if the couple saved half of what we suggested, their net worth at retirement would still well exceed the marker of $1 million. Ultimately, it's their task—your task—to decide how many of the available opportunities will be converted into financial wealth. It is our intent to insist and illustrate that the opportunities *are* there.

Even if the couple decided to live on $60,000 a year after taxes and misfortunes—which is a fairly generous living allowance, given that it is 42 percent above the median family income (which was $42,300 before taxes in 1996, the latest year of available data)—the couple would still have a retirement kitty of over $6.5 million at seventy years of age! Yes, you should be astounded.[10]

Indeed, the couple could spend 97 percent of their after-tax income and still reach our "rich" net worth standard of $1 million at retirement time. The couple could have the current median net worth for retirees of $106,000 even if they spent over 99.7 percent of their after-tax income.

The moral of our examples, one to which we will return time and again throughout the book, is straightforward: *Great wealth is POSSIBLE in America*. All that most Americans need to do is exploit the income opportunities available to them and then control their expenditures.

Management consultants Thomas Stanley and William Danko, who have studied the buying practices of affluent Americans for two decades, make a point that is fully congenial with our theme: "Many people who live in expensive homes and drive luxury cars do not actually have much wealth: Many people who have a great deal of wealth do not live in upscale neighborhoods."[11] Contrary to what so many people seem to think, the run-of-the-mill American millionaire is pretty ordinary, as is evident from the profile of millionaires in the box close by. Moreover, Stanley and Danko add that the wealthy rarely get their wealth through luck or inheritance; most become wealthy in the good old-fashioned way: They earn what they make, and they save a reasonable portion of what they earn.

There is a great deal of hope in the Stanley/Danko statistical profile of millionaires and in our calculations; you don't need to start with all that much annual income to build a fortune. Indeed, if our couple in the United States had not gotten their MBAs and, as a consequence, had only $40,000 in combined annual income, paid 15 percent of their income in taxes, paid out 10 percent of their income to cover misfortunes, and lived at the Polish standard of living, they would still have a net worth of over $4.5 million at age seventy (assuming they started working *and* saving at age twenty-eight). We understand that living on $20,000 would be tough in most areas of the country (and *very* tough in places like Los Angeles and New York City), but the point is that building wealth often requires that you make tough choices. One of the toughest of all choices is how much to save, given our income, which implies a choice between consuming now and consuming later.

In a later chapter, we will measure the cost of various ways of living conspicuously not in the usual way, by price, but in terms of how much they subtract from the future portfolio. Just as you are rightfully amazed at how rapidly a portfolio can build to astronomical levels, you will be astounded at how much things cost in terms of lost accumulated wealth later in life.

You can spend your time and you can spend your money in all sorts of ways in this country. From the perspective of this book, you can also spend your opportunities. In doing so, you effectively determine your future net worth. Fritter away excessive hours at the bowling alley or on the golf course or even in school, and you will pay the consequences in the long term. But there is promise in the calculations. In creating a life that makes you happy as well as rich, there is a lot of wealth to fritter away, and it is still possible to reach retirement well off by common American standards. The bottom line: You can *choose* to be rich in this country, and you stand a good chance of making it happen—even while having fun. It's up to you.

Stress on What's Possible

Americans have been repeatedly reminded of what they can't do and how exceedingly tough it is to become wealthy—supposedly, becoming wealthy is getting tougher year by year. *New York Times* reporters mused in the mid–1990s that, in spite of the economic recovery that had been under way for five years at the time their articles appeared, many Americans had reacted to the "downsizing" of their firms by "downsizing their expectations of material comfort and the sweetness of the future." Moreover, the sense of "gloom" about their futures was especially "emphatic among prosperous and well-educated Americans."[12]

The Profile of American Millionaires

You could very well be living next door to millionaires, and never know it, according to Thomas Stanley and William Danko.[13] Although there is the usual variation among the 3 million to 4 million millionaires in the country, the profile for millionaires as a group looks something like this.

Millionaires tend to be males who have been married for a long time, are in their fifties before they become millionaires.

They typically have between $1 million and $5 million in net worth (with their median net worth about $1.6 million, which means that half of all millionaires have between $1 million and $1.6 million in net worth and half have more than $1.6 million).

Most millionaires built their fortunes through owning and running their own businesses.

They are frugal and live much more modestly than might be expected. The overwhelming majority of millionaires (85 percent) clip coupons. They tend not to live in upscale neighborhoods, and they tend to drive older domestic cars, not the foreign-made luxury models (BMWs and Mercedes, for example).

Millionaires tend to have far less income than might be expected, with a median income level of $131,000 (with some millionaires with very modest incomes).

Most millionaires are first-generation millionaires.

Our research has indicated a radically different reality, concluding that the assessors of economic doom and gloom have many of their facts all wrong. The economy has had spells of recessions (like the one in the very early 1990s), but has done reasonably well over recent decades in just about all regards, most notably in terms of increased production of goods and services, and steadily rising real incomes and net worth for the over-whelming majority of Americans.[14] The American economy is poised to do even better in the future, and the run up in stock prices in the mid–1990s indicates a long-term confidence in the country's future. That is to say very simply, building wealth in the future will be even easier than it is now.

And make no mistake about it, getting rich in this country does not depend on a continuation of the type of stock market boom that investors have experienced over recent years. The stock market is unlikely to continue to advance at a rate of over 20 percent a year, and as a result, we base our calculations on far less optimistic rates of increase.[15]

Throughout the book, we intend to stress what is *possible* to do, not what you will or must do. Indeed, if these rules were followed to the letter, they could be called a formula for lifelong wealth and success. But by virtue of the fact that they are rules and they do restrict behavior, and we are human beings who tend to resist restriction, we do not expect readers to follow our rules exactly. They necessarily require "patterns" of behavior, though the details of behavior can be filled in by you. Ironically, however, our rules are liberating in the sense that, if they are followed, they allow for greater success, greater fortune, and greater freedom.

We've heard all the pundits' claims that our opportunities are restricted by genetics and the social and economic "environment" in which we live. We recognize that success is "path dependent," to use a pat phrase of some social scientists. That is, the steps in building a substan-tial retirement portfolio of assets build on one another. Not all people are able to make it to the same degree because they are not equally endowed with the same physical or mental abilities, nor are they blessed with the same luck. Yet there is much we can control in this life.

Advancement indeed depends in part on the career and financial paths that you initially take. It is because of that very fact that our rules should be heeded. Follow them and you will put yourself on the path to good fortune, no matter who you are. You can depend on it.

Unheralded Past Progress

Every time you hear the refrain, "Times are tough and getting tougher," you should consider famed radio host Garrison Keillor's point: "All in all, there is more self-pity available to wallow in now than there was during the Great Depression when your grandparents lived in grimy little houses with newspapers stuffed in the cracks and worked so hard their bodies hurt at night. Complaining was against their religion, though. They believed that if you smile, you'll feel better."[16] We think readers should start this book with a smile.

We know you've heard many well-respected journalists, scholars, and policy makers fret that hard data supposedly show that it's tougher now to make it in America than ever before. They will point to measures of workers' wages that appear to prove their contention.[17] According to their calculations, real worker wages rose more or less consistently in this country until the early 1970s, after which real wages fell. Between 1973 and 1995, the buying power of workers' wages supposedly fell by more than 15 percent.

Should you believe these figures? Are Americans really worse off now than they were two or three decades ago? Is your future going to be less prosperous than your parents' or grandparents'? Will getting rich get tougher?

The answers to these questions are complex. Granted, after adjusting worker wages for changes in the cost of living over time using the Consumer Price Index (CPI), worker wages have trended downward since the early 1970s. However, this line of analysis is seriously flawed for two reasons.

- First, since the early 1970s, workers have taken a progressively greater percentage of their earnings in fringe benefits, giving up money wages in the process, a tradeoff that has effectively hidden worker income gains over time.
- Second, as many experts have come to realize, the CPI has overstated inflation, mainly because it does not adequately account for the quality improvements of goods and services over time. As a consequence, using the CPI to adjust for inflation unnecessarily depresses income growth.

In our own evaluation of what has been happening to American wages and family incomes, we have come to the conclusion that American worker incomes have actually risen significantly (by as much as a third) over the past two decades, not to mention the past half century and more.[18]

Michael Cox, an economist at the Federal Reserve Bank of Dallas, and Richard Alm, a Dallas journalist, have come up with perceptive ways of settling the "better or worse" debate, mainly by asking, "Does it take Americans more or less time at work to buy what they want than it did decades ago?"[19]

Cox and Alm consider the changing cost—measured in dollars and work time—of an array of goods and services from the 1950s to the 1990s. Among the many goods and services they evaluate for signs of economic progress for Americans, they found that the median-priced house cost $14,500 in the 1950s and $140,000 in 1997. A dishwasher cost $250 in the 1950s and $370 in 1997. A soft drink carried a price of 7 cents in the 1950s and 33 cents at the supermarket in 1997, and so on.

While most of the prices of the goods on their extensive list went up, so did worker wages, facts that taken together made Cox and Alm wonder if it took the average American worker more or less time at work to buy the goods and services on their list. Their answer? For the most part, it now takes less work time—often far less time. Granted, it takes more time at work for an American worker to buy the "typical" house today than it did in the 1950s. However, the reason is that Americans are now buying much larger houses than they did in the 1950s. Now it takes only 5.6 hours of time at work to buy a square foot of housing, whereas it took 6.5 hours of work time (or 16 percent more) in the 1950s. Even then, these figures understate the decrease in the cost of housing, given that today's houses are packed with far more expensive features—for example, air conditioning and dishwashers—than the typical house had in the 1950s.

In the 1950s it took an American worker 562 hours of work to buy a color television. Now it takes only 23 hours (96 percent fewer hours). In the 1950s it took 71 hours of work to buy a coast-to-coast airplane ticket, but it took only 16 hours in 1997 (77 percent fewer hours). A gallon of gasoline cost 6.4 minutes of work time in the 1950s and 5.7 minutes of work in 1997 (11 percent fewer minutes). Just go down through the list and see if you don't agree that in terms of what we can buy, most Americans are better off now than ever. Because of these kinds of opportunities, Americans have a far greater chance of getting rich than ever before.

The American Future: More Progress

It is important to recognize the considerable progress the country has made over recent decades for two very important reasons:

- First, it allows us to set aside the claims of the pessimists and the nay-sayers who constantly warn that economic Armageddon is just around the corner. When you hear them in the future—and they will continue to beat their drums—remember they were sorely wrong in the past.

- Second, we can see in the data on rising incomes and declining prices of goods (measured in the hours of work required to buy them) a reason to believe that the country stands to make even more progress in the future.

That is not to say that the economy won't continue to have its ups and downs—periods of prosperity followed by periods of recession. It will, and no one is ever able to predict those very accurately. But there are several solid reasons to expect the country's economic progress to continue, perhaps at a more rapid rate of growth than the country has experienced in the immediate past:

- America today is blessed with low rates of unemployment, inflation, and interest. While there is no promise that these very favorable conditions will remain in place for very long, they certainly will contribute to continued progress in the immediate future.
- The country is producing nearly two-thirds more goods and services (after adjusting for the effects of inflation) than it did two decades ago. There are no apparent caps on how much the country can produce. We continue to increase our productivity and industrial base.
- The country has nearly 50 percent more real assets in the form of business machinery and structures than we had at the start of the 1980s. Those assets can be used to produce even more assets and goods and services in the future.
- Technological progress continues apace, especially in computers, telecommunications, and the Internet. There are in existence today a number of key technologies that will likely power the economy for several decades to come, not the least of which are
    Optics (information transmission with light).
    Holography (three-dimensional images).
    Photonics (use of light's energy).
    Artificial intelligence (programming computers to think).
    Recognition technology (programming computers to recognize shapes, sounds, and smells).
    Virtual reality (use of computers for undertaking remote surgery and training pilots, as well as playing games).
    Robotics (use of machine to replace repetitive work).
    Integration technology (the connection of computers, televisions, and microwave systems).
    Nanotechnology (the manipulation of matter at the molecular level).

Micro electronics (the engineering of machines small enough to operate inside the body).

Material sciences (the science of creating stronger, lighter, and more durable composites).

Genomics (the study of human DNA that will allow for new medical breakthroughs).

Bionomics (the merging of mechanics with biology that has the promise of allowing the deaf to hear and the blind to see).[20]

There is simply no telling what new technologies are now being developed in labs around the world that will eventually make their way into common use in the first quarter of the twenty-first century.

The economy has moved gradually from a world in which the value of goods was locked up in the *materials* that are used in the goods to a world in which the value of goods is locked up in the *ideas* that give birth to the goods. For example, only 2 percent of the value of a computer chip is in the material (basically sand) that is used to produce it. In this new economic world, our future opportunities are much more unbounded, unchecked by material constraints, because the critical resource in this universe—ideas— "are not used up as they are used," as futurist George Gilder has written. In this new economic world, "the inventive inputs of producers launch a spiral of economic growth and productivity at steadily declining cost in every material domain: land, energy, pollution, and natural resources."[21] And the real prices of most physical resources—most notably, energy—have been on a steady decline for decades.

- The federal government seems to have significantly improved its fiscal affairs through constrained growth on its expenditures and dramatic reductions in its deficit spending. Indeed, government expenditures as a percent of total domestic production has actually been on a downward trend in the 1990s. The federal Treasury now projects budget surpluses for several years.

- Integration of the world economy through trade and telecommunications will likely continue far into the future, which means that the American economy can continue to grow by drawing on resources from around the world.

- The liberation of the former Soviet Bloc countries means that the productive energies of over half a billion people will no longer be checked by the communist ideology. Over a billion people in China are gradually being given their economic freedom from state planning. The freeing of all these people will mean that they will produce and earn more, and there will be, as there have already been, more economic opportunities for Americans to buy from and sell to the newly freed people of the world.

Clearly, the country has problems, many of which are social (with teenage pregnancies, crime, and racial tensions being several of the most serious) and economic (with the nation's saving rate declining to a post–Great Depression low in 1997[22]), but it has always had problems.[23] As a country, we will work our way through them, as we have done in the past. But unlike the past, in the future we will have more resources, goods, and services to help rectify the problems that we encounter. Progress may be abated by the problems we face, but rest assured that progress will not likely be halted. To grow rich, you need to plan to be a part of the progress that is the country's future.

One of the most important attributes for making it in America is *attitude*. Those who are convinced they can't make it because they have bought into all the claims about how little they can do to improve their lives probably won't grow rich, or have a very satisfying life. Those who wait on others or the government for aid, because they are convinced that relief from their unfortunate circumstances will come only that way, will be doomed to dependency. These Americans will, in effect, live a self-fulfilling prophecy.

Those Americans who believe the contrary—that all is possible, that they are the "captains of their fate"—and behave accordingly will, as we show, have a good shot at doing well in life. Don't be discouraged by the fear of failure, and don't count on avoiding failures altogether. Failures—large and small—are inherent to progress and can actually energize it. We can learn important lessons from failure, not the least of which is what not to do next time.

Eddie Diaz, founding partner of New Mexico Chili Products in Deming, New Mexico, understands the role of failure in his business: "My father taught my brothers and sisters and me that to succeed in a land of opportunity, you've got to create opportunities for success where others might only see a chance to fail." He also advises, "You can't dream the American Dream, you've got to live it."[24]

Everyone has an *attitude*, sometimes to his detriment because he is stifled by it. Diaz has the attitude we had in mind when writing this book. So did Joseph Schumpeter, a highly respected Harvard professor, now deceased, who more than half a century ago observed, "The report that a given ship is sinking is not defeatist. Only the spirit in which this report is received can be defeatist: The crew can sit down and drink. But it can also rush to the pumps."[25] We intend to show you how to man the "pumps," not to save a sinking ship (the American economy is not going under), but to take full advantage of the available opportunities to build a fortune that, without some "pumping" on your part, will never get built.

Practical Advice for Achieving the Good life

The central admonition of this chapter is one you've heard before: Think positively and optimistically. When you don't have everything you want, think of your glass as half full, not half empty. We suggest the following day-to-day tips for making that admonition work in your life:

- Organize your life with the future in mind. Engage in some strategic planning for your whole life. Set some priorities. Lay out some goals for, say, the next year, the next five years, and retirement. Don't just think about your goals, write them down. Make your goals realistic and achievable, but be sure to make them tough, worthy of being "goals." Then add concrete ways you plan to achieve them. Better yet, take a few minutes to go through the exercise that follows this section. You will be amazed how writing down your thoughts will sharpen your thinking and add a sense of personal commitment to the goals you specify.

- Develop several internal "counters" (degrees, business accomplishments, people you have helped, etc.) that will allow you to assess on a regular basis how well you are moving toward the fulfillment of your strategic plan. Don't allow money to be your only "counter," simply because dollars are so easily counted. If you do, you might build a fortune, but we suspect that you won't feel good about what you have done in life.

- Take note of the wisdom in the adage, "There's a season for everything." Recognize that your life cannot always, at every moment or during every year, be satisfying if you are ever to build a fortune. There must be a "season" in your life for a lot of hard work and long hours at endeavors that can be painful to get through. In your season of work, be prepared to arrive at work before everyone else and leave after everyone else has gone for the day. Such "seasons" can be gratifying, but only if you understand there will be other "seasons" that follow in which life will be more comfortable.

- Realize that few people have been able to endure the "season" of hard work at things they don't enjoy doing or are not good at. Make a serious inventory of your skills, talents, and likes and dislikes, and be choosy over what you do in your career.

- Understand that your own personal constraints in your own life can be liberating. They ensure that you will not have to live by the constraints that others (family and friends, employers, and creditors) impose on you. This means recognize the values of budgets as constraints. When you don't know where your money has been or will be going, you very likely will not be building much wealth or a satisfying life.

- Realize that opportunities don't just "exist" independent of what you do; they are, for the most part, discovered and made. Opportunities to create opportunities are not always obvious and they are not evenly distributed in time or place. You must search out opportunities, and you must be prepared to move to them. This means you must be prepared to change your skills and your location. And because opportunities have a tendency to arise unexpectedly, be "opportunity ready."

- See the *problems* you and other people complain about as unrecognized opportunities to provide solutions. Fortunes are made by people who provide value to others, and solutions to problems are valuable.

- Remember that it takes far less in the way of "material resources" to get rich in America than is commonly believed. Both Gates and the Joneses understood one of the more basic prerequisites for building a fortune in this country or anywhere else: *Start with a good idea.* That's an optimistic observation because no one—absolutely no one—can corner the market on good ideas. Good ideas can come to anyone, and everyone, and they have a tendency to build on themselves.

- Appreciate the value of "networks," given that the only way most people can create value in this world is through working with others. Make as many friends and business contacts as possible. But choose your friends and contacts carefully. Associate with people who are optimistic, who have a sense of their own futures, and who understand the value of hard work and commitment.

- Identify one or more mentors, older people who seem to have done what this book is all about—who have built a fortune and have, at the same time, led a satisfying life. (One clue for identifying such people: They are not always complaining about what they don't have and did not do in life.) Ask them for their own tips for the "good life." You will be amazed at how consistent their advice is.

- Above all, don't forget that the greatest good fortune you will have lies within you—your knowledge, skills, and attitudes that take constant cultivation and upgrading.

An Exercise for Achieving the Good Life:
Taking Stock and Setting Goals

To build a fortune and satisfying life, you must have some goals. Here, we ask that you become an active participant in achieving the "good life" by specifying where you are today, what your goals are, and what opportunities are available to you. You will use this information to make some calculations at the end of the following chapters. You can also compare your calculations at the end of later chapters with the answers your provide here. Expect to have revised your answers substantially by the time you reach the end of the book.

1. What is your job (or main daily activities) now?

2. What job do you want to be doing
    A year from now?
    Five years from now?
    In the five to ten years before you retire?

3. What is your annual income now?

4. What do you realistically want your annual income (estimated in today's dollars) to be
    A year from now?
    Five years from now?
    Just before you retire?
    Just after your retire?

5. How much have you saved over the past year?

6. What percentage of your annual income do you now save? [(5)/(3)]

7. At what age do you plan to retire?

8. What is your current net worth (add up your debts and your assets that have a market value and subtract your total debts from your total assets)?

9. What do you realistically want your net worth to be when you retire?

10. Describe briefly what you consider your realistic goals for the next five years in the areas listed below. Then indicate briefly how you intend to achieve your goals. Feel free to extend the exercise for longer periods of time.
    Savings per year
    Education
    Health
    Self-restraint (to achieve other goals indicated above)

11. What opportunities (financial and otherwise) are available to you that you have not exploited as you should?

12. Which of the available opportunities that you listed in your answer to question 11 would help you achieve your goals?

Take the Power
of Compound Interest
Seriously—and Then Save

Getting rich has always been an American tradition. That tradition will continue in this country if for no other reason than that many Americans who were either born here or who immigrated here have opportunities to develop and use their talents and energies that are unequaled in most parts of the world. Americans at all income levels continue to use their imaginations to convert their opportunities into financial wealth.

When you feel that you may not be one of the fortunate Americans who can get rich, just remember that Southern California abounds with immigrants who started life in this country with literally nothing but the shirts on their backs and, if they were lucky, very low incomes. Still, many have managed to create and build thriving businesses. These businesses range from gardening and maid services to software and high-tech firms to restaurants. Indeed, Hispanic-owned businesses in this country grew by 76 percent between 1987 and 1992, and that growth and the considerable success of many Hispanic businesses has given rise to a new catch phrase, *"El Millionario* Next Door."[1] The Hispanic millionaires no doubt share many of the same characteristics of American-born millionaires. They tend to be hard workers, frugal, willing to take risks, age fifty or older, entrepreneurial, and married (to frugal spouses).

Consider the experience of Bartolo Lopez, who crossed the Mexican border into California in 1970 at the age of seventeen. At first he worked menial farm jobs (picking strawberries), but then he acquired landscaping skills while working for a Japanese gardener. When the recession of the early 1980s hit and Lopez lost his job with another Los Angeles landscaping firm, he started his own landscaping business, 3 Pinos Landscaping. Within a year, he had ten employees. Now Lopez's business has annual revenues of $2 million, which leaves him with an annual salary for himself of close to $100,000, for designing and creating, as one writer put it, "opulent backyard Xanadus for the San Fernando Valley's upper crust."[2] Lopez is rich today by the standards of this country, and he is extraordinarily rich by the standards of his home country, Mexico.

How do the rich get rich? Surely, some people are rich because their parents were rich. Senator Ted Kennedy is surely rich. Just as surely, he would not likely have lived the lifestyle he has or achieved his high office if his parents had been of modest means. Of course, Ted Kennedy is not alone in his good fortune, and considerable wealth is passed from generation to generation. John Kennedy, Jr., is following in the Kennedy tradition, living the American Dream in style with lots of money inherited from his parents. But relatively few Americans get their wealth from extravagant inheritances. Fewer still gained their wealth though luck, as in gambling. From the statistics in the box in the first chapter, it is a sure bet that precious few American millionaires got their fortunes by winning the top prize in state lotteries (you have a six times greater chance of being struck down by lightning than winning a state lottery).

We tell you about Bartolo Lopez because he is more representative of the "rich" in this country than are the Kennedys, and the way he achieved his riches can be studied and replicated, whereas the Kennedys' way, unfortunately, cannot. No doubt, Lopez worked very hard and took some risks when investing much of his savings back into his business, but he has also done what most other American millionaires have done. He has taken the power of *compound interest* seriously.

What this means, in a few words, is that he has allowed his savings and investments to build upon themselves by not spending the interest income (or profit) his investments have generated. Accordingly, the interest income (or profit) has earned interest income, which has begotten more and more interest income with the passage of the years.

Most Americans are not capable of building a substantial fortune from work alone; their wage rate is not high enough and there aren't enough hours in the day for them to work for their fortunes. They need help, which more often than not comes in the form of compound interest.

While many Americans are not aware of its power to help amass modest, if not huge, fortunes, compound interest is no trade secret. Investment experts and entrepreneurs have known the "magical" powers of compound interest for a very long time. (See the nearby box, which dramatizes the power of compounding.) What Lopez and many other rich people in this country have generally done is take the power of compounding to heart; and they have lived by its underlying principles. Succinctly, these principles are:

1. Save and invest something of what you earn persistently.

2. Achieve a reasonable rate of return each year on your investment, which requires that you take some risks.

3. Be patient, allowing your savings and investments to grow for a long stretch of time.

The Importance of Saving Something

Again, how can ordinary—even low-income, if not poor—Americans become rich? The answer to that question is as simple as it is mandatory: Start by saving and investing something regularly, even if it is a modest amount—in anticipation of big returns in the future. Your persistent savings will add up with time. One hundred dollars saved each year will cause your total savings to rise from $100 to $1,000 in ten years.

However, your net worth (or financial wealth) should grow, over time, by much more than the sum of your savings. This is because of the power of compound interest. This means that you should expect to receive on your savings some rate of interest (or return or appreciation) each year. If you leave the interest in your account, your interest will "compound" because you will then receive in subsequent years interest on your savings, plus interest on the interest that you received in previous years. Again, if you save $100 for ten years and receive an interest rate of 10 percent, your total savings with interest will grow from $100 the beginning of the first year to $210 the second year ($100 of savings the first year plus $10 of interest on the first year's savings plus $100 of new savings), to $331 the beginning of the third year, on to $1,594 the beginning of the tenth year. In short, with compound interest you will have close to 60 percent more in net worth at the beginning of the tenth year than you would have had from the savings alone.

You can imagine with "interest on interest"—or compounded interest—your net worth will build progressively more rapidly with each passing year. With sufficient savings, enough patience, and a reasonable rate of interest on your savings (or return on your investments), you can

Confounding Compounding

The power of compounding can be confounding. To see how, take a short quiz related to the consequence of doubling payments (which is, admittedly, a very high rate of compounding):

- **Question 1:** If you were a king of long ago who had a debt to one of your subjects, would you be pleased if the subject asked to be paid in wheat the total of the following payments made with reference to the squares on a chessboard: one kernel on the first square, two kernels on the second square, and so on, with the kernels doubled for each succeeding square?
- **Question 2:** Which would you prefer to have, the combined current fortune of the four hundred richest Americans (as estimated by *Forbes* magazine) or the wealth you would receive from being paid weekly in the following manner: 1 cent for the first week, 2 cents for the second week, with your weekly payments doubled for each succeeding week of the year? Suppose that under the second option, you had to give away your wealth accumulated for the first fifty-one weeks, which would you then prefer?

With reference to the first question, the king was (according to legend) very pleased at his subject's "modest" request for payment—until he had to pay up! The king had to supply a total of 9,450,000,000,000,000,000 grains of wheat (in round numbers). Those grains amount to roughly 17.4 trillion bushels of wheat. That's a lot, equal to the total wheat production of the United States for 16,000 years (assuming an annual production over a billion bushels). We can only guess that the king lost his temper and the subject lost his head long before the sixty-fourth square of the chessboard was reached.

You probably now suspect that your wealth would be much greater if you take the second pay option, and you would be right by a sizable margin. If you took the combined wealth of all four hundred of the world's richest people, your fortune would be a "mere" $940 billion. If you took the second option, your total pay for the year would be about $45 trillion! Even if you gave away the first fifty-one weeks of pay, you would be left with over $22.5 trillion in wealth.

imagine that your net worth (and resulting income level) in the future will be the envy of those who have chosen to spend all their income year after year on many things they could do without, or do with less of.

To dramatically illustrate just how powerful compound interest can be in building wealth, suppose that you are a newly minted twenty-two-year-old college graduate, with a starting salary of, say, $30,000 a year, and you salt away a mere $2,000 the first year—*and only the first year*—on your job (which means that you will then save only 6.6 percent of your annual pretax income that one year). Assume that you are able to secure an annual rate of return on the investment (above the inflation rate) of 15 percent until retirement. Amazingly, your onetime investment will be worth, in the purchasing power of today's dollars, $814,774 at age sixty-five and over $1.64 million at age seventy.

If at age sixty-five you put your savings in an interest-bearing asset (say, a low-risk government bond) earning 4 percent in interest income (which is about what you could earn after inflation at this writing on long-term government bonds), you could have an annual retirement income of $32,591 in *today's dollars* without reducing the real dollar value of the principal (or the amount invested). You could have an annual income of $59,952 if you were willing to draw on the principal, leaving a zero balance in your investment account at the time of your expected death, which we assume (for illustration purposes) is age eighty-five.[3] If you held off retiring until age seventy, your income would be nearly $65,600, assuming you draw out only the interest each year, and $147,503, assuming you plan to draw down the principal to zero at the time of your expected death, which is again assumed to be age eighty-five.

Not bad, is it? We suspect that you will agree that these income levels are quite attractive, given, as noted earlier, that the median family income in America (including all races) was about $42,300 in 1996. The median income of American families headed by retirees (including their Social Security checks) was about half that amount.

Of course, most retirees would not likely seek to draw down their principal to zero at the expected time of their death, fearing the ever-present prospect (and serious threat) that they would live longer than expected. But that doesn't mean that they—and you—would necessarily want to leave the full principal intact at the time of death. You can draw down some of the principal on the installment plan, with the expectation that a portion of the principal would be left at death (although you would have to accept the risk of living longer than planned). Alternately, you can actually buy an annuity at retirement that would provide a fixed income every year until death (with the seller of the annuity taking the risk of when you would die). Whatever you plan to do (and we can't tell you how much you should draw after retirement), don't let these more sophisticated calculations obscure our central point, which is that by saving a little and doing it early, you can have a very nice, substantial net worth and income at retirement.

Okay, our assumed rate of appreciation for the onetime $2,000 contribution to your savings—15 percent—may be an unreasonably high rate of appreciation for such a long period of time (forty-three years, with retirement at age sixty-five, and forty-eight years, with retirement at age seventy). However, notice that we have been talking about a *onetime* saving of only $2,000. Surely college graduates could do better than that over the course of their careers, if they wanted to do so.

The Importance of the Rate of Return

The amount you save each year is crucial to how much wealth you will have at retirement. However, the rate of return you get on your savings and investments, as well as the length of time you save, are just as important to how much of a fortune you build as how much you save each year. Indeed, the amount you save may be less important than the rate of return and period of time over which you allow your net worth to build in determining your net worth at retirement.

Here we can make that point by laying out several saving scenarios, assuming three rates of appreciation on your savings and investment— 15, 8, and 5 percent (after adjusting for inflation). The results are in Table 2.1. In the top part of that table, we extend our analysis of the one-time investment of $2,000 at age twenty-two. The table shows that if the rate of appreciation in your investments were limited to 8 percent (after inflation), you could have a net worth of $54,733 in *today's dollars* if you retired at age sixty-five and a net worth of $80,421 in *today's dollars* if you retired at age seventy. If your rate of return was a mere 5 percent, you wouldn't have much net worth, only $16,299 and $20,803 at ages sixty-five and seventy, respectively.

The difference in net worth with rates of return of 8 percent and 5 percent rather than 15 percent is stark. At age sixty-five, your net worth with a 15 percent return ($814,774) is nearly fifteen times your net worth when you receive an 8 percent rate of return ($54,733). At age seventy, your net worth at 15 percent ($1.64 million) is twenty times your net worth at an 8 percent return ($80,421). At age sixty-five and a 15 percent return, your net worth is nearly fifty times your net worth at 5 percent ($16,299). At age seventy and a 15 percent return, your net worth is 79 times your net worth at 5 percent return ($20,803).

The lesson of these calculations is obvious; it pays big-time—even for a onetime saving of $2,000—to secure a slightly higher rate of return. Still, we must not lose sight of the fact that the person who makes a onetime saving of only $2,000 at age twenty-two and who receives only a 5 percent return will have at retirement a net worth ($20,803) that is about one-fifth of the median net worth of Americans at retirement age. That

Table 2.1.
How Compound Interest Works Under
Different Saving and Retirement Plans

ONETIME SAVING OF $2,000 at Age 22

| Retirement Age | Rate of Appreciation of Investments | | |
	15%	8%	5%
65	$814,774	$54,733	$16,299
70	$1.64 million	$80,421	$20,803

SAVING OF $2,000 EACH YEAR from Age 22

| Retirement Age | Rate of Appreciation of Investments | | |
	15%	8%	5%
65	$6.23 million	$713,899	$302,286
70	$12.55 million	$1.06 million	$396,853

SAVING 10% OF INCOME,
Starting with an Annual Salary of $30,000 at Age 22 and
Receiving 1% Real Annual Increases Thereafter

| Retirement Age | Rate of Appreciation of Investments | | |
	15%	0%	5%
65	$10.01 million	$1.20 million	$525,588
70	$20.16 million	$1.79 million	$696,974

might not sound like a big accomplishment, but notice how limited the saving and the rate of return are.

There is absolutely no need for you to restrict your net worth at retirement by a onetime saving of a mere $2,000. Instead of putting aside $2,000 only one time in your life at age twenty-two, suppose you put aside $2,000 a year every year from age twenty-two until you retire. How much would you then be worth in today's dollars at retirement?

Consider the results in the middle section of Table 2.1. You would be worth $6.23 million in today's dollars at age sixty-five and over $12.55 million at age seventy, assuming a real annual appreciation of 15 percent; $713,899 at age sixty-five and $1.06 million at age seventy, assuming

How to Run the Numbers

You can compute your expected net worth (given your own selected set of assumptions on income, saving, and rate of return) using Microsoft Excel or Lotus 1,2,3, relatively easy-to-use spreadsheet programs for personal computers, which is what we did, or a hand calculator. These are the steps to follow to compute your net worth at retirement for a fixed amount of saving each year using Excel:

1. Fill in column A of the spreadsheet with the years you intend to include (if you plan to start saving at age twenty-two, then the cells in column A should read "22, 23, 24 . . ." up to your target retirement age).
2. Enter in cell B1 the amount you intend to save each year (for example, $2,000).
3. Enter the following formula in cell B2, assuming you save 2000 each year and receive rate of interest of 8 percent: =2000+(B1*1.08).
4. Enter the following formula in cell B3: =2000+(B2*1.08).
5. Select cells B2 and B3.
6. Place the pointer on your screen over the lower right-hand corner of the selected area. Depress the left button on your mouse and pull down until you reach your selected retirement age (as indicated in column A).
7. Your computed net worth for every year will be automatically computed when you release the left mouse button.
8. Repeat the exercise by changing the amount of saving and rate of interest.
9. You can make more complicated calculations regarding the percent of income saved by simply replacing the formulas used.

You can also make these calculations on any one of several available financial (or business) hand calculators. Most of the available financial calculators have the same identifying keys that we indicate below (in square brackets). We used the Texas Instrument BA II (or Model 35) (which is inexpensive, just under $21 at this writing). To make the above calculations, you can consult the directions for computing annuities that come with the hand calculator, or follow these steps:

1. Press [2nd] and then press [MODE].
2. Enter 2000 (for the annual saving) and press [PMT].
3. Enter the number of years until your target retirement age and press [N].
4. Enter 8 (for the interest rate) and press [%i].
5. Press [CPT] and then [FV], which will give you the value of the accumulated savings at your target retirement age. (Ignore the minus sign in the window of your calculator.)

an annual appreciation of 8 percent; and $302,286 at age sixty-five and nearly $396,853 at age seventy, assuming an annual appreciation of 5 percent.

If you were even more aggressive in saving between age twenty-two and retirement, your net worth at retirement would be dramatically higher. For example, suppose that you were able to raise your skills and the market demand for your services so that you start work at age twenty-two with an annual salary of $30,000 but receive a very modest 1 percent annual raise (above the rate of inflation) for the duration of your career. Suppose also that you save 10 percent of your (before-tax) income. This means that at age twenty-two you will earn $30,000 and save $3,000. By the time you reach age seventy, however, you will be earning $48,367 a year and saving $4,837 a year. Your net worth at age sixty-five will be slightly more than $10 million, assuming an appreciation rate of 15 percent; $1.20 million, assuming an appreciation rate of 8 percent; and $525,588, assuming an appreciation rate of 5 percent.

Your net worth, of course, will be significantly more at age seventy, mainly because you will then be saving for more years and the compounding process has more years to work. At age seventy, your net worth will be $20.16 million, assuming an appreciation rate of 15 percent; $1.79 million, assuming an appreciation rate of 8 percent; and almost $696,974, assuming an appreciation rate of 5 percent.

Obviously, the rate of appreciation (or interest or return) is important, mainly because of the power of compounding. But there is really nothing "magical" about that power. Your wealth builds not only because of the savings that you add each year, but also because of the appreciation in your wealth from all the prior savings. In this way you get *compound* growth, which is why we write about the *power* of compounding.

Your net worth grows by increasing amounts as you get closer to retirement. The greater the rate at which your wealth builds (or the greater the rate of interest or appreciation you get), the greater your wealth at retirement will be. Anyone interested in building wealth should, of course, be concerned with the rate of appreciation as well as the rate of savings, and should also be concerned with starting a saving plan as early as possible. It should surprise no one that any millionaires who live next door to us tend to spend more time than most other Americans working with their finances; they understand the power of compounding, which means they know it pays to pay attention to the rate of interest or rate appreciation on their investments. A very small increase in the interest or appreciation rate can translate into sizable increases in net worth years down the road.

What is truly remarkable about the compounding process is how the *increase* in your net worth can eventually surpass, first, your level of saving and, then, your entire pretax annual income. Let's reconsider our earlier example, in which we assume you start with a salary of $30,000 a year, receive 1 percent real increases thereafter, save 10 percent of your salary, and receive a real appreciation of 8 percent a year in your net worth. The increase in your net worth starts at age twenty-two at 10 percent of your annual salary (or $3,000), but then at age thirty the increase in your net worth ($5,882) will move up to 18 percent of your salary ($32,486). At age forty, the increase in your net worth ($13,187) will be 37 percent of your salary ($35,884), and at age fifty the increase ($29,013) will be 73 percent of your salary ($39,639). By age fifty-five, we note with special emphasis, the increase in your net worth ($42,866) will for the first time be slightly higher (3 percent) than your annual salary ($41,661).

At a retirement age of sixty-five, the increase in your net worth ($93,171) will be slightly more than twice your last year's salary ($46,019). If you delay retirement to age seventy, the increase in your net worth ($137,173) will be close to three times your last year's salary ($48,367).

The "Rule of 72"

Throughout the book we will be calculating the value of everything—for example, the income you set aside in stocks or the cost of a car you might buy—in terms of how much your net worth will change at retirement time. These calculations will be based on very precise assumptions about what you do—how much you save or what you buy—and the rate of return you can get on your investment. You might not agree with our assumptions, and this does not bother us. We develop our examples to illustrate broad principles that we want you to grasp. You can make your own calculations using a hand calculator or a popular spreadsheet program for personal computers (as we described in an earlier box in this chapter).

There is a simple but rough way you can figure what an investment today will be worth in the future. All you need to do is divide 72 by a rate of return you consider reasonable. The quotient will be the number of years it will take your investment to double. For example, if you think a reasonable rate of return on your investment is 8 percent annually (after inflation) on your investment, then you can divide 72 by 8, which tells you that it will take about nine years for your investment to double. For example, if you invest $5,000 today at 8 percent a year (after inflation), your investment will be worth $10,000 (in today's dollars) nine years from now. It will be worth $20,000 eighteen years from now, and $40,000 twenty-seven years from now. If you retire thirty-six years from now, the $5,000 you invested today will be worth $80,000 at retirement.

The Importance of Saving Early

As you can now understand, your net worth late in your career or at retirement will depend critically on when you start saving. To see the impact of starting your saving late in your career, consider the findings in Table 2.2. In that table we recomputed your net worth at retirement, assuming you have the same earning power each year of your career as in the above illustration and that when you do start saving, you save 10 percent of your annual income. However, in contrast to our early illustrations in which we assume you start saving right out of college, we assume in the upper half of Table 2.2 that you delay saving 10 percent of your income until age forty.

Table 2.2.
How Compound Interest Works When
Saving Is Delayed Until Age 40 and Age 50

SAVING 10% OF INCOME,
Starting with an Annual Salary of $35,884 at Age 40 and
Receiving 1% Increases Each Year After Age 40

| Retirement Age | Rate of Appreciation of Investments | | |
	15%	8%	5%
65	$937,136	$312,763	$202,784
70	$1.92 million	$487,328	$284,986

SAVING 10% OF INCOME,
Starting with an Annual Salary of $39,639 at Age 50 and
Receiving 1% Increases Each Year After Age 50

| Retirement Age | Rate of Appreciation of Investments | | |
	15%	8%	5%
65	$231,746	$127,601	$100,117
70	$498,008	$215,263	$153,954

What a dramatic difference the eighteen-year delay can make! When you start saving at age forty, your net worth at age sixty-five is only $937,136 at a rate of return of 15 percent (and equals less than 10 percent of what your net worth would have been had you started saving at age twenty-two). Your net worth at age seventy is only $1.92 million (again, less than 10 percent of what your net worth would have been had saving started at age twenty-two). At lower rates of returns—8 and 5 percent—the drops in net worth are not as dramatic, but they are still substantial.

In the second half of the table, we assume you don't start saving until age fifty. Your net worth then drops further to $231,746 at age sixty-five and to $498,008 at age seventy, assuming an annual appreciation rate of 15 percent; to $127,601 at age sixty-five and $215,263 at age seventy, assuming an annual appreciation rate of 8 percent; and to $100,117 at age sixty-five and $153,954 at age seventy, assuming an annual appreciation rate of 5 percent.

Our calculations lead to two insights that should be remembered:

- First, a high rate of return (interest and/or appreciation) on your accumulated wealth can take the place of a lot of saving, and vice versa. One reason many smart investors study and keep track of their investments is that they know that their efforts can pay off in terms of more net worth or in terms of having to do less saving.

- Second, if you *don't* start saving early in life, you can count on having to save more later in life and/or be more concerned about getting a higher rate of return when you do start saving just to reach any given level of net worth at retirement.

Recovering from a Late Start: Easier Now Than Ever

We don't mean to suggest that "all is lost" if you wait until you are middle-aged to start saving. Nothing is ever lost—totally. As Table 2.2 reveals, even the person who waits until age fifty to start saving 10 percent of income, retires at age sixty-five, and receives only a 5 percent return will still have close to the same net worth than the typical American retiree today (and we remind you that all our figures are in today's dollars). Our point is that to reach our standard for being rich—$1 million—at retirement, a fifty-year-old who has saved little or nothing will have to take some combination of the following courses of action:

Save more than 10 percent of income.
Extend the years of work and saving.
Increase the rate of return.

There is good and bad news in those options. The good news is that it is generally much easier for a fifty-year-old to save than it is for younger people, given that the incomes of people in their late forties and fifties may still be increasing while their family responsibilities may be contracting, not expanding as is the case for many younger people. People in their late forties and fifties may also know more about where to find investments with higher rates of return.

The bad news is that as people approach their retirement years, they have to be more concerned with the ups and downs of the market value of their investments, mainly because they don't want to confront a downward spiral in the market just as they need their financial assets as a source of retirement income. Older people have to be concerned with the safety of their investments, which means that they may not be in a position to seek as high a rate of return, if it means greater riskiness of their investments.[4]

Investment advisers have long argued that as people approach their targeted retirement age, they should seek greater security in their portfolios by gradually shifting the mix of their investment from stocks, the income on which is highly variable, to bonds, the income on which is fixed. There is even a rule of thumb that goes along with this advice: To figure out the appropriate mix of stocks and bonds, subtract your age from one hundred, which gives you the percent of your portfolio that should be in stocks. For example, if you are fifty-three years old, then you should have 47 percent of your portfolio in stocks and 53 percent in fixed income securities. If you follow this advice, your rate of return should gradually contract as you approach retirement, which means the advice will make it all the harder for you to achieve any net worth target if you start saving late.

But there is still some more hidden good news for late starters that is not considered by a blind application of the formula: Life expectancy has risen over the years (from about seventy in 1970 to seventy-six today). This means that older Americans can take more risks for a longer period of time than they could decades ago. In practical terms, the longer life expectancy means older Americans do not need to follow the formula as closely as they once did. They can delay making the shift from equities to fixed-income securities to some later point in their working careers and they can work longer and still have the same number of retirement years. While it may have been appropriate for Americans fifty-three years old to have 47 percent of their portfolios in stocks, they can now have, for example, 53 percent in stocks, which means that older Americans can now continue to receive a higher rate of return on their portfolios for a longer period of time. Because they can live longer and therefore work longer, they can let their portfolios compound for a longer period of time.

In short, people who now start saving late may not be able to achieve the same net worth as younger people. However, they can have a greater net worth to draw on during their retirement years than could their counterparts decades ago. Alternatively, they don't need to save as much as they once did to achieve the same targeted net worth.

To see this point more clearly, let's reconsider an example developed earlier in this chapter. A person starts her career at age twenty-two with an annual salary of $30,000, and she receives an inflation-adjusted annual raise of 1 percent a year. This means that her real annual income rises to $39,639 at age fifty and then to $48,367 at age seventy. However, this time we assume that she doesn't start saving 10 percent of her income until age fifty. Let's now consider how much net worth she would have at age sixty-seven if she receives a rate of return that declines (because of the gradual shift of her investment portfolio from stocks to bonds) from 8 percent at age fifty to 6 percent at age sixty-seven. Her net worth will be $140,008 when she retires at age sixty-seven. However, suppose that her life expectancy rises by three years, causing her to delay the start of the gradual shift in her portfolio from stocks to bonds by three years, or to age fifty-three, and to delay retirement by three years, or to age seventy. Because of the greater rates of return during every working year from age fifty on and the extended career, her net worth at age seventy will rise $185,700, or by 29 percent from what it would have been in the absence of the longer career and life.

Opportunities for Everyone

Some may argue that building net worth is easier said than done. "Doing it" of course requires that you first make the income that will allow for saving. It also requires some modicum of denial, not to mention foresight, patience, and persistence, which are topics taken up in greater detail in later chapters. You will need foresight simply because you must be able to imagine the gains to be had in the distant future if you save today—and next year and the next. Patience is required because you can't expect to see the rewards immediately. If you can't wait long to spend the gains from your savings, don't expect to be able to build much in the way of net worth. If you save one day, only to draw out your savings in the days or years immediately ahead, don't expect to gain much from the power of compounding.

Some may also argue that the ability to accumulate wealth in America is limited to the well off. Indeed, there are some Americans who are so poor that they have very limited prospects of ever "making it" in this country in terms of financial wealth. However, based on more than a half century of collective experience and research, we remain unconvinced that those Americans represent a sizable percentage of the population. As indicated, the previous examples were based on a starting income level that, while allowing an impressive amount of wealth to be accumulated, is still over 25 percent below the median annual income level for American families. The person's average career income in our example is only $38,470, 9 percent below the median family income for 1996.

But we have found that saving and wealth creation is even possible for much lower-income individuals and families. Low-income Americans may not have much income, but they do have *time* that, through another job, they can convert into income and then savings—and finally a sizable net worth at retirement.

To see this point, consider a very conservative case, a high school graduate who at age eighteen and for the rest of his working career earns $15,000 a year, or about $7.21 an hour for working the usual forty-hour week throughout the year.[5] How can he build a fortune?

Granted, his options may be very limited (if he does not extend his income through education). However, instead of working the usual forty-hour weeks, he can extend his work week by putting in overtime at his job or by getting a second job at the same rate of pay. To keep the illustration conservative, let's assume that he increases his workweek by only ten hours a week through age forty (after which he reverts to the standard forty-hour week). In other words, we assume here that for twenty-three years he works fifty hours a week, which is what the average American worker worked every week in the late 1920s (the average workweek in 1997 was about thirty-five hours for all workers and forty-two hours for manufacturing workers). Finally, let's assume that he uses half of his extra income to pay taxes (mainly in the form of Social Security taxes) and to boost marginally his standard of living. Assuming he is not paid at the overtime rate, he will save the rest of the additional income, or $3.60 per hour of extra work.

How much would he be worth at retirement? If he retires at age sixty-five, his net worth would be $9.82 million at an appreciation rate of 15 percent; $780,673 at an appreciation rate of 8 percent; or nearly $262,638 at an appreciation rate of 5 percent. If he waits to retire until age seventy, his net worth would be $19.74 million, $1.15 million, or $335,201, respectively, at the three appreciation rates we've been using. Not bad, we'd say, especially since we've not allowed for overtime pay (which, by law, requires employers to compensate workers for all hours over forty a week at one and a half times the worker's regular pay rate).

Lives of Poverty—and Riches

Do you doubt the ability of poor people to accumulate sizable fortunes? Consider the story of Oseola McCarty, who made a gift of $150,000 to the University of Southern Mississippi when she was eighty-seven years old. It was a significant gift, but not one that normally makes national headlines as this one did. You see, Oseola McCarty never attended the University of Southern Mississippi. Indeed, she had to drop out of school in the sixth grade to help care for a sick aunt. She made her living taking in washing and probably never made the minimum wage. Without question, she had to work her way through and around the maze of racial prejudices in the South, given that she was an African-American. Yet when she made her gift, she had almost $250,000 in the bank—two and a half times the average net worth of American retirees, most of whom probably earned several times what she did.

How did she do it? Early in her life she started making the choices that would make her wealthy. She summarized her approach to saving this way, "I started saving when I was a little girl just to have candy money. When I got grown, I started saving for my future. I'd go to the bank once a month, hold out just enough to cover my expenses, and put the rest into my savings account." She adds, "The secret to building a fortune is compounding interest. It's not the ones that make the big money, but the ones who know how to save that get ahead. You've got to leave your investment alone long enough for it to increase." And maybe Oseola's wisest advice is "you can't rely on government to meet all your needs. You have to take responsibility for yourself."

Oseola McCarty was obviously a very special woman. But as impressive as her saving program was, what really makes her so special is that she gave most of her wealth away. There are far more people who manage to convert small incomes into large wealth holdings than there are people who give most of it away after building the large wealth holdings. Oseola McCarty is not unlike many other low-income Americans. She chose to make it financially, and she didn't let a low income stand in her way.

Neither did Zygmunt Arendt. Mr. Arendt was an immigrant with a sixth-grade education who, when he died at the age of ninety-two, left his entire estate valued at $4 million to the City of San Francisco to help the poor, the elderly, and disabled children. No one knows where he got his money. We would like to be able to give you the details of how Mr. Arendt did it, but he seemed to live his life in total obscurity. All that reporters could uncover at his death and the announcement of his bequest is that he had worked for fourteen years as a car inspector for the Southern Pacific Railroad. What is known is that he lived frugally and saved much of what he earned. Also, like Ms. McCarty, Mr. Arendt had a long life. A long life makes it easier to accumulate a fortune since it allows you to take advantage of compound interest for a longer period of time. As we will see later under Rule 6, it pays handsomely to take care of yourself to live a healthier *and* wealthier life.

Do you think our saving requirements are too high for someone earning so little income? Then let's assume he works only ten extra hours *a month* (or saves $36 a month), and then run the numbers. At a rate of return of 15 percent, he will have a net worth of $2.27 million at age sixty-five and $4.56 million at age seventy. With an 8 percent return, he will have a net worth of $180,155 at age sixty-five and $264,707 at age seventy. With a 5 percent return, he will have a net worth of $60,609 at age sixty-five and $77,354 at age seventy.

No matter how you change the examples, the point remains: Even many low-income Americans have the chance to be well off at retirement. All it takes is a willingness to work hard and an early appreciation of compound interest. Few Americans get rich in America by taking it easy, or by

The Rise from Orphanage Life

If it were not possible for Americans to substantially improve their economic lots in life, then the children who grew up in orphanages decades ago would not have done well. The children who lived in orphanages in the 1950s and before began their lives in distressed, if not sordid, family circumstances. Many child-welfare experts are convinced the children were "damaged" by their orphanage experience. However, a survey of 1,600 alumni of nine orphanages in the South and Midwest contradicts popular presumptions of how the grown-up children should have done.[6] Compared to their counterparts in the general population, the orphanage alumni as a group have

- 40 percent higher college graduation rate (as well as more advanced degrees).
- 10 to 60 percent (depending on age group) higher median family income.
- Far higher level of self-assessed "happiness."
- Much lower rates of unemployment, poverty, incarceration, and dependency on public assistance.

How did the orphans do so well? The alumni recognize the disadvantages of their way of growing up, but they also attribute their relative success to several key attributes that were evident in their homes:

- Strong work ethic that was instilled in them.
- Religious and moral nurturing that was provided.
- Strong sense of responsibility for how far they went in life.
- Camaraderie they built with others through education, sports, and work.[7]

avoiding giving up something. Most well-off Americans who get rich do so by putting in, for some stretch of time in their lives, extra hours in school and on the job. Indeed, researchers have found that at least 26 percent of the income gap between the top and bottom 10 percent of all income earners in the 1973–91 period is explained by the fact that the top 10 percent of income earners simply worked longer hours each year. And don't think that a college education will allow you to get by with less work. The hours worked by college-educated workers is higher than the hours worked by the non-college-educated workers.[8] Many people who make high salaries late in their careers are merely collecting on the considerable investment of their time early in their careers and education.

The Rise to the Top

To find examples of people who have made it in this country through hard work and long hours, all you have to do is look around. They are everywhere. Our favorite mentor, economist James Buchanan, has made it in America in grand style, given that he was awarded a Nobel Prize in economics late in his career. How did he do it? Certainly, not through inheritance. He grew up in rural Tennessee very modestly (conditions that some might construe today as poverty level).[9] No doubt he is a brilliant man, but when we were in his graduate classes or working with him, we couldn't help but notice that he was always first in the office in the morning, before the sun came up, and always one of the last to leave in the evening (after taking his regular midday nap). He contributed mightily to his professional abilities through long hours of work. Over his career, he has pumped out a veritable avalanche of articles and books, many of which are some of the most frequently cited works in modern economics, all the while remaining a dedicated teacher. He literally converted plowshares into the best and most enduring of all kinds of "swords"—those that are intellectual. He did it in a good old-fashioned way, by being willing to put in the time and dedication to a job he loved doing.

We believe our analysis of what the low-income worker can accomplish is conservative, mainly because we have assumed no real improvement in the worker's income level. For most Americans, incomes rise over time because of the accumulation of experience on the job, if nothing else. And workers can do a lot to improve their lot, not the least of which is to actively develop their skills and obtain more formal education (a subject to which we devote a whole chapter, Rule 4). Of course, low-income (and high-income) workers can also worsen their lots in life, as we will also show later (Rule 6), simply by not taking care of themselves.[10]

There is much evidence to counter the repeated refrain that low-income Americans can't make it. Roberto Goizueta fled Cuba in 1961 after Fidel Castro started the slow process of destroying Cuba. Goizueta had very little when he arrived, but he eventually became CEO of Coca-Cola. During his tenure at the helm of Coke—1981 until his death from cancer in 1997 at the relatively young age of sixty-five—Goizueta became very wealthy, mainly because the stock market value of Coke rose by $141 billion during his tenure at the head of Coke. In building Coke's market value, Goizueta and the 32,000 employees under him generated value in quenching the thirsts of a multitude of people in this country and around the world. Ironically, the increase in Coke's market value in the 1981–97 period was enough wealth that, if spread evenly among all Cubans in 1997, it could have doubled Cuba's average standard of living.[11]

We grant you that Goizueta's rise to power and wealth is extraordinary. However, his tale is repeated on more modest scales by other immigrants. Several years ago Richard McKenzie hired a young Vietnamese immigrant, then a college student, Lynda Li, as his research assistant. She was assigned an endless number of menial office and library tasks. She took each assignment as a challenge to do it right, and she always went the extra mile. She had learned well from her parents, who came to this country with little more than the shirts on their backs after the fall of South Vietnam to the communists. Her father went into farming because that is what he did in Vietnam. You have to believe that he put in extra long hours, given that he and his wife had nine children. All nine children now have college degrees. Lynda Li's parents are not rich today, but you can bet that their children are on their way to becoming well off. Lynda Li is now working her way up in the insurance brokerage business, and be assured that she understands the value of saving, which she is doing aggressively. The Li story shows what you can do in this country even when you start with little or nothing.

For far too long, poor Americans have been presented with a defeatist message, that improvement is beyond their means and can come only from the goodwill of higher-income Americans. Not true. Poor Americans should look to themselves for their own improvement, where they can be the beneficiaries of 100 percent of their *own* efforts to improve their *own* lot.[12] First, however, they need to *believe* in a prosperous future, and in the value that their savings, however small, will bring over many years if invested wisely.

Practical Advice for Achieving the Good Life

In building a fortune, the first order of business is to save, and do so regularly. Here are some tips as to how you can do that.

- Learn how to make the type of calculations we have made in this chapter and run the numbers to fit your own economic circumstances. Periodically rerun the numbers to remind yourself of the long-run benefits of savings.
- Look upon saving as an obligation, on par with other monthly bills, and heed the advice "pay yourself first."
- Select a saving rate that is slightly higher than what you think you are capable of saving. Start with a saving rate of 10 percent of your annual income before taxes and break up the saving into monthly installments.
- In choosing your employer, seek one who contributes monthly to your retirement fund. Your employer may not pay as much as other employers without retirement plans, but don't fret. Look upon the reduction in wages as forced saving (and a long-term benefit to you).
- Make saving automatic. If possible, have your employer deduct from your paycheck some specified amount each pay period with the proceeds going into a bank account or mutual fund that you establish. If your employer can't make the deductions, ask your bank to transfer a fixed amount each month from your checking to your savings account or to a mutual fund established by the bank (and many banks do have such funds). Recognize that once you have made saving automatic, outside of your day-to-day control, you will adjust your lifestyle. You will be surprised how rapidly the "pain" of the saving will fade with time.
- Reduce the cost of saving by taking advantage of tax laws that make savings in 401(k) and 403(b) and IRA retirement plans nontaxable income.
- Remember that you may be able to raise your savings as much through wise expenditures as through more work or a higher rate of pay.
- However you increase your saving, leave it alone for a long stretch of time.

An Exercise for Achieving the Good Life: Taking Stock and Setting Goals

This exercise will help you estimate how much you will need to save each year to achieve your financial goals for retirement. To complete the calculations, you will need to use one of several available financial hand calculator (for example, Texas Instruments BA II or Model 35) that have keys similar to the ones identified below.

1. How much annual income (measured in today's dollars) do you want at retirement?

2. How much retirement income do you expect to receive from the following sources (measured in today's dollars)?
    Social Security (you can estimate the annual payments from this Web site: http://socialsecurity.com).
    Work-related pension.
    Other income (not including your income from your financial wealth, which will be considered below).

3. Now, total the above sources of income.

4. Compute the amount of income (measured in today's dollars) you will need to generate from your financial wealth to achieve your income goal by subtracting the total in item 2 from the amount in question 1.

5. Compute the amount of financial wealth you will need to have at retirement in order to have the real interest income computed in item 3 (assuming a real interest rate of 4 percent on safe government bonds). This can be done by dividing your answer for question 3 by 0.04.

6. Determine your financial net worth today (add your financial assets and subtract your debts).

7. Determine the amount you need to add to your financial net worth to achieve your required retirement financial wealth computed in question 4, by subtracting the amount in the fifth question from the amount in item 4.

8. Determine the amount you need to save on average each year between now and the time you retire, assuming you invest your savings in a stock index mutual fund that earns an average of 8 percent a year, computed in the following way with the Texas Instrument BA II calculator (the calculator keys that must be pressed are inside square brackets):
    Press [2nd] and then press [MODE].
    Enter the amount from question 6 and press [FV].

Enter 8 (or any other the rate at which you expect your investments to appreciate) and press [%i].

Enter the number of years between now and the year of your retirement and press [N].

Compute the amount you must save on average each year by pressing [CPT] and then [PMT].

9. *Compare the amount you have been planning on saving each year with the amount computed in item 8 and determine how you will be able to bring to two amounts into agreement. Recognize that if your current annual saving falls short of what you computed in item 8, you have four basic options that can be used in various combinations to make your savings equal to what you will need to save to achieve your retirement income goal given in question 1:*

Reducing your desired income at retirement.

Increasing the percentage of your income that you save.

Increasing your income, which will allow you to continue to save at your current rate.

Increasing the rate of appreciation on your investments.

RULE 3

Resist Temptation

One of the most persistently acclaimed personal virtues is frugality—save, don't waste your money. We have all heard Benjamin Franklin's famous aphorism: "A penny saved is a penny earned." Franklin was actually understating the case for saving. As we emphasize in the second chapter (Rule 2) and throughout this book, a penny saved can be many pennies earned. Like most advice that lasts for generations, there is wisdom in the advice to be frugal and save. Saving a certain percentage of your income is an important part of taking control of your life, paying yourself first, and improving your psychological and financial well-being in the process.

But frugality clearly requires some sacrifice. The money you save obviously cannot be currently spent on things you are tempted to buy. Everything we do in life requires some kind of tradeoff, and saving is certainly no exception to this elementary fact. The key is to sacrifice those things of lower value and to do so in such a way as to acquire the most value. Most people can save more than they do, far more in many cases, by resisting temptations to buy things that add little satisfaction to their lives. And the payoff for resisting these temptations can be very large.

The key to resisting temptation is in recognizing:

1. That there are plenty of things we can easily do without, or with less of.

2. That tremendous benefits can be achieved from being frugal.

Most people believe that they are just getting by on what they are now spending, when only a little thought would reveal that there is plenty they could eliminate and hardly miss. Do you really need that new CD, or the new cell phone just because it's a little smaller than the one you have? And most people are unaware of just how much they could realize over the long haul by cutting back on things that are largely superfluous to their well-being. Certainly we are in no position to determine what tradeoffs you should make. The costs and benefits of doing anything are, at their core, subjective, and so only you can really know the costs and benefits of saving. But we can recommend some temptations that most people can resist, and point out the impressive returns that can be realized as a reward for resisting them. Resisting temptation also creates more than just financial gains.

Resisting temptation establishes a sense of self-control that is an integral part of any satisfying life. It is summoning the strength to take control of your choices and choosing wisely and deliberately, rather than responding to things like a feather in the wind. It also helps to establish, in your own mind, a hierarchy of importance, enabling you to realize just what matters in your life.

Marshmallows, Resisting Temptation, and a Satisfying Life

The difficulty of resisting short-run temptations for the long-run gains of enjoying a more satisfying life, as well as doing better materially, has been born out in experiments with children.[1] The experiments started with four-year old children who were each taken into a room and given a marshmallow. Each child was told, "You can eat this marshmallow as soon as you want, but if you wait and don't eat it until I return in a little while, then I will give you a second marshmallow." When the experimenter left, the children were observed through a one-way window. Several of the children ate their marshmallows immediately, others tried to resist temptation but soon devoured theirs as well. And others were determined to wait, and soon received a second marshmallow.

The result of each child's experiment was recorded, and then the children's academic performance was followed through their later school years. Those children who had saved their first marshmallow until they received the second were later found to be, according to the researchers, better adapted and more popular, and they exhibited more confidence and responsibility than those children who could not delay gratification. Also, those who had resisted temptation scored an average of 20 to 25 percent higher on the Scholastic Aptitude Test (SAT), the test most widely used by colleges and universities to help predict academic success.

Needs vs. Wants

There are some things we all need. Food, clothing and shelter are basic and obvious needs. But even when considering the most basic needs, it is important to distinguish between what we *need* and what we *want*. There is a natural tendency for people to claim that they *need* certain things, such as a new car, a stylish coat, or a Caribbean vacation, when what they are really saying is: I *want* them. Not surprisingly, the urgency of such "needs" tends to be tied in to how much one has to pay for them. People tend to *need* a lot, for example, when they believe someone else is picking up the tab. Their needs generally become more moderate when they themselves are paying.

We both have children, so we developed firsthand knowledge about the difference between needs and wants as our children grew up. We both had the experience of taking our children shopping and being informed that they needed, for example, the most expensive outfit. Becoming weary of trying to explain why a less expensive brand would be just as serviceable, we have, on occasion, made our point in a more compelling and long-lasting way. We have given our children the cash to buy the items they claimed to need, letting them know that they could then spend it on those items—or anything else. This made it impossible for them to get the "needed" item without giving up other valuable alternatives. Most of the time, though not always, the children would decide that they could do without the item that they absolutely needed when it wasn't their money paying for it. When we agreed to pay for whatever clothing items they chose, it was our sacrifice and therefore painless to the kids. When we gave *them* the money in the form of an allowance to buy the clothing they chose, their choices changed—suddenly the cost was theirs to bear; and they had to decide just how important the "much needed" items were. With our children, we saw a rule at play that you should always keep in mind if you want to get rich: Make a clear distinction between what you need and what you want.

Clothes purchases can almost always be pared down, given that most of us have more changes of clothing than we really need and can always get by (for a short time, at least) without making new purchases. But what about the most basic of needs, food? Even here there is more latitude for saving than most people realize. Food is essential to maintain life, but almost all of us could spend far less on it than we do, and still get all the nutrition we need (perhaps even more than we do now). The supreme pizza with double cheese, delivered to the door, tastes awfully good with your favorite drink, followed by extra-rich ice cream. You might definitely want it, but you certainly don't need it. It has been estimated that a nutritious diet for an average adult male living alone can be purchased for $1,704 a year.[2] That is how much we *need* to spend on food, which is far less than the $3,268 that the average adult living alone actually spent on food and alcoholic beverages in 1995 (the latest year of available data).[3]

Please don't think that we are recommending that you switch to a diet of powdered milk and day-old bread. Neither of us has been near any powdered milk lately (we both were forced to drink the stuff in our youth). Nor are we really expecting anyone to spend no more than $1,704 a year on food. The point is: There is money to be saved in those food bills, without being deprived. A filet mignon tastes just as good, maybe even better, prepared at home on an outdoor grill rather than in a restaurant, and it costs a lot less. In addition, preparing a delicious meal at home, with that charcoal-flavored steak as the centerpiece, can be a pleasant family experience, with everyone helping out. And when you do go out to eat, choose a treat that you wouldn't ordinarily make a home (like lasagna instead of plain pasta) and consider resisting the alcoholic beverage with your meal, and the dessert after it—the drinks and desserts typically carry the largest markups. You can always enjoy a nightcap or a bowl of ice cream once you get home. Food is a basic need, but there are lots of creative ways to spend less on food with little real sacrifice.

It is important to note that frugality is not an all-or-none proposition. Like most things, it is measured along a continuum, and yes, people can be too frugal just as they can fail to be frugal enough. It makes no sense to eat boiled cabbage every night for years so you can feast on filet mignon when you have made a million. That's not just sacrificing to save, that's sacrificing satisfaction. Treat yourself and your family to a nice meal out on a special occasion—but think twice about the five-star restaurant. The key is in achieving balance—and as the Greeks would say, "Everything in moderation."

Life, Enjoyable at All Ages

"All right," you say, "I can get by on less than I spend, but what if I don't want to? I work hard, and the things I buy add a lot of pleasure to my life. Why shouldn't I spend my money while I can enjoy it?" And you're right; the decisions on spending or saving are ultimately yours. But as we said earlier, life is full of tradeoffs, and getting rich is no exception. You can spend everything you earn now and have nothing later. Or you can choose how to spend wisely, knowing that by spending a little less today you can spend a whole lot more tomorrow. The reality is that cutting back on spending will do little to reduce the pleasure of life, so the sacrifice required to significantly improve your future wealth isn't as painful as you

Time and Gratification

A fundamental problem in building a fortune and a satisfying life is that all too often the costs of what we do are incurred in the near term while the rewards are realized only in the distant future. This is the case when we consider denying ourselves cars or boats or drinks today in order to save and invest. The pain of the self-denial is immediate; the gain in the form of a larger net worth and higher income at retirement is, at least for young people, way off in the future.[4] The press to reap immediate gratification is so strong that we often buy things fully aware that we will regret the purchase later.

Psychologists and economists alike have documented people's bias toward immediate gratification, and their distorted decisions, in a variety of experiments. In one such experiment that has been widely replicated, the subjects in the experiment are given the choice of $100 to be received twenty-eight days from now or $120 to be received thirty-one days from now.[5] The subjects consistently choose the second option, perhaps reasoning that they would effectively get a 20 percent greater reward by waiting a mere three additional days. They apparently make that choice only because of the remoteness of the reward; three extra days of wait doesn't mean very much when tacked on to the minimum wait of twenty-eight days. We say that because when given a choice between $100 today or $120 three days from now, the subjects tend to choose the former. They don't want to wait an extra three days in spite of the fact that the 20 percent greater reward amounts to a return that is greater than they could get on any other investment (with the annualized rate of return on their delay in excess of 2,400 percent!).

It seems that people are hardwired to seek immediate gratification (perhaps because of our evolutionary history in which survival was the central daily problem). And the more immediate the gratification is received and the more remote in time the costs are incurred, the more likely the option will be taken. Similarly, the more immediate the costs and the more remote the gratification, the less likely the option will be chosen.

Building a sizable fortune can be a tough assignment simply because it requires us to go against our basic inclinations. This is where our allegiance to rules (or principles) of behavior become important. The act of committing ourselves to rules means that we have acknowledged their long-run value; it also means that we will be going back on what we know is the *right* thing to do when we go against the established rules. In this way, committing ourselves to rules creates the prospect of guilt and helps us to stand stronger against our nature to take immediate rewards when the costs are remote. Violations of the rules have their own immediate discomfort, if not pain. The trick is to make the *commitments* themselves count for something apart from the future gains; that is to say, the commitments must be valued in themselves.

believe. And the young readers out there who assume that life ceases to be much fun once you're really "old"—say, over forty—are simply wrong.

There are many things that older people enjoy more than the young. Take it from us, some of the better pleasures of life don't kick in until after fifty! McKenzie enjoys working in his yard far more now than he did twenty years ago. Rather than paying someone else a lot of money, he enjoys the pleasant pastime of landscaping and putting in a fishpond, which also adds value to his home. Lee enjoys taking long walks with his wife three to four evenings a week. The exercise is healthy, and the opportunity to have an uninterrupted conversation is wonderful. But all our pastimes aren't so cheap. We also enjoy golfing on resort courses and traveling to foreign countries, things we couldn't—and wouldn't—have done when we were half our current ages. And we can spend the money we do, while still saving for retirement, because when we were younger, we recognized the big financial payoff that could be realized from relatively small sacrifices.

The Cost of That New Car Smell

Let's now consider some temptations that most people can resist with little real sacrifice, but which, when they are resisted, allow savings that can accumulate to a significant amount of financial security over time. Let's begin with cars.

How much is it worth to have a new car instead of a used car? That new car smell is worth something, as is the satisfaction of driving the latest, right-off-the-showroom model. Unfortunately, the new car smell soon dissipates and the new car soon becomes used, if only by you. And you can end up paying quite a lot more for a new car than for an equivalent, or almost equivalent, used car.

For example, you would have paid about $26,000 for a brand-new 1998 Ford Taurus SHO (the midpoint between dealer invoice and suggested retail price on a 1997 model). You could have sold it one year later for about $16,225 (trade-in value in 1998 if it is in excellent condition), for a yearly depreciation cost of $9,775. On the other hand, if you buy a two-year-old Ford Taurus GL (a somewhat cheaper model than the SHO), you will pay about $12,400 (the midpoint between Blue Book suggested retail price and the trade-in value of the car in excellent condition). If you drive your used GL five years and then give it away, your yearly depreciation cost is only $2,480—a total saving of $7,295 a year over the one-year loss on the new more expensive Taurus SHO.[6]

Even if you choose not to buy a cheaper model, you can still save a lot by buying it used. For example, you can buy a top-of-the-line Toyota Camry brand-new for about $26,000. Although not considered a prestige car, the Camry is nice-looking and highly reliable. By driving sensibly and doing the routine maintenance, you can easily get 150,000 to 200,000 miles of service from a Camry. But when you drive your new $26,000 Camry off the lot, it depreciates quickly. If you sell it after 30,000 miles, you will get about $16,000, for a depreciation cost of 33 cents per mile.

Instead of buying a new Camry, you could buy the same model used with 30,000 miles on the odometer for about $18,000—$2,000 more than the original owner can sell it to a dealer. Assuming you take good care of it, you could easily drive it for 130,000 miles, at which time you can probably sell it for $1,000. So your depreciation cost is $17,000, for a per-mile cost of 13 cents, or 20 cents per mile less than the original owner paid.

Bob Becomes Serious About Saving

Bob loves to play golf. Indeed, Dwight Lee first met him when they were matched up in the same foursome. At fifty-three Bob is a millionaire, and so is able to play his favorite game frequently at nice resorts around the country and at his local country club. Bob's financial success would not have been predicted earlier in his career. At age thirty-two Bob was a college graduate, had done some graduate work, and had a steady job, but he had no savings and a net worth of almost zero. It was at that point in his life that he got serious about saving. He went to work as a representative for a large company helping individuals establish saving and retirement plans. Since he was advising his clients on the importance of being frugal, Bob decided to practice what he preached, and started his own saving program.

He did well at his job, making $65,000 to $80,000 a year by the early 1980s, and he consistently saved a little over 20 percent of what he made. In the mid–1980s he started his own financial consulting business with a partner, and, after a temporary dip, his income increased steadily and is now in the $150,000 to $175,000 range. And he kept up with his saving program, investing most of it in the mutual funds he was recommending to his clients. On his fifty-third birthday in 1998, Bob had a net worth of a little over $1.3 million.

Bob's financial success is impressive, but not that unusual. Since he didn't start his saving program until he was in his thirties, he lost some of the advantage that comes from letting compound interest start working its magic as soon as possible. But Bob did what most financially successful people do when they get started a little late. He became a prodigious saver. Bob is also happy to report that as his net worth has gone up, his handicap has come down.

This means that, if you drive 15,000 miles a year, you save $3,000 a year in depreciation cost if you buy the used car. Your repair costs will no doubt be higher with the used car. Making the pessimistic assumption that you have to pay $750 more a year on the used car than on the new car, you still save $2,250 per year with the used-car option.[7]

Before responding that buying used cars is demeaning, consider that millionaires commonly purchase them. Indeed, when millionaires buy a car, about 37 percent of the time they buy a used car.[8] This may be one reason they are millionaires. Buying used cars helps them do the saving that enables them to become millionaires. To see this point, consider an example. Instead of buying a new car and driving it for two years, assume you bought a used car and drove it a little over eight and a half years (as in the above example of the Camry) and invested the $2,250 savings every year at an 8 percent real return. If you began this practice at age twenty-three, about the time you get your first job out of college, when you are age sixty-seven you will have an addition to your total net worth of $869,638 (see Table 3.1).

Table 3.1.
Cost of Current Purchases in Terms of Lost Retirement Wealth at Age 67 at 8 Percent Rate of Return

PURCHASE	INCREASE IN RETIREMENT WEALTH
Buying a used Camry instead of a new one from ages 23 to 67	$869,638
Not buying a second car from ages 30 to 67	$440,632
Cooking steak dinner at home once a month from ages 25 to 67	$197,750
Buying a regular cup of coffee rather than a latte and taking a brown-bag lunch to work from ages 25 to 67	$282,700
Buying a $1,000 computer instead of a $3,000 computer every three years from ages 25 to 67	$219,832
Not making a one-time purchase of a $4,000 Rolex watch at age 30	$68,983
Spending $2,500 instead of $5,000 on an engagement ring at age 22 and saving until age 67	$79,801
Saving $5 a week redeeming coupons from ages 25 to 67	$85,692
Buying two pairs of $40 sneakers instead of $165 sneakers a year from ages 14 to 19	$73,745
Saving $1.50 a day on junk food, alcohol, and tobacco from ages 18 to 67	$290,363
Not spending $200 a year on lottery tickets from ages 18 to 67	$ 106,068

With that additional net worth at retirement, you could increase your retirement income by $34,786 a year (assuming an interest rate of 4 percent, after adjusting for inflation, on safe government bonds). With that income you and your spouse can afford to take a moderately priced round-the-world cruise every other year. Is the new car worth that? Think about it.

Some may argue that you can save money by leasing rather than buying a car. This can be true if you are considering a new car. With a leased car you don't pay sales tax on the entire value, only on the monthly lease payments. Also, for those who use their cars mostly for business, it is possible to write off as a business expense almost all of the lease payment, which is typically more than the depreciation and expense write-off possible if you buy a car. So if you are in a business in which it is important to show clients around in a new car, leasing can be a good idea. But leasing a new car is still far more expensive than buying a used car and driving it for several years.

You might also consider not buying that second car. Of course, in some circumstances a second car can be close to a necessity. But often there are ways to get by with one car with less inconvenience than you might think. Most second cars are for getting to and from work, and often commuting by public transportation or by carpooling with a friend are convenient, cheaper, enjoyable alternatives. Also, those who live within a mile or two of their offices, and many do, are often able to walk to work. A two-mile walk can be a pleasant activity that does more to get you going in the morning than drinking a strong cup of coffee, and it doesn't take much longer. Furthermore, you'll probably get more healthy exercise than some people do at their health clubs, and the walking is actually saving you money.

Not buying a second car is not a reasonable option for everyone, and even under the best of circumstances it can require some inconvenience. But the financial payoff can be great. Even if the car is used, the cost in depreciation, insurance, maintenance and repairs, gasoline, and parking is difficult to keep below $2,000 a year. Saving that $2,000 a year at 8 percent interest beginning at age thirty (an age when a couple is likely to be thinking about a second car) gives you an extra $440,632 at age sixty-seven.

Adding Up

The little things, as they say, do mean a lot—in love and in saving. Cutting back on some of the little expenditures can make a big difference. We now consider a number of small savings that are possible, but savings that can add up to far more than most people realize.

WHAT WE EAT

Let's return to food. We do not expect you to spend only $1,704 a year. But we suspect that many readers just might spend more than the average $3,268 a year on food. By resisting minor culinary temptations most people could save more than they realize over the course of a year, and convert that saving into a real bonanza at retirement.

For example, by grilling that steak in the back yard instead of going out to an upscale steak house, a couple can easily save $50. Make that change just once a month beginning at age twenty-five and you save $600 a year by cutting back a bit on dining out. That amount of yearly saving translates into an extra $197,750 at age sixty-seven, as shown in Table 3.1. Or assume that you resisted that $1.35 cup of Starbucks coffee every day (or save the $1.35 a day by buying the regular coffee instead of paying $2.70 for a latte, mocha, or cappuccino), plus another $7 a week by taking a brown-bag lunch to work one day a week, rather than eating lunch out. That would amount to a saving of $857.75 a year. If every year, beginning at age twenty-five, you invested this amount at 8 percent, at age sixty-seven your net worth will have grown by an additional $282,700 as shown in Table 3.1.

When it comes to resisting temptations, there are lots of possibilities where food is concerned. You can still eat out and treat yourself to that latte, and save elsewhere, giving up things that are less important to you. How much you cut back, and where, is your choice. But if you exercise your "wealth power" when it comes to spending on food and drink in ways that make you look and feel better, your saving can add up over time.

TOYS AND TRINKETS

Many people buy computers with far more capacity than they need to do the things they do. If, for example, you do basic word processing and computing, you might consider buying one of the super affordable computers every three years, which at this writing were priced at $999, instead of the high-price, high-performance model with all the bells and whistles, which was running about $3,000 at this writing. If you did this, and invested the yearly saving of $667 a year (assuming the computer lasts for three years), beginning at age twenty-five, you would have an additional $219,832 in net worth at retirement.

Or consider how, by spending less on telling time, you can make time do more to increase your wealth. Often people who are doing well financially like to tastefully advertise their purchasing power by wearing expensive watches. A $4,000 Rolex, for example, makes a statement about the discretionary income of its owner. But a $35 Casio electronic watch keeps time more accurately, and can also serve, among other things, as a calculator, a calendar, and an alarm clock. And you can replace electronic watches every couple of years, getting new and ever more useful models, for what it costs to have your Rolex serviced.

So let's assume that, instead of buying that $4,000 Rolex at age thirty, you invest the $4,000 at 8 percent and use the money you would have spent having the Rolex cleaned and serviced on an electronic watch. This one-time $4,000 investment will be worth $68,983 when you reach age sixty-seven, which means that your single resistance to buying the Rolex one time will enable you to have two-thirds the net worth of the median retiree.

Although we aren't making a recommendation here, you should also know that if you buy a $5,000 engagement ring at age twenty-two, instead of a $2,500 ring, the difference will cost you $79,801 in terms of lost retirement net worth. (We don't consider here the possible appreciation of the diamond because there are typically steep discounts when trying to resell). We're not trying to be unromantic, but consider how much difference that $79,801 can add to your golden years together.

Buying low-mileage used cars rather than new cars; not buying that second car; eating dinner out one time less a month; taking a brown-bag lunch once a week and consuming a little less specialty coffee, buying a less expensive engagement ring and electronic watches instead of a Rolex; purchasing the cheaper home computers are all manageable sacrifices. But the savings from just these consumption adjustments will, over a normal working career, increase your wealth by over $2.15 million (as can be added up from Table 3.1). That's a lot of money. It is enough money that you don't have to follow every suggestion and you'll still do just fine.

More Little Things

Of course, there are lots of people who are already driving a used car (or relying on public transportation), and who aren't buying specialty coffees, Rolex watches, high-powered computers, expensive diamond rings, or eating at fancy restaurants. And perhaps you're thinking that most of these people are not getting rich. True enough. But even these people typically spend money on lots of little things that can add up, and a surprising portion of this money could be saved with little inconvenience if you are alert to the opportunities. A little inconvenience can lead to a large payoff for those who are alert and patient.

Every weekend your local paper has pages of money-saving coupons that are redeemable at nearby stores. Seldom are these coupons worth more than 50 cents off, and many of them are for products you aren't interested in anyway, so it is easy to ignore them. This can be a big mistake. Of course, you shouldn't buy something you don't need just because you can "save" money on it. But it takes only a few minutes to find coupons adding up to several dollars on items you are going to buy. Cutting out those coupons and saving them for your next trip to the store is no more difficult than bending down to pick up a few dozen quarters lying on the sidewalk. So why not do it? Assuming that you save just $5 a week with coupons, or $260 a year, that small amount can add plenty to your retirement wealth. Saving $260 a year from ages twenty-five to sixty-seven at 8 percent will add up to $85,692, as shown in Table 3.1.

Teenagers, often from families without much money, commonly buy expensive sneakers that are more for fashion than function. Instead of buying that $165 pair of Air Jordans, you could purchase a pair of equally useful and maybe as durable sneakers for $40. Assuming the purchase of two pairs of sneakers a year from ages fourteen to nineteen, the money saved by purchasing the cheaper sneakers would, at 8 percent, grow to $73,745 by age sixty-seven, again shown in Table 3.1. We understand the value teenagers place on being fashionable, and a pair of generic sneakers might seem unacceptable. But it is worth considering the cost of fashion and how much fashion is really lost by buying a somewhat cheaper shoe.

By making some of the little savings today that can add up over time we could be physically healthier as well as financially wealthier. The money we could save by just cutting back (not eliminating entirely) on soft drinks, alcoholic beverages, junk food, and tobacco could easily add up to $1.50 a day, or $547.50 a year.[9] Saving this amount every year at 8 percent, beginning at age eighteen, adds up to a total of $290,363 at age sixty-seven.

Many people who are convinced they lack the income to save somehow find the money to buy lottery tickets on a regular basis. According to Duke University economists Charles Clotfelter and Philip Cook, "The average person in the lowest income class spends 2 percent of his household income on state lottery tickets."[10] This comes to $400 a year for someone with a household income of only $20,000 a year. Of course, gamblers get, on average, about 50 percent of their lottery wagers back in "winnings," which means we are talking about a loss of $200 per year. And this is the average, meaning that many people with incomes in the $20,000 a year range lose more every year gambling. If instead of losing $200 a year gambling, a person beginning at age eighteen saved that amount at an 8 percent return, he would have $106,068 when he reached sixty-seven.

There are many other possibilities for small saving that can add up to a significant amount of wealth over time. And yet, out of an exhaustive list of savings possibilities, only a few are necessary for accruing big long-term savings. And, of course, those sacrifices that are right for your neighbor may not be right for you. The saving of just $5 a week with money-off coupons; buying cheaper sneakers during the teenage years; cutting back $1.50 a day on junk food, alcohol, and tobacco; and not gambling can easily accumulate to well over half a million dollars ($555,868 to be exact) by the time a person retires at age sixty-seven (see Table 3.1).

You may be thinking that few people, particularly young people from modest backgrounds, will choose to start, and continue, to save the kind of money necessary to accumulate the significant sums we are talking about. And you are right. For many, the immediate gratification derived from spending what they have now will be more tempting than the long-run rewards of financial success. But surely the number who do decide to save and invest, or who save and invest a little more than otherwise, can be increased by an increased awareness of what can be gained by resisting temptation and delaying gratification.

Strengthening Your Resolve

While we hope to give you helpful suggestions for resisting temptation today for long-run gain, the most important factor in saving money is the dedication that can come only from you. The advantages of saving and investing are tremendous, but we know they can occasionally pale next to immediate satisfactions. Fortunately, there are ways of strengthening your resolve in the face of temptations by concentrating on the immediate advantages of savings, and reducing the immediate costs.

Psychologically it can be best not to think of saving as a sacrifice at all, but rather as a way to pay yourself first. As a caller from Green Bay, Wisconsin, said to Dwight Lee on a radio talk show, "I don't think of my savings as a sacrifice, I think of it as purchasing financial freedom." That sense of financial freedom is realized immediately, and it is a benefit that is not measured entirely by the increased ability to buy more things in the future. The knowledge that with increasing wealth come increasing options on such things as when you can retire, the type of job you can take, is valuable right now.

Obviously, the additional purchasing power is important. But there is great value to being frugal quite apart from the money you accumulate. There is a sense of security that comes from saving and investing. It is difficult to put a value on the peace of mind that you get from knowing that you have a financial cushion in case of unforeseen problems. But the value of that comfort is not insignificant, and is best appreciated by comparing it with the mental anxiety that comes from constantly being in financial distress.

- Establishing a saving and investment plan also provides the immediate satisfaction that comes from taking more control over your life. The frugal person who resists the temptation to spend to the limit is actively taking charge of her prospects, and a number of studies suggest that such control is a major factor in how happy we are. Those who see their situations determined primarily by "internal" control are found to have happier and more satisfied lives than those who see themselves largely subject to "external" control.[11] Charles Dickens's Mr. Micawber was surely correct when he famously said, "If a man had twenty pounds a year for his income, and spent nineteen pounds nineteen shillings and sixpence, he would be happy, but that if he spent twenty pounds one he would be miserable."

- Make a game out of saving. People get enjoyment out of collecting things and keeping count of what they have. So think of your saving program as a game in which you are keeping score of how well you are doing. Your score can quickly take on a significance that is largely independent of the monetary value of your saving. This explains why setting a goal is such a good idea. A goal makes your count more meaningful and thus provides additional, and immediate, motivation for making progress toward the objective. So establish saving goals, short-term and long-term goals, and keep count of how your savings grow. When you achieve one goal, reevaluate and establish new ones. If you do, your ability to resist spending temptations will be fortified by the immediate satisfaction of the progress you are making.

- Reduce the immediate cost of saving. The federal government learned a long time ago that more taxes could be extracted from the public if paying taxes is made to seem less costly. That is the explanation for withholding taxes directly from workers' paychecks. Since workers never see the money, they don't miss it, at least not as much as they would if they had to write a big check at the end of the year. Indeed, some workers have their tax withholdings increased so they will get a refund from the government—they don't miss the withholding but they enjoy the refund. A far better idea is for you to have the minimum legal amount deducted by the government and have your employer start deducting money that goes directly into an account that pays. Most employers have plans for doing this, and you won't miss the money going directly into your account any more than you will the money going directly to the government. Then, if you owe taxes at the end of the year, you can pay it somewhat painlessly and have the interest left over.

- Many employers offer what are known as 401(k) plans—or 403(b) plans for those in education—in which money is deducted from your paycheck and invested, with the savings deducted from your taxable income. And no tax is imposed on the savings and accumulation until after you retire, assuming you leave it invested until then. Not only do you not miss the money because it is deducted, but because it isn't taxed, your take-home income falls by less than your savings. For example, if your marginal income tax rate is 35 percent, putting an additional $100 in a savings plan will reduce your taxes by $35, and so your take-home pay declines only $65. If you salt away $2,000 a year in one of a variety of ways to avoid taxes, your take-home pay will fall by only $108 a month, or about $1,300 a year. Often employers will supplement employee contributions to a 401(k) or 403(b) by matching some percentage of the employee's contribution, which makes it an even better deal—check with your employer for details. And while there are limits on how much you can save with before-tax dollars, the limits are generous enough to allow people to save an amount that can make them quite wealthy at retirement if they start saving early. As of this writing the maximum contribution to a 401(k) or 403(b) is $10,000 a year. By taking full advantage of this tax-reducing way to save, you can significantly reduce the immediate cost of saving.

Another way to make it easier to save is by making it harder to yield to spending temptations. One of the best ways to do this, particularly for those who run up credit card debt, is by simply getting rid of credit cards. Not only does credit card debt make it easier to spend more, it adds 14 to 18 percent more in interest payments to the cost of what you buy. There is almost no way a person who keeps a big balance on her credit cards can get rich. The best thing such a person can do, if she is serious about getting rich, is to cut up every credit card she has and tear up every credit card application she receives in the mail. For every dollar you don't spend because you have no credit card, you will have $1.22 to $1.26 more at the end of the year—the dollar you saved, plus an 8 percent return, plus the 14 to 18 percent you didn't have to pay in interest to the credit card company. This represents a 22 to 26 percent return on your savings.

Individual Retirement Accounts (IRAs)

The purpose of resisting temptation is not to resist temptation per se, but to add to your savings and to build your net worth. We anticipate that the less costly it is for you to save, the more you will save. If you save in ways that make the savings tax deductible, the savings are less costly to you in terms of spendable income. If you are in a 30 percent tax bracket and you save an additional $1,000 in a tax-deductible way, the cost of saving $1,000 will be only $700. This is because you can deduct the $1,000 from your taxable income, which means your required tax payment will go down by $300 ($1,000 in savings minus $300 in reduced tax payments equals $700 reduction in spendable income).

In addition to 401(k) plans mentioned in the body of this chapter, in which your money is deducted from your paycheck and invested without being taxed, there is also the possibility of contributing to an Individual Retirement Account (IRA), which can be invested in a wide variety of ways, and deducting the contribution from taxable income. Each taxpayer can contribute up to $2,000 a year (a taxpayer with a nonworking spouse can contribute $2,250), and the tax deduction is gradually phased out when your income exceeds certain amounts— the amount depends on your marital status and whether you file singly or jointly (see a tax accountant for the current details). Your IRA investment grows tax-free until you retire, at which point you pay taxes on your withdrawals at the tax rate that applies to your retirement income.

In 1997 Congress added another IRA option, called the Roth IRA. Again you can contribute up to $2,000 a year, but the contribution does not reduce your taxable income. But with the Roth IRA the investment not only grows tax-free, but beginning at age fifty-nine and a half it can be withdrawn tax-free. For people who are in a low tax bracket now, but who expect to save a lot, retire wealthy, and be in a high tax bracket during retirement, the Roth IRA can be a better deal than a regular IRA. Keep in mind that the Congress has a tendency to keep changing the details of these retirement options, so check with a tax accountant for the latest details and to find out which option is best for you.

For those who are self-employed, there are also ways to save with dollars that are not taxed. A Keogh plan allows a self-employed worker to save as much as 20 percent of his income, up to $30,000 a year (again, provisions of the tax law are subject to change any time the Congress is in session) and deduct that saving from his taxable income. As with the regular IRA, the growth in your Keogh investment is not taxed until you start withdrawing it at retirement.

Of course, credit cards are almost essential for some things, like renting a car away from home. For those who need a credit card for such occasions, but who are prone to run up debt, consider freezing the card in water so you have to plan ahead to use it. For those who aren't as tempted by credit card debt as some, but who want to reduce the temptation without giving up the convenience of a credit card in their wallets rather than in a bowl of frozen water, there are other possibilities. Most American Express credit cards, for example, require you to pay off the entire amount every month, which means you pay no interest at all. Or instead of a credit card, you can carry a bank debit card that allows you to spend only as much as you have in your checking account. Again, you are not subject to interest charges on your purchases. Another, though less constraining possibility, is to carry a credit card but ask for a small debt limit. The bottom line? If you want to get rich, don't carry any credit card debt.

By taking advantage of some of these suggestions you are not only more likely to start and stay with a saving and investing program, you will find it possible to maximize the savings possible for every dollar reduction in current spending. Set a saving goal, make it challenging, and consider it a challenge worth accomplishing.

Always keep in mind that by meeting rather modest saving goals each year, you can purchase a surprising amount of financial freedom over a lifetime.

Saving Is Productive

Resisting temptation to increase your savings pays, and it pays for very good reason. Saving is a productive activity. By being patient, savers produce more than they currently consume and make the difference available to borrowers who are not so patient—those who place a higher current value on extra money than the saver. In other words, saving is productive because it allows scarce resources to be moved from lower-valued to higher-valued uses. Some borrowers want more now because they are impatient to consume. Other borrowers want more now to invest in what they believe are profitable opportunities. In both cases, the borrowers are willing to pay a premium, in the form of interest or ownership in appreciating (they hope) corporate stock, for the savings of others. And by reinvesting the return, the saver increases his productivity exponentially over time, as the total amount she contributes to others is continuously compounded.

Those who become wealthy through saving do so the way most people become wealthy in a market economy: by contributing to the general wealth of the economy and to the welfare of others. A person may not earn much on the job, but if he saves enough for long enough, his saving will allow him to *earn* a high income. The income from saving is often called "unearned" income. Don't believe it. There is nothing unearned about the income generated by the productivity from saving.

Expenditures as Investments

In extolling the virtues of saving, it's important not to belittle the significance of spending. Indeed, the primary purpose of working and saving is to have *more* money to spend. What's the point of having lots of money if you aren't going to enjoy it? It is a really a question of when to enjoy it, a little now, a lot more in the future, or some compromise between the two.

If you want to accumulate more money, it is worth keeping in mind that not all expenditures are the same. Most expenditures are best thought of as consumption, which, no matter how justified they are, reduce the amount of money you will have in the future. On the other hand, some expenditures (on education or even an annual vacation, for example) allow us to be more productive in the future and so they add to, rather than subtract from, our future income and savings. Such expenditures are really investments and can provide a significant rate of return.

For example, if you buy a personal computer for your home, it might seem like most other expenditures; you deduct it from your bank balance and potential savings. But the computer can be much more like saving because it can add to your future income stream by enabling you to do additional work for your employer or develop your own business. What you do with your own computer now can affect your credentials and market value in the future. If you do nothing more than play games on the computer, the purchase is pure consumption; if you write books or do reports on it, it is an investment.

Many people wonder if they should buy a personal computer or if they can *afford* one. A computer is a big-ticket item, and people are smart to give the purchase of one careful consideration. But the reality is that many people cannot afford not to have personal computer. Whether you can afford to buy a computer (or a fax machine or a modem connection to the World Wide Web) depends on whether the current value of the increase in your future income from your use of the computer would be greater than the computer's cost. (See the box on page 68 for a discussion of why you might even want to use your own money to buy a computer for your office.)

There are other examples of expenditures that can pay for themselves financially, plus pay dividends in quality of life. Hardworking people in high-pressure jobs need to take time off occasionally to recharge if they are to maintain their productivity over the long haul. So, however much there is to do, take periodic vacations to relax, read a novel, and try to forget about work for a while. The cost of these leisure activities is more than returned in the increased energy and productivity that results. Membership in a health club, if it motivates you to get more exercise, can be both an enjoyable consumption expenditure and a good financial investment in good health and future productivity. And one of the most important expenditures you can make is on education. Getting a good education and continuing one's education are excellent investments in the future. As deeply satisfying and enjoyable as learning can be, a good education will also almost always more than pay for itself in higher future income.

How much financial freedom you purchase by resisting temptation and saving is up to you. But always keep in mind, wealth is not something that just happens to some and not to others. You have a lot of control over how wealthy you become. How you exercise that control is your choice.

Don't Let Your Boss Hold You Back

Should you buy a computer upgrade (or any other office machine) for use on the job when your boss will not? Yes—don't let your boss hold you back if the estimated gains that you can expect to receive over your career from buying the computer exceed the cost of the computer. If the computer costs $1,500 and you estimate the gains over several years to be $2,500 in today's dollars, buy it! To do otherwise would be to leave $1,000 of net gains to you on the table. Imagine how much that $1,000 of additional savings can add to your net worth at retirement (better yet, run the numbers yourself). And don't fret about the gains your boss will receive from your purchase.

What are the potential gains to you from something you use in your firm? Improved computer skills that are marketable is one potential benefit, given that other employers will likely pay you more if you know more. The cost of the computer can easily be recovered by a minor increase in your market wage. If other employers are willing to pay you more because of your greater computer skills and experience, then your employer will have to do the same to keep you.

Back in 1981 personal computers were still an oddity and a luxury in university offices, and they also were not very good by today's standards. Nevertheless, we were all amazed at what they could do. My (McKenzie's) university did not have the funds to buy me a computer. Nevertheless, I bought my own, an Intertech Data System "Superbrain." It had 64K of RAM and two large floppy disk drives. Plus I bought a printer (which was no more than a reconfigured IBM Selectric typewriter) and a word processing program. The entire system cost me about $12,000 in today's dollars. But never mind, I made the purchase with some pleasure because I figured that the computer would enable me to write and publish more articles and books, the value of which would more than cover the considerable cost of the system—and it worked! I have never regretted the purchase of that first system, or any of the ones I bought throughout the 1980s. I'm sure I would be poorer today by tens of thousands of dollars had I let my university hold me back.

Don't be scared off by how much something costs or by the fact that someone else won't buy what you think you need. If it doesn't pay *on balance*, resist the temptation, or you will be poorer as a result. If it pays *on balance*, buy it. You will be richer if you do. Just don't let your boss (or firm) hold you back.

Practical Advice for the Good Life

Saving for the long term requires financial discipline. Ultimately this discipline comes from within you and is rooted in willpower, determination, and desire. But there are some things you can do to reduce the external temptations that can undermine your financial discipline.

- Reconsider your life's goals that you may have developed after reading the first chapter, and let those goals guide your choices about what expenditures to curb partially or altogether. Always remember that exercising control over your life is far more satisfying than being manipulated by outside distractions and temptations, and responding to the whims of the moment.
- Make a list of your monthly expenditures and identify cuts that are consistent with your goals. Estimate how much the cuts can boost your savings on a monthly and yearly basis. Then, using the methods for calculating your net worth at retirement that were developed in chapter 2 (Rule 2), estimate how much the cuts in your expenditures will boost your retirement net worth.
- Tie your saving goal to a resolution to give up something that you have been wanting to give up anyway, such as smoking, gambling, or eating all those between-meal snacks out of the vending machine. This can help you do two good things at the same time: Give up a bad habit and free up more money to save.
- Once you have estimated how much you can increase your monthly savings, make your savings automatic, and take advantage of tax-deferred saving programs.
- Pay off any credit card debt. Reducing that debt is the same as receiving a 14 to 18 percent return on your savings, which is probably better than you can consistently get on alternative investments.
- If you have trouble resisting the temptation of using your credit card, cut up your cards, and use a bank debit card.
- If you feel that you must use a credit card for convenience but still worry about being unable to control your expenditures, use a credit card that requires the entire balance to be paid off at the end of the month or call your credit card company and ask for a credit limit that is less than the company will allow and well within your ability to handle.
- Always keep in mind that even little additions to your savings will add up to big increases in your retirement wealth. Save your leftover change every night and watch it add up at the end of each month. Adding your saved change to your monthly saving can make a big difference over the long run. (Indeed, to see what we mean before you start saving your change, assume

that you put aside 65 cents a day in change every day and figure out how much more net worth you will have at retirement time. You will likely be surprised at your calculation.)

- When you go shopping (especially in grocery stores), bring a shopping list. Carry a hand calculator to keep a running total of your intended purchases. Remember that most people who go shopping invariably spend more than they intended to before they reached the stores.

- Establish financial goals for the next year, the next five years, and retirement. Buy a copy of a personal accounting program like Quicken on which you can keep records of your purchases, savings, and net worth. Make a game out of your saving program and achieving and exceeding your goals, a process that can be of value apart from the money being saved. Become a little compulsive about saving.

- Save any money you receive over and above your normal income, say an inheritance, a holiday gift, a bonus at work, a garage sale, or an insurance reimbursement on a medical bill. Consider such "windfalls" a bonus, which you can multiply several times over through saving and prudent investments.

- If you live with someone, make separate budget allocations, after some agreed-upon amount has been set aside for saving. Separate budgets ensure that the cost of expenditures will not be shared, hence, that each person will incur the full cost of the purchases. Separate budget allocations can encourage each person to be more frugal than he would otherwise be.

- Concentrate on the feeling of security, personal freedom, and satisfaction that comes from having a growing financial base as you move toward retirement. Retirement may be a long time in the future, but the security and satisfaction of knowing you are achieving your financial goals for retirement can be enjoyed right now.

An Exercise for Achieving the Good Life: Finding Ways to Cut Back

We all buy things on the spur of the moment, and we all have bad habits. This exercise will help you lower your expenditures on a monthly and yearly basis by simply cutting out "excesses. It will also help you realize how much more you can have in the way of added net worth at retirement by simply resisting a few temptations. To make the calculations, you will need the hand calculator used in the exercise at the end of the second chapter (Rule 2).

1. Make a list of six things you buy on a monthly basis but could do with less or do without altogether (for example, movie tickets, meals out, soft drinks, and candy). Roughly estimate how much you spend on each item per month. Then indicate how much less you can spend on each item.

2. Now, add the total savings possible and multiply by twelve (feel free to extend your list beyond six items).

3. Determine the potential increase in your net worth if you make the cuts in your purchases each year indicated in question 2, assuming an annual return of 8 percent. Follow these steps on your Texas Instrument BA II or 35 hand calculator:

> Press [2nd] and then press [MODE].
> Enter the total from question 2 and press [PMT].
> Enter 8 and press [%i].
> Enter the number of years until retirement (your target retirement age minus your current age) and press [N].
> Calculate the potential increase in your net worth by pressing [CPT] and then [FV].

RULE 4

Get a Good Education

Probably the most common advice kids get as they grow up is: Get a good education. That means stay in school, study hard, learn as much as you can, and get good grades. And it's good advice. Education is one of the best foundations for financial success.

But getting a good education is a worthwhile idea even if your goal is not to get rich. There are many reasons to stay in school and study hard that have nothing to do with becoming financially well off. A good education can be the springboard to a life rich in knowledge and appreciation of a wide range of physical and intellectual wonders. And while our primary concern is with the financial gains derived from education, we believe that those gains are most likely to be realized when education is pursued first for the love of knowledge and second for financial reasons. As with all of our rules for building a fortune, getting a good education is also a good rule for living a satisfying life. It is a wonderful way to develop interests and insights that will enrich your life, and will make it possible for you to realize more enjoyment from the extra money that normally comes with more education.

There is plenty of evidence showing a positive relationship between education and income. For example, consider Table 4.1, which shows the median income for families whose heads have different levels of education. Based on this table, the best financial advice we could give a tenth grade student who is thinking about dropping out of school to get a job and buy a car is: Stay in school and forget the car, as it will cost you *several million dollars*. This is the advice (adjusted for inflation) that Dwight Lee's father gave him quite a number of years ago when he was thinking about dropping out of high school (yes, even people who go on to get Ph.D.'s often didn't do that well in, or like, high school). Table 4.1 suggests that completing high school will increase your annual income from $24,575 to $38,563, or an extra $13,988 a year. That is a lot of income to sacrifice to start working at a job that will almost surely be less enjoyable than school, and less enjoyable than the higher-paying jobs available to those with at least a high school diploma.

Table 4.1.
How Education Adds to Income

EDUCATION	MEDIAN HOUSEHOLD INCOME (1996)
Less than 9th grade	$20,781
9th to 12th (no diploma)	$24,575
High school graduate	$38,563
Some college (no degree)	$44,814
Associate degree	$51,176
Bachelor's degree	$64,293
Master's degree	$76,065
Professional degree	$102,557
Doctorate degree	$92,316

Source: U.S. Bureau of the Census, Current Population Reports, P60–197, Money Income in the United States: 1996 (Washington, D.C.: U.S. Government Printing Office, 1997), p. 18.

Of course, Table 4.1 gives the "median incomes" of those who have achieved various education levels. This means that half of the people in each educational category make more and half of the people make less than the amounts indicated, so not all high school graduates will earn more than some high school dropouts. But you are taking a very unwise risk by thinking you will be the exception to the rule. Let's consider one measure of what you will likely lose.

The average high school graduate would not immediately upon graduation make $13,988 a year more than the average dropout. Some of the extra pay would come only with years of experience on a job requiring a high school diploma. Moreover, some of the income gains from having a high school diploma will be soaked up in taxes.

Still, by making some conservative assumptions we can give you a preliminary idea of what the high school diploma is worth. We assume that the take-home (or after-tax) difference in earning between the high school graduate and the dropout is $8,000 a year at age eighteen. Also, let's assume that this difference increases at 1.5 percent a year until retirement at age sixty-seven, at which point the difference in after-tax earnings is $16,593 a year.[1] Finally, let's assume that the difference in take-home pay is invested each year from ages eighteen to sixty-seven in assets that earn 8 percent each year. Would you believe that the high school graduate's net worth would be almost $5.5 million dollars ($5,496,806 to be exact) more than it would be if he dropped out of high school? Now we don't expect that high school graduates will spend no more than high school dropouts earn, and invest the difference. Much of the advantage of the extra income comes from the joy of spending it before retirement. But that means that the benefit of the extra education is actually greater than the almost $5.5 million at retirement, because if retirement wealth is what a high school student valued most, he can have it.

Table 4.1 suggests an even higher payoff to continuing an education beyond high school and earning at least a college degree. As can be seen in the table, the median difference in annual family income between a high school and college graduate is $25,730 ($64,293 minus $38,563). Assuming conservatively that this difference, after taxes, begins at $13,500 at age twenty-two and increases by 1.5 percent a year until retirement at age sixty-seven, at which time the difference will reach $26,382. If these after-tax differences are invested at an annual return of 8 percent from ages twenty-two to sixty-seven, they will have accumulated to almost $6.75 million. These figures indicate that education pays off big time financially.

Again we want to emphasize, we do not expect that a college graduate would ever save all the difference between her income and that of a high school graduate. The biggest advantage of making more money is being able to spend more money and, as we have noted earlier, there is little sense in living the life of a miser for most of your life so you can spend enormous sums after you retire. But our figures provide a rough measure of how much a high school and college degree *could* be worth at retirement. It's not surprising that "Get a good education!" is such common advice.

Some Qualifications

We don't think it is a good idea, however, to make the case for education entirely in terms of the financial advantages. You should never forget the other advantages of education. A good education can provide satisfactions that no amount of money can buy. And the return to education in the form of a better understanding and appreciation of the many amazing features of the world around us is a return that government has not yet figured out how to tax. Also, as great as the financial advantage to education is, there are four qualifications that bear mention.

First, just because those with higher education earn more money does not mean that the additional education necessarily *caused* all of the higher income. Those with the talent and ambition to do well in school find that those attributes also help them succeed financially even if they don't get a lot of education. Consider Microsoft chairman Bill Gates. He dropped out of Harvard soon after founding (with Paul Allen) Microsoft in the summer of 1975. Who can believe that Bill Gates would have done better financially by staying in school and earning a Ph.D., instead of dropping out to become an entrepreneur? The point is simple: The financial success of those who stay in school cannot be attributed entirely to schooling.

Yet, for most people, getting a good education remains the surest path to a higher income. Education affords people an opportunity to uncover and develop their talents. Education can open new vistas for students and excite their ambition. Also, always keep in mind how the sheer enjoyment of your work can affect how much money you will make. According to a *Fortune* magazine article on those who become wealthy, "A striking number of wealthy entrepreneurs interviewed . . . had the same advice on how to get rich. As one [entrepreneur] put it, 'Do what you like and the money will come.'"[2] Of course what you like can have a significant influence on how much money comes your way. But if you go into an occupation, say accounting, just because you hear that most accountants make lots of money, you are unlikely to be very successful or highly paid if you don't enjoy the work. So an important advantage of getting a good education is that it exposes you to a wide variety of subjects and possibilities, and this exposure can increase your chances of discovering what you really enjoy.

Second, the additional income associated with more education, even if attributed entirely to the education, is not all gain. Like everything else, education is costly. Much of the cost is obvious, such as expenditures for tuition, books, and supplies (expenses for food and lodging are not all costs of education since much, if not all, of that expense has to be paid regardless of what you are doing). Usually the greatest cost of education (particularly a college education) is the earnings that are foregone while in school. For a high school graduate with good job prospects, the opportunity cost of going on to (or staying in) college can be quite high (remember Bill Gates), and it is really high for a college graduate thinking about going to graduate school. When figuring the financial gain from additional education, all the costs of that education have to be taken into consideration.

A third qualification concerning the connection between education and income is that at some point additional education can actually *reduce* your potential lifetime income. For example, those who pursue Ph.D.'s in eighteenth-century English literature or ancient languages will generally make less money than those who spend less time in college getting a professional degree such as a master's in business administration or a law degree. Looking at Table 4.1, for example, we see that the median family income for a family headed by a person with a doctorate was $92,316 a year, while the median family income for a family headed by a person with a professional degree was $102,557 a year.

Fourth, you should not forget that the longer you stay in school, the later you start earning income, and the less time there is to earn an income before retirement. As we saw under Rule 2, missing out on a few additional years of the magic of compound interest can have a very large impact on wealth accumulation. The potential benefit, in terms of retirement wealth, of having an MBA over a Ph.D. does not come only from the added annual salary. Some of the difference is that it takes more years for someone to earn a Ph.D. than an MBA, and that means less time for the power of compound interest to work on your savings. So Table 4.1 can give a misleading sense of the actual financial advantage of education because it doesn't account for the delay in receiving the higher earning from additional schooling.

The Rate of Return on Education

When considering the financial value of college, keep in mind that when given a choice between a dollar today and a dollar of the same purchasing power (after adjusting for inflation) a year from today, nearly everyone will choose the dollar today. The dollar today is worth more because people are impatient; they would rather have things now than have to wait for them. This impatience explains the positive rate of return, or interest, on savings. People are willing to pay for the privilege of spending now rather than later, so those who are patient enough to postpone their spending are paid a bonus for making their savings available to those who genuinely need it—or think they need it—now. This is why being patient by resisting short-run temptations is one of the keys to becoming rich. By being patient, you can satisfy the demands of the impatient people and, in the process, receive a rate of return that, when compounded over a career, can cause your savings to grow into millions of dollars.

But a positive rate of return on saving means that education is not quite as good a deal financially as indicated earlier. The money that is spent on the additional education, plus the earnings that have to be sacrificed, could have been invested in assets and generated a return that somewhat offsets the higher income from education.

To illustrate the importance of comparing the money foregone in getting additional education to the additional money earned when considering the financial value of education, we extend one of our previous examples. As shown earlier, if a college graduate began, immediately upon graduation, saving all the added after-tax income that she earned (above what could have been earned with a high school diploma), those savings would be worth about $6.75 million (assuming an 8 percent annual return) at age sixty-seven. This example, however, is incomplete because it ignores the cost of getting a college degree.

Instead of going on to college, a high school graduate could have immediately started working and earning an income, and also have saved the money paid by the college student on books and tuition. Assume that the high school student can make an after-tax income of $18,000 a year for the first four years out of high school.[3] Assume also that if she had gone to college she would have had to pay out $7,000 a year for four years for books, tuition, and supplies that otherwise would not have been spent.[4] If the high school–educated worker had invested the $25,000 each year at 8 percent from age nineteen (one year after graduating from high school) until she would have graduated from college four years later, and never saved another dime after that, she would have about $3.6 million at age sixty-seven. This is an investment the college student cannot make since she is foregoing the $18,000 a year income and paying out $7,000 a year while in college. Of course, upon graduation from college her additional income will let her spend as much as the high school graduate and save enough to have $6.75 million at age sixty-seven (as figured earlier). So the difference between $6.75 million and $3.6 million, or $3.15 million, can be thought of as a measure of the value of a college education.

Clearly, going to college pays off financially, but not by as much as indicated by our earlier discussion. We should emphasize once more that this example is not meant to suggest that a high school graduate will save every after-tax dime earned for the first four years after graduation, plus an additional $7,000 a year to account for the out-of-pocket expenditure if she had gone to college. And neither is a college graduate going to live on a high school graduate's income in order to save the rest of her after-tax earnings. But with our examples we are able to obtain a ballpark measure of the value of a college degree in terms of potential added wealth at retirement.

Another way of evaluating education is by comparing its rate of return to the rate of return from other investments. The earnings you forgo while in college, and all that money spent on books and tuition, are really an investment; they represent a sacrifice you make now in the expectation that you will receive a future return. The extra income you make in the future because of the education is the return to that investment. The *rate of return*, expressed as a percentage, is the actual annual dollar return divided by the investment made to get the return.

How does the financial rate of return from education compare with the rate of return on other investments, such as investing in the stock market? In the above example, the rate of return to the college education is clearly higher than 8 percent since saving the cost of going to college at 8 percent until age sixty-seven came to less than saving the extra earning from going to college at 8 percent until age sixty-seven. A large number of studies have attempted to measure the financial return to education.[5] These studies are never completely accurate,[6] but most of them conclude that the financial return of an *additional* year of education is somewhere in the range of 6 to 9 percent.[7] This rate of return may not seem that great since (as mentioned under Rule 2 and will be explained further under Rule 7) you can get around 8 percent return just by investing in a Standard & Poor's Index mutual fund. So what is so great about education, at least financially, if it doesn't pay any better than an investment in the stock market? That's a good question, and there's a good answer.

When you get an 8 percent return on your money in the stock market, that is the *average* return; you get the same 8 percent on every dollar invested. But the 6 to 9 percent return on education cited above refers to the return to investing in *one more year* of education. For example, the rate of return a student receives from going to the fourth year of college may be 8 percent. But this is not the same as an 8 percent average return for *all* four years spent in college, or the years of education before college.

In general, the return to the early years of education is higher than the return to the later years. For example, the return on the year of education during which a future accountant learned to read at a basic level and to do basic arithmetic is very high, as it is for all of us. And so is the return on the next few early years of education when we rapidly improved and expanded our skills. Indeed, that extremely high return on the early years of education explains why most people would stay in school until age sixteen, even without laws requiring them to do so. But as we stay in school longer the financial return on an additional year eventually starts declining. For any number of reasons, some people find that after, say, a high school education, the expected rate of return to another year of education becomes low enough that they have little motivation to continue. Most people who go on to college find that the return to another year of education beyond their college degree has declined to the point where it does not pay to continue. And for almost everyone, the return to another year of education beyond a professional degree or a Ph.D. has declined to the point where it doesn't pay to continue as a student.[8] So the financial return a person receives from all of his years of education can be quite high, say 20 to 25 percent, even though the return to their last year of education may be as low as, say, 6 percent.

The fact that most people tend to continue their education until the return on an additional year has fallen to 6 to 9 percent is not surprising. It makes sense for people to increase their investment in education until the return on the additional dollar is about the same as it would be on the best alternative investment. If the rate of return on the last $1,000 spent on education is 12 percent and the return on the money invested in the stock market is 8 percent, it makes sense to shift the funds invested in the stock market to the purchase of more education.

So until the return on another year of education is about the same as, say, the 8 percent a person can earn by investing in the stock market, it pays to continue investing in education.[9] Furthermore, since much of the return on education is not financial, but measured in terms of the personal satisfaction realized from improving our understanding of the world and learning useful skills, many people will continue their education even though the *financial* return to the additional year is less than available on alternative investments.

So the *total* return to education is much higher than academic studies seem to suggest. By concentrating on the return to the last year of education, those studies ignore the much higher return on all the previous years. And by considering only the financial return to education, those studies ignore the fact that some of the most valuable benefits from education have nothing to do with money.

Discovering What You Like

It is important to keep emphasizing that the return on education extends beyond the financial gains, however substantial those gains may be. The educated person will lead a richer, more satisfying life than the uneducated one, even if their incomes are exactly the same. This is worth noting, even in a book about financial success, because those who are motivated in school primarily by the joy of learning will tend to have a richer life both financially and in general than those who are pursuing an education only to make more money. Getting a good education requires a genuine excitement about the ideas and topics being studied, and that excitement should be an important guide when deciding what to study. But it should also be emphasized that not all educational paths are equal in their financial impact. Those who become interested in accounting, electrical engineering, or medicine will, *on average*, do far better financially than those who become interested in drama, dead languages, or dance history.

How Financing College Education Has Changed

The chart below indicates that times are a-changin' in the way incoming college freshmen have paid for their education. The biggest change is the percent of freshmen who say they paid for college themselves. In 1967 a third paid for college themselves. In 1997 only a tenth of freshmen covered their college costs. In 1997 some 37 percent indicated that they primarily paid for college with student loans, whereas only 15 percent used student loans thirty years earlier. The same percentage of freshmen—18 percent—in both years had the good fortune of having all the cost covered by their parents.[10]

The more than two-fold rise in the percentage of students who covered their college costs with student loans can be in part attributed to the greater availability of student loans and to the rise in the real (or inflation-adjusted) cost of college education over the past three decades. Just between 1985 and 1996, real college tuition rose by 60 percent. However, part of the explanation for the greater dependency on student loans may be the growing number of students who take computers, stereos, and mini-refrigerators to college. In 1967 some 69 percent of freshmen took zero to ten stereo albums to college; only 4 percent took fifty to one hundred albums to college. In 1997 some 24 percent of freshmen took zero to ten music compact discs to college with them. However, 22 percent had fifty to one hundred CDs, statistics that should force students and their parents to ask, "Are the college loans going to pay for college or CDs (and other things of lesser importance)?"

HOW DID YOU PAY FOR COLLEGE? PRIMARILY BY . . .

1967	1997
34% Paid for it myself	31% Student loans
22% Parents paid for most	22% Parents paid for most
18% Parents paid 100%	21% Scholarships
15% Student loans	18% Parents paid 100%
12% Scholarships	10% Paid for it myself

Source: Survey undertaken by Best Buy, as reported by Dawn C. Chmielewski, "Gearing Up for School," Orange County Register, August 30, 1998, p. business 5.

Consider Table 4.2, where we list the average annual starting salaries for 1998 college graduates with bachelor's degrees for several different majors. A student's choice of major obviously makes a big difference in annual salary, and an even bigger difference when considered in terms of potential wealth. To pick the biggest difference in Table 4.2, the person who majors in chemical engineering will, on average, earn a starting salary of $45,236, which is $19,737 higher than the starting salary of $25,499 made by the person who majors in psychology. How much can this difference be worth?

One way to measure is to determine how much more the engineer could have at retirement if he decided to save and invest all the after-tax difference between his income and that of the psychology major. Let's assume that, after the erosive effect of taxes, this engineer's additional income amounts to about $13,000 a year in extra take-home income. And let's make the conservative assumption that this take-home difference stays the same throughout the careers of the two graduates. If the chemical engineer saved the $13,000 each year from age twenty-two, and invested it at an annual return of 8 percent, it would accumulate to $5,439,539 at age sixty-seven.

Table 4.2.
Starting Salaries for Different Majors, 1998

MAJOR	STARTING SALARY
Accounting	$32,872
Economics and finance	$34,043
Management information systems	$38,830
Letters (including English)	$27,608
Psychology	$25,499
Chemical engineering	$45,236
Electrical/electronic engineering	$42,931
Mechanical engineering	$40,931
Computer science	$41,561

Source: National Association of Colleges and Employers, July 6, 1998 Salary Survey (http://www.jobweb.org). This survey compiles reports from more than 350 college and university services offices nationwide.

Of course, we are not suggesting that students major in chemical engineering over psychology. If you love psychology and hate chemical engineering, you will likely make more money as a good psychologist than as a poor chemical engineer, and will have a more fulfilling career even if you don't. But those who are interested in financial success should keep in mind that intellectual interests are not preordained, although people have different talents that can cause them to favor some topics over others. But what you become interested in depends in large measure on what you choose to become interested in. You will not find every course you take exciting. But by exposing yourself to a wide range of academic topics, and by studying them seriously, you can increase your array of choices for career paths. And the wider the range of subjects you investigate and study, the greater will be your chances of discovering a field of study that is both intellectually satisfying and financially rewarding.

Be Well-Rounded and Send the Right Signal

There is another reason to take a wide range of subjects while in school that has nothing to do with discovering your intellectual interests. Even if making a high salary is your sole concern, and you already know that you love the field of management information systems (a lucrative field as seen from Table 4.2), it would still be a good idea to take a wide range of liberal arts courses in college before beginning your specialization in MIS. It takes more than knowledge of the latest MIS techniques to truly succeed in that or any other field. For example, the ability to communicate effectively, both orally and in writing, makes everyone, including MIS specialists, more productive. Subjects such as history, political science, and geography broaden your perspective and improve your ability to productively interact with a wider group of people. Employers generally prefer employees who are well rounded so they have the interests and versatility to advance through an organization and add value in ways that narrowly trained specialists cannot. In other words, many employers prefer to hire those graduates with attributes that are enhanced by a broad education.

Indeed, employers may rather hire specialists who have emphasized their general education, even if this means they have not taken as many specialty courses as possible. While this may seem surprising, it follows from the fact that much of the knowledge a person needs on the job comes from training provided by the employer. Businesses with fifty or more employees annually spent almost $8 billion on the wages and salaries of in-house trainers and $5.5 billion on outside trainers for their workers in the mid-1990s. When you add the wages and salaries paid to workers while they receive training, the total cost came to about $80 billion a year.[11] Businesses don't spend this kind of money unless there is the promise of a big payoff in terms of higher productivity. And this payoff is captured in large measure by employees as well, since the more productive the worker, the more pay the worker generally earns.

However, even though employers may place a high value on employees with a strong "general education," and the general skills that it develops, that's not the type of training employers will tend to provide. The problem employers face with providing general education is that the education is costly and the skills acquired by the employees are also useful to many other firms. General education skills improve the productivity of people *no matter where they work*, so workers can easily take the benefits of that training to other companies. For example, you are not likely to convince your employer to give you training in English composition. However, increasing the technical skills of an MIS specialist with a training program tailored to the company's specific problems makes the specialist more valuable to his current employer without doing much to increase his value elsewhere.[12] It follows that students with deficiencies in general education tend to be less valuable to employers than students with deficiencies in a specific technical field because it makes less sense for employers to remedy the former educational deficiency than the latter.

And it's not enough simply to have a degree. You won't do as well taking a lot of easy courses as by pursuing a rigorous program of study. Courses that do the most to increase your productivity, and your value to employers, are generally the most demanding. It stands to reason that workers with the kind of knowledge and skills that are easily mastered are in greater supply than workers who have developed the knowledge and skills that require greater effort, and so those who have worked their way through difficult courses of study will generally be able to command more pay.

But there is an important advantage to a more rigorous program that has nothing to do with whether it makes you more productive. Because much of what you will need to know on the job will be taught after you have been hired, employers want some assurance before hiring you that you can learn what needs to be learned. They also want to know if you have the ability and willingness to work hard and stay with tough assignments to their successful completion.

An employer can ask a prospective employee these questions, but there is no particular reason to believe the answers given by the prospective employees who are diligent will be any different from the answers given by those who are indolent. The best way you can indicate *credibly* to a prospective employer that you are the type of person who can and will get the job done is by having completed a demanding assignment, such as finishing a tough academic program with respectable grades. In other words, a good *and* tough education provides a valuable signal, sent with credibility, that you are a person who can be depended on. And it goes without saying that those people who can be depended on are worth far more than those who cannot.

How do we know that the type and quality of an education serves as a signal that a person can stick with and complete a task? Employers have made the point to us in casual conversations when they come to our campuses to recruit. Moreover, consider the importance of actually getting a diploma as a measure of one's ability to stick with a task. When comparing the earnings of people with the same number of years in school, those who have actually completed their degree requirements are found to make significantly more than those who have not. For example, those who complete a high school degree can expect to earn 18 percent more over the course of their working careers than those who attend school for twelve years without earning the diploma, and those who complete a bachelor's degree can expect to earn 33 percent more than those who attend school for sixteen years without earning a college degree.[13]

Networking Works

Studying hard, performing well, and completing your degree pay off financially, but there is far more to school than the daily grind in the classroom and library. Interacting with your fellow students is an important part of an education. Teachers and professors may like to think that they are the primary source of their students' education. They are important, but students probably learn more from one another through classroom discussions and after-class socializing than they do from lectures. The International Institute for Management Development recognizes the importance of this "peer group" effect in an advertisement for their master's of business management (MBA) program in Lausanne, Switzerland. The advertisement begins in bold letters, "Who's that sitting next to you?" and then continues, "In any quality MBA program, the people you sit next to are a key source of your learning."[14] The positive peer group effect may partly explain why acquiring the equivalent of a high school diploma after dropping out of school by passing the General Equivalence Diploma (GED) exam does not increase a person's income to the level of a regular high school graduate.[15] And graduates of the nation's elite universities no doubt have higher starting salaries on average than their counterparts from lower-ranking universities in large part because of the network of well-placed alumni available to those graduates, in addition to the educational advantage from associating with other students good enough to get into the elite schools.

The educational gain that comes from interacting with fellow students is not the only advantage from the social side of going to school. The old saying, "It's who you know, not what you know," is an exaggeration of what counts at work, but don't dismiss the truth it contains. Networking is an excellent way to expand your opportunities. One of the most important, and difficult, things for a smart, hardworking person just out of school to do is to convince others that he is indeed smart and hardworking and can be trusted with responsibility. Graduating with good grades is one way of communicating to others that you are responsible enough to take on a tough job. But the more information people have about you, the more opportunities you will have, assuming you really are capable and responsible. And the wider the network of friends and associates you develop while in school, the larger the number of people who can come to know your positive attributes.

One of the most valuable things you can *earn* as you go through life is a network of people who have a high regard for you as a person of character, and for your dedication and willingness to work hard. A good time to start developing such a network is in school. The payoff can be enormous financially, but more importantly, the friendships that are formed create a value that goes beyond financial considerations.

Going Back to School

We all too often think of an education as something we complete before moving into the world of work. But a good education is never finished, rather it is a continuous process of developing new skills, acquiring new interests, and opening up new windows of knowledge and appreciation. Few things are as important to a satisfying life as the enjoyment of learning. This helps explain why, as longevity increases, more older people are returning to college campuses. Between 1991 and 1995 the number of college students who were sixty-five years old or older increased 27 percent.[16] Of course, those who continue to learn are also best able to create and take advantage of opportunities to progress financially.

We have already examined the advantages of training on the job. This is often training that builds on the knowledge acquired in school. But what should be emphasized is that the training obtained on the job is often a great prerequisite for going back to school. Academic courses can take on more relevance and meaning, and be extremely useful, to those who have experienced the real world of work firsthand. This no doubt explains why, after graduating from college and spending a few years working, many people are going back to school for a master's of business administration degree. It also explains why most good MBA programs have a strong preference for students who have a few years of work experience. Based on the salaries being paid to new MBAs, businesses

The Payoff to Getting Through College Quickly

One way of increasing the financial payoff of a college education is by getting it quickly. It is possible to get a bachelor's degree in three years or less, and students do have some choice in the matter. For example, Chris Sorrow, a student at the University of Georgia, received his degree in economics in two years by taking heavy loads and summer classes, and graduated with a 4.0 grade point average. Granted, Chris was an unusually gifted student; in fact most students aren't able or willing to put in the hours he did to finish so quickly. And there is a downside to passing through college so rapidly, since there is more to a successful college experience than attending class and studying. But a student doesn't have to race through college to graduate early, he can get a college degree at a younger age by finishing high school ahead of schedule. This is what Michael Russell did by graduating from James A. Garfield High School in Cleveland a year early. According to Russell, "I decided to work toward graduating early because I was thinking about college . . . I saw this opportunity to get into college and a job one year early."[17] This compares to an increasing number of undergraduates who are taking five and six years or more to finish their degrees, which costs them far more than most realize.[18]

Consider the financial advantage a student can realize from graduating with a college degree in management information systems in three years as opposed to five years. The three-year graduate earns two additional years' salary, which for an MIS major is $38,830 for the first year (see Table 4.2), and, being conservative, we assume the same income for the second year as well. This means that after taxes the student will have approximately $27,000 dollars a year for two years that the five-year graduate doesn't have. To determine the potential gain from the early graduation, consider investing the $27,000 at age twenty-two (one year after starting to work) and again at age twenty-three at 8 percent and letting it accumulate until age sixty-seven, the three-year student will have $1,659,863. Also, the three-year student saves the out-of-pocket cost of going to college for two years, which we assume is $4,000 a year. This is money that the student could also invest at ages twenty-two and twenty-three, which, at 8 percent, would equal $245,906 at age sixty-seven, totaling $1,905769. But this is not all gain. The three-year student no doubt paid somewhat more tuition and sacrificed some summer earning during the three years he was in college to graduate early. Assuming that this came to $8,000 a year, if this saving had been invested at ages nineteen, twenty, and twenty-one and left to compound at 8 percent until age sixty-seven, it would be worth $895,333. But this still leaves a net gain of $1,010,436 at retirement for finishing college two years earlier than is now common.

obviously believe that the combination of work experience followed by academic training in business provides a real boost to a person's productivity.

Freshly minted MBA's from solid schools almost always go back to work with substantial salary increases, and for some, the MBA is a springboard to the fast track to top management. But getting an MBA is not cheap. The biggest cost to MBA students is forgoing the income they would have made if they hadn't dropped out of the work force for the two years it takes to get their degrees (some schools offer a one-year MBA option). And tuition can be high (in some cases over $20,000 a year), although many state universities offer reasonable tuition to in-state students. So is an MBA worth the cost? For those who are willing to work hard and make the most of the opportunities an MBA opens up, the answer is yes. To illustrate, consider the costs and benefits of the average twenty-six-year-old going back to get an MBA at the University of Georgia.

According to student surveys, the average student entering the University of Georgia MBA program in the fall of 1996 had about four years of work experience, was about twenty-six years old, and was making about $37,000 a year. In-state tuition was $3,000 and out-of-state tuition was $9,500 a year. To bias the case against the MBA financially, we will assume the higher tuition figure. But this tuition can be ignored since most students receive more than $9,500 each year in Assistantships and internships. We will also assume that the students would have made $40,000 in each of the two years they were in the program. So the students, on average, gave up $40,000 each year spent in school. But when they graduated in 1998 the new MBAs took jobs that paid an average of about $57,000 a year. To compare the costs against the higher income, we ask whether getting the MBA increased the student's potential wealth at retirement.

If $40,000 were invested at age twenty-six and the same amount again at age twenty-seven, and allowed to grow until age sixty-seven, it would be worth $1.81 million. On the other hand the student is making about $17,000 a year more than he would have because of the MBA. Making the conservative assumption that this difference doesn't increase over the student's career, this means that he has about $11,000 more after taxes that could be invested each year, beginning at age twenty-eight. At 8 percent, that series of investments would be worth $2.85 million at age sixty-seven. In other words, the potential value of the MBA at retirement is the difference between $2.85 million and 1.81 million, or a little over $1 million. Of course, we don't expect the MBA to save all the extra earning for retirement, but neither do we expect the person who doesn't go back for an MBA to save all she earned and saved on tuition for the two

Tom Hits Pay Dirt with an MBA

For many students, going back to school for an MBA is spectacularly rewarding, both personally and financially. Consider the case of Tom, who Dwight Lee met through one his students. Tom graduated in 1994 with a degree in economics from a leading liberal arts college in a southern state. He worked two years for a major international insurance broker, making $30,000 ($25,000 in salary and another $5,000 in commission) during his second year. In 1996 Tom decided to take his work experience back to school, and he entered a MBA program at a large state university. He worked hard, performing well academically and taking an active role in campus activities. Upon graduating in 1996 Tom was offered a job by a major securities firm in New York, with a starting salary of $75,000, a $25,000 guaranteed annual bonus, and an extra $30,000 up front, of which he keeps $10,000 for each year he stays with the firm. Assuming Tom stays with the firm, it is expected that his pay will escalate rapidly, with his compensation soon consisting solely of commissions and bonuses. Financially, Tom's decision to go back for his MBA looks like a big winner. But when talking about his MBA experience, he gets the most animated when discussing the friends and the plans they all have for staying in touch.

Tom's story is obviously one of success. But it's not an unusual story. It is one that is repeated tens of thousands of times every year as people take their on-the-job experiences back to school.

years she could have been an MBA student. But the $1 million is a reasonable estimate of what an MBA *could be* worth at retirement for a twenty-six-year-old.

Attributes That Count

A good education clearly does more than provide a signal that you possess attributes that make you productive. In the process of taking your education seriously you develop productive attributes. Doing well in school requires learning the importance of such things as:

- Showing up on time.
- Paying close attention to assignments.
- Completing assignments on time.
- Doing more than the minimum required.
- Expressing your views forcibly, yet reasonably.

- Treating the views of others with respect and consideration.
- Struggling with difficult tasks rather than giving up in frustration.
- Organizing your time and activities to satisfy a number of pressing demands.

The principles of behavior you develop as a good student also make you a dependable and productive member of the workforce.

Securing and succeeding in a good job that pays well, one in which you contribute significant value to others, is a necessary step along the road to financial success. A good education is the most effective way of preparing for that step. But more than a good job is required if you hope to get rich. Other essential steps to building a fortune include deferring gratification and being willing to resist current temptations to better save and invest for future payoffs. Those who cannot control the impulse to have as much as possible now are unlikely to ever have much in the way of wealth, either now or later. Those who stay in school and get a good education are deferring gratification and making one of the most productive investments they can make. They are also learning the practice of patience and persistence, therefore increasing the chances that, after they start working, they will follow a saving and investment program that will make them financially well off.

Finally, there is another big advantage in getting a good education, one that increases your prospects for a deeply satisfying life, as well as a prosperous one. School is where people commonly meet the person they will marry. People who go on to college increase the number of people they meet with similar interests and aspirations, which increases the chances of meeting a compatible marriage partner. And the choice of your marriage partner, while obviously important to your general happiness, is also crucial to your financial success. Married people are generally more successful in almost every imaginable way than are those who remain single.

The rule "Get a good education" is not only a good one for building a financial fortune. Get a good education and you increase your chances of achieving many other wonderful things that life has to offer.

Practical Advice for the Good Life

Education pays—and pays handsomely. And the added pay from additional education can give rise to more savings, which can generate a substantial net worth by retirement time. Here are some tips for getting the most out of your education:

If you are in college:

- Take professors, not courses. In college the word gets around about who the best professors are and who the easy ones are—they are seldom the same. Take the best professors even if it sometimes means taking courses that don't always fit your planned course of studies. Remember that easy professors will lose your respect (if you remember them) as the years go by. Good professors can turn a subject that seems boring when taught by most professors into an inspiring and exciting adventure.
- Search out professors who are actively trying to create and pass on to students new knowledge from their discipline. (Ask professors which professors they would want their children to take.)
- Most college graduates can think back to one or a few professors who made a big difference in their lives. Don't let this happen just by chance.
- Take a reasonable but challenging course load each term and graduate on time, if not early.
- Estimate the financial benefits of an early graduation, both in terms of current savings (from not having to pay college expenses and from being able to enter the workforce early) and the impact of the savings on your eventual net worth.
- Give every course a chance to excite you. Take it seriously and act as though it is interesting. This will not always work, but you'll be surprised how often a course you expected to find boring becomes interesting if you give it a chance. And you will generally learn more in those courses you find interesting.
- Don't neglect the importance of friendships and a social life. Campus is a great place to form networks that can provide personal satisfaction and financial opportunities for a lifetime. Remember that networks of friends and contacts are important because so much business is a matter of cooperation.
- Don't focus so much on your major courses that you neglect the importance of courses that have nothing to do with your major. Remember that employers will tend to provide training that is specific to your job; they will tend to avoid paying for training that can be used at other firms.
- Consider going back to school at night to get an advanced degree, for example, an MBA. Don't judge degree programs solely by their costs.

Recognize that many schools charge more than others for a good reason: Their graduates' salaries are higher. What you must do is balance your current out-of-the-pocket expenditures on tuition and books at different schools with the potential increase in your salary upon graduation. Treat your school expenditures as an investment, and judge schools as you would judge other investments, by the expected rates of returns.

- Consider that most of your education in life will occur outside your formal classroom studies. Use opportunities to learn on the job both by taking on additional on-the-job responsibilities and by taking formal training that is offered.

- Try to read at least one book every month (fiction or nonfiction). Develop a reading list by asking friends and associates what one or two books had the greatest impact on them.

- Get a computer and get on-line. (Recognize that in today's world the relevant question is not whether you can afford a computer; it is whether you can afford *not* to buy one.) Look on the Internet as one great growing "library" of educational resources that can be tapped for both pleasure and work. Moreover, look on the Internet as one of the cheapest ways to meet and stay in touch with contacts. (For college students, not to be able to use the Internet would be similar to their parents not knowing how to use the telephone.)

- Remember that you will have to compete in job markets throughout your career with people who are capable of using with ease the vast and growing electronic resources on the Web. If you are a "technophobe," get over it.

- Recognize that you will likely have three or more careers during your working life, with each career requiring substantial retooling. Try to anticipate your career changes, and look forward to them.

An Exercise for Achieving the Good Life: Learn More, Earn More

No matter how much education we have, there are always new things we can learn that will make us more valuable as employees or business owners. Sometimes those things are best learned by going back to school for more formal education. But often they are things that you can learn on the job from training opportunities, from being willing to take on more responsibility, or from just being alert to opportunities in the workplace. Also, it is sometimes possible to develop an enjoyable hobby that, as a nice side benefit, makes you more valuable on the job. For example, many people are fascinated by the things they can discover on the Internet once they develop the skills necessary for surfing the World Wide Web. That skill and the information it makes available can enhance your earning potential.

1. List three things you could learn, on the job or at home, that would make you a more valuable employee. Write down what you estimate learning each thing would cost you financially. Finally, estimate how much the additional knowledge would add to your yearly after-tax income beginning two years after you acquired it.

2. Next, use your cost estimates and additional income estimates to estimate whether learning each thing pays financially—remember, even if learning something doesn't pay financially, it may still be worth learning for the satisfaction it adds to your life.

3. Assuming the money spent learning a skill is a onetime cost incurred when the skill is learned, figure out how much that money would be worth if, instead of spending it on education, you invested it at 8 percent until you retire. Follow these steps on your Texas Instrument BA hand calculator.
    Press [2nd] and then press [MODE].
    Enter the cost and then press [PV].
    Enter 8 and then press [%i].
    Enter the number of years until retirement and then press [N].
    Now calculate the amount the money could be worth at retirement by pressing [CPT] and then [FV].

4. Next calculate how much your additional yearly income would be worth if invested at 8 percent until you retire. On your Texas Instrument BA calculator:
    Press [2nd] and then press [MODE].
    Enter the additional income and then press [PMT].
    Enter 8 and then press [%i].

Enter the number of years until retirement minus 2 (remember we are assuming your income doesn't increase until two years after you do the learning).

Calculate how much the extra income could be worth at retirement by pressing [CPT] and then [FV].

5. If the value obtained from question 4 is greater than that obtained from question 3, then the additional learning is estimated to pay for itself financially.

6. Repeat the calculation for each item of learning listed in question 1.

RULE 5

Get Married and Stay Married

Marriage is one of those marvelous, long-standing social arrangements that many Americans love to hate. Marriage has variously been described as hell and as divine—maybe both at the same time. The poet Robert Louis Stevenson quipped, "Marriage is like life in this—that it is a field of battle, and not a bed of roses," while Ralph Waldo Emerson asked, "Is not marriage an open question, when it is alleged, from the beginning of the world, that such as are in the institution wish to get out, and such as are out wish to get in?"

We are here to argue that notwithstanding all its other virtues and detractions, marriage is definitely a legal and social institution that, for a variety of reasons, can lead to wealth accumulation. The evidence is clear: Married couples earn disproportionately more and have disproportionately more wealth than single people living separately or together.

Clearly, many married couples may be better off than their single counterparts because men and women who choose to marry may have more advantages, that is, they may be more educated and better-looking, may be inclined to work harder and longer, and may be smarter and may remain more alert to economic opportunities—not because of the advantages per se of marriage as an institution. Married couples may accumulate more wealth than single Americans, in other words, simply because the married partners individually tend to be like all the residents of radio host Garrison Keillor's fictional town of Lake Woebegone, "above average." But as we will explain in this chapter, marriage should help even well-educated and good-looking people (as well as not so well-educated and good-looking people) earn more income and accumulate more wealth than they would otherwise.

And yet despite the positive data about marriage, we want to assure you that marriage is not *essential* to making it in America; many of our well-off friends are single, and some of our married friends are as poor as church mice both in spirit and in wealth. But marriage can greatly *improve* your chances of making it in this country, which is reason enough to consider the economic, emotional, and physical advantages it offers. There are reasons for believing that marriage, because of its social, moral, and legal foundations, can enable you to earn more and save and invest more, as well as improve your chance for leading a satisfying life. It may also help you to live longer, which can definitely have an impact on your ability to take the long view—and reap the rewards of compounding in your distant future.

At the same time, before you think that we propose to consider marriage exclusively through rose-colored glasses, we stress that you must be cautious about going into marriage. Divorce can heap financial disaster onto the emotional pain of breakups, especially when lawyers start sucking up the wealth of splitting and feuding couples. (And we both speak from experience here, given that we are all too aware of the blessings of marriage *and* the pains of divorce.) For many Americans—especially women with children—divorce is a surefire gateway to poverty from which it may be difficult to escape.

Marriage: The Facts

As shown in the box on page 97, marriage remains popular in America, given that nearly 56 percent of American adults in 1997 were married and living with their spouses. However, it is also clear that more and more Americans are choosing to live together without being married. In 1970 there was one unmarried couple living together for every one hundred married couples in the country. By 1997 there were eight unmarried couples for every one hundred married couples.[1]

To appraise the impact of marriage on people's lives, consider a few facts on the income and wealth of married couples and singles. Married men earn up to 26 percent more than unmarried men do. Married women earn more than unmarried women do, but only as long as they don't have children.[2] In 1994 (the latest year of available data), all American families taken together had a median income of just under $39,000. However, married-couple families had close to $45,000, or 15 percent more than all families. Families headed by males (with the wives not in the home) had a median income of $28,000, while families

Profile of American Living Arrangements in 1997

- 109.2 million adults (or 55.9 percent) were married and living with their spouses.
- The median age at first marriage was 26.8 years for men and 25.0 years for women.
- Among people twenty-five to thirty-four years old, 13.9 million (or 34.5 percent of all people in that age group) had never been married.
- 19.3 million adults (or 9.9 percent) were currently divorced.
- Nearly half (46.3 percent) of women sixty-five years old and over were widowed.
- There were 4.1 million unmarried couple households. Over a third of these households (35.6 percent) had children under eighteen.
- 19.8 million children under eighteen (27.9 percent of all children under eighteen) lived with one parent.
- 84.5 percent of all children who lived with one parent lived with their mother, and about 40 percent of these children lived with a mother who had never been married.[6]

headed by females (husbands not in the home) had a median income of slightly more than $18,000. This means that married-couple families had a 61 percent higher median income than families headed by males and two and a half times the median income of families headed by females.

Male single-person households had a median income in 1995 that was about $26,000, or only 58 percent of the median incomes of married-couple families. Female single-person households had a median income of $16,000, or 36 percent of the median of married-couple families. The income gap between white American and African-American families can be explained to a substantial degree by the greater percentage of intact families among white Americans than among African Americans. In 1997 all black families had a median income that was only 62 percent of the median for all white families. However, black intact married couples had a median income that was much higher relatively, 87 percent of the white median income.[3]

Not surprisingly, given their higher incomes, married people have far more wealth later in life than unmarried couples. From a National Institute of Aging survey of 12,000 people fifty-one to sixty-one years of age, researchers found that married couples have on average twice the wealth of unmarried couples.[4] Not surprisingly, in surveys of married, single, and divorced Americans, the National Opinion Research Center at the University of Chicago has found married people to be happier than singles or divorcees.[5]

Our comparisons are not completely fair to singles, as some of the differences are related to the age distributions in different groupings. There are more very young and very old people among the singles group than in intact families. Some of the differences in income exist because the more skilled and educated Americans are likely to be married. Still, who doubts that some of the income difference is a function of the fact that intact families often work better in producing income? The added income from husbands and wives working together can, of course, translate into an enormous advantage when it comes to accumulating wealth.

Why Marriage and Wealth Go Together

Why should we not be surprised that married Americans tend to do better financially than their nonmarried counterparts? There are actually a number of ways to answer that question.

Obviously, two people should be able to produce and earn more than a single person, but there is every reason to believe that two people united in marriage should be able to earn more than two people working separately. Married people can cooperate, and the cooperation should be as important in their work around their home as it is in any business. They can also achieve economies of scale, however limited, given that they can combine their households and not have to suffer the consequences of double rents and double expenditures on things like furniture and pots and pans.

Economists have long argued that production can be improved if workers specialize in what they do—that is, limit their work to a few well-focused activities with the result that they are able to accomplish these activities with more efficiency and greater speed. For example, one spouse can do the cleaning around the house and build an outside career, while the other concentrates on doing the yardwork and rearing the children. Each can become more proficient at the chosen tasks than if they each tried doing everything or switched off frequently. Moreover, by specialization, each would not have to waste as much time constantly changing skills, tools, and jobs. Just imagine your skill level and the time you would waste if you tried to learn to do everything in any complex production process, from running the various pieces of machinery on the shop floor to keeping the books in the back office and doing the legal work in another office. The same goes for "home work," because in many ways a home is much like a firm. Families produce a number of things, not the least of which are meals, companionship, entertainment, and security.

Workers in firms and members of families who specialize can use the time saved to produce more output—and earn more income. If you are wasting an hour a day changing assigned tasks in an unspecialized work environment, in a specialized work environment you would have an additional hour of time to work—to produce—translating into higher wages. Similarly, in a marriage the husband and wife (or any two adults living together) can do different things around the home, and do them with greater productivity, while having more time to work at their assigned tasks.

It's important to note that we are not suggesting that there be predefined tasks according to gender (aside for the obvious fact that women must bear the children if the couple chooses to have them).[7] What is important about specialization is not that it encourages separation of work along any lines, but that it forces cooperation. In short, marriage helps people achieve the benefits of cooperation and specialization simultaneously. It enables them do what they need to do at home more efficiently, allowing more time to do other things (among them, work, which creates more disposable income to hire people to cut the grass and clean floors, thereby allowing the couple more quality or leisure time together).

Many single people have another decided *dis*advantage. They often spend an inordinate amount of time searching for companionship in various forms, including sex. Singles bars and clubs exist and are profitable because they offer singles a service, reducing the cost of their search for a companion. Although married people still seek friendships beyond the family, they tend to spend less time searching for companionship than single people. When it is acknowledged that mate searching is costly in terms of time and dollars, it becomes obvious that married people would tend, on average, to have more time to earn an income and pay attention to their long-term investment strategies than singles. Married people, on average, can make it in America with greater ease.

Put another way, because of the economies of being married, a married couple should be able to earn more and save more over the course of their married lives, the net effect of which can be a substantial buildup of retirement wealth. Suppose for example that a married couple can save $2,000 more a year from age twenty-two than they would be able to save as singles. At an annual rate of return of 8 percent, the added wealth from being married amounts to $836,852 at age sixty-seven.

However, married people may lose a measure of their comparative advantages from specialization with the gradual developments of markets. Markets now provide services that were once largely provided in homes—cleaning, laundry, meals, yard maintenance, and entertainment. Singles can get many benefits of specialization from buying what they need from specialists in the market. Where you may once have had to rely on a spouse to cook, you can now buy virtually any form of meal you want in restaurants, or you can buy already prepared meals at the grocery store. Singles often have a major share of their laundry done at cleaners, and can just as easily "outsource" their housecleaning and yard-work.

Because of the advantages of specialization that previous generations of singles didn't have at their disposal, making it in America for singles or couples has never been easier. Holding marriages together has, as a consequence, never been more difficult, a point to which we will return later when we consider the growth in the incidence of divorce.

The Many Dimensions of Marriage

Marriage is necessarily a set of commitments that two people make to each other. As such, marriage is a complex undertaking under the best of circumstances, mainly because of the somewhat natural human ten-dency to shirk responsibilities and commitments. And marriage is a chal-lenge, given the most basic need of the spouses to fortify repeatedly their commitments to each other despite all the temptations to do otherwise. As a consequence, a married couple must be prepared to work together in any number of relational dimensions, the most prominent and impor-tant of which are the personal and social dimensions. Many people seem to think of marriage as an event or a state, and it is surely both. We see marriage as a process, one that can be terribly gratifying, given a lot of work on both spouses' part. Unfortunately, all too many people seem to understand their need to work at their jobs, but not their marriages.

Because of the potential for divorce (if for no other reason), we can-not overlook the importance of the legal dimension of marriage that may explain why people continue to marry in large numbers. God may view marriage as holy (which many people see as *the* overwhelming advantage of marriage), but the courts view aspects of marriage as a legally enforceable contract. Each spouse explicitly or implicitly makes certain commitments about personal responsibilities within the family and to the other. Each spouse agrees to recognize certain rights and priv-ileges of the other, and both agree, again explicitly or implicitly, to a set of rules by which household decisions and changes in the contract are to be made. The last provision is necessary to state because not all issues concerning the relationship are likely to be settled before the vows are stated and because conditions of the partners do change.

Such provisions of the contract may be only vaguely understood and recognized as such, but they are nevertheless generally present in one fashion or another. The couple may simply have an understanding that they will work things out together, tacitly realizing from their knowledge of the other's behavior what this means.

Divorce often occurs because spouses devote insufficient resources (time, energy, and emotions) to developing and maintaining the marriage contract. Admittedly, many provisions of a marriage contract generally do not have the force of law. Occasionally there are cases in which one spouse takes the other to court (for example, for lack of support), but these are relatively rare events. One reason many disputes cannot be settled by the court is that a couple's mutually agreed-upon contract is usually vague and rarely written down. Another reason is that the cost of one spouse taking the other to court over many disputed issues can be considerable.

If the provisions of the marriage contract have any meaning, it is mainly because of the moral obligation such agreements engender, the pressures that can be brought to bear on the party involved by the other spouse and by friends and relatives, and the threat of one party retaliating by shirking responsibilities.

Another underappreciated reason for an extended dating and engagement period is that dating affords time for the partners to test each other, to see if the potential spouse will likely live up to the agreements. Each likely wants to avoid marrying anyone who constantly calculates the costs and benefits of everything the couple do in their relationship. Such a person may simply walk out when things get tougher than expected when the vows were exchanged. In their dating, the couple evaluates each other for signs of commitment that go beyond the particular costs and benefits of the moment. The couple needs to know that the legal enforceability of the marriage contract is, for the most part, irrelevant.

One explanation for why men give their fiancées diamond engagement rings is that such extravagances indicate a form of irrationality, given that most men see little personal benefit in the gesture, beyond sending a message that says: "I'm literally crazy over you; see what a stupid thing I'm doing!"

Understandably, both parties in a marriage hope to marry someone who truly loves them, mainly because that love ensures a strong degree of irrational commitment and trust, both of which are crucial to each spouse's willingness to abide by the contract they have devised—and invest in the development of the relationship and the mutually owned family assets. An unloving—and, worse yet, hostile—marriage is not likely to be a committed and trusting relationship, which is to say that it is not likely to be a relationship that has promise of much wealth accumulation.

Plus such a marriage cannot possibly offer the personal security and satisfaction people everywhere want and need.

The Role of the Courts

The main role of the courts has been one of refereeing the division of the family assets (children included) between the husband and wife at the time of divorce. This limited role of the courts in the divorce process, however, is crucially important—and has definite implications for the expected wealth accumulation of the couple. The court's intrusion ensures that the husband and wife each has some property rights to the family assets, both tangible and intangible. To this extent, the husband and wife have a greater incentive to invest their time and other resources in the development of the family assets and in building a strong—and trusting—family relationship. The "family" itself can be viewed as a long-term investment project, given that many of the costs must be incurred up front and the returns are received over a span of years, if not decades.

Consider the role of property rights in a business investment. Suppose you are an entrepreneur who is considering an investment in an office building you plan to build. Would you be willing to make the investment if you knew that after doing so, you would have no property rights in the building—that is, someone else could take it over without any objections from the courts? More to the point of the topic of this chapter, would you invest in the project if you feared your business partners would run off with your share of the investment? Although you might be willing to make some investment in the enterprise and to protect it by your own means to some extent, you would probably be more willing to invest a larger amount in the project if you had some rights that were protected by a third party, such as the state.

There is a rule here in our examples relating to business investment: Where property rights are not protected, investment is often impaired. Many households in depressed or ghetto areas of central cities often look run-down not because the residents couldn't invest more in their homes or communities, but because they have to fear the criminals in their midst, who could take or destroy their property with relative ease.

Near where Richard McKenzie lives is a dilapidated beachside community. The problem the residents have is that the land their houses are on is state property, and the state has for decades been threatening to reassert its rights over the land, which would be made a part of an adjoining state park. The residents have simply not been able to predict how long they all will be able to live in their homes. And you can bet that because of that fear, they have done little to improve their homes. As a consequence, the homes are little more than shacks. The homeowners have maintained their properties well enough to live in them, but they have tried to ensure that when the state takes over the land, they will be out as little as possible in terms of the investment in their homes. By way of contrast, the beachfront homes in nearby Laguna Beach and Corona Del Mar, where property rights are reasonably secure, are beautiful, well-maintained, upscale homes.

In the first chapter (Rule 1), we introduced you to a real-life couple who lives in Poland with their three children on a very low income for their level of education. The husband confessed that his family saved little during the communist era not so much because they had little income to save, but because they were fearful that their savings would be drastically eroded by the passage of some new capricious tax law or, more likely, would rapidly depreciate with a new round of hyperinflation. Now that the communists have been deposed and democracy has returned to Poland, his family's income is rising with a falling inflation rate, but he simply hasn't been able to shake old concerns about what the government will do in the future to erode the value of his savings.

We recognize that marriage is far more than a legal document to most people. At the same time, we talk in terms of "contracts" and "property rights" as applied to businesses and homes because those attributes are a part of what we call "marriage," and those attributes can affect the willingness of the partners in a marriage to invest in their union—and their mutual assets. To the extent that the stability of the marriage is favorably affected by such investments, the legal status of the marriage can be expected to yield a variety of financial and emotional benefits to the entire family.

Marriage can also be expected to extend the time horizon of the spouses in two important ways: First, marriage can, apparently, extend the spouses' life expectancy over and above what the wife and husband could expect as single people. The most general reason for this is that married couples have better health than single and divorced people, as is obvious in the following research findings:

- Divorced men have twice the lung cancer rate of married men. Divorced men also have three to four times married men's rates of genital, buccal, and pharyngeal cancers. The cancer rates among divorced and single women is also higher than that for married women, although the differences are not as great for women as for men.
- Divorced and single men and women have from two and a half to three and a half times the married men's rate of death from hyper-

tensive heart disease, and when their heart diseases are not fatal, divorced and single people tend to stay longer in the hospital.

- Not surprisingly, married people have fewer problems with anxiety and depression than unmarried people. (Marriages between mentally ill women and men also seem to relieve some of their emotional problems.)
- Marriage increases the likelihood that women will have children, and women who have given birth tend to have a lower rate of breast cancer.[8]

At one time it was thought that men definitely benefited from marriage, given that married men lived longer than single men but that women might, on balance, be harmed health- and wealth-wise by marriage, mainly because of studies on the economic and physical consequences of marriage for women that were published in the early 1970s. In recent years, however, the research evidence has begun to mount that women's physical and emotional well-being is helped by marriage, causing a higher percentage of married women (90 percent) than never-married and divorced women (60 to 70 percent) living until age sixty-five (and remarkably widowed women fared almost as well as married women in terms of living to age sixty-five).[9]

Why married people have fewer health problems and live longer, no one knows for sure. Obviously, healthy people make more attractive partners and are, therefore, more likely to get married. But also, married people eat better, are more settled and content, monitor each other's health, and have more income to take better care of themselves and to obtain the needed medical treatment in the event of accidents and ailments. Married people also seem to be slightly happier, are less prone to depression, develop fewer "bad behaviors," and have sex twice as often as single people.[10] Moreover, cohabiting women (as distinguished from married women) are twice as likely to be victims of domestic violence and three times as likely to suffer from depression as married women.[11] The second reason marriage can be expected to extend a couple's (investment) time horizon is that the contractual nature of marriage gives each spouse more assurance that the other spouse will be around for a longer period of time.

The superior health of married people caused one researcher to conclude that marriage has the same effect as "jogging and lowering cholesterol intake" and caused another to deduce that "being divorced and a nonsmoker is slightly less dangerous than smoking a pack or more a day and staying married."[12] The positive health effects of marriage mean that married people can save more not only because they earn more, but also because they do not have to spend as much on health and medical care.

Whatever the reason (or combination of reasons) that married people live longer, the longer life expectancy can mean that married retirees will need a larger retirement net worth just to maintain themselves during their extended retirement, if they continue to retire at, say, sixty-seven. Thankfully, given their better health, the married elderly should be able to work longer, if they need the additional years of saving, to garner more benefits from having more years over which compound interest can work. We noted that a married couple that from age twenty-two is able to save $2,000 a year more than they would be able to save if they were single would have $836,852 in additional net worth at retirement. If the couple was able to work an additional five years before retirement, allowing their investments to continue to expand at 8 percent a year compounded, the couple's net worth benefits from marriage would rise an additional 48 percent, to $1,241,344.

Children and Wealth

A major reason people marry is to have children, and geneticists reason that women have a special biological interest in the marriage contract, given that children require long periods of nurturing. The man may have a biological interest in "sowing his seeds" wherever he can, given that that by doing so, he can increase the chances that at least some of his supposedly "selfish genes" will survive for any number of generations into the future.[13]

The "selfish genes" of the woman, on the other hand, assure a different strategy for increasing their survival into future generations: Be choosy about the father and ensure, to the extent possible, that the father sticks around to help with the nurturing and rearing of the children. The woman should seek high quality, and should see the marriage contract as a means of increasing the likelihood that the father will remain with her, which can be expected because the marriage contract increases the cost of his leaving. Like it or not, women have a greater interest in binding marriages than men simply because they are the ones who generally do the lion's share of the rearing of the children in the event of divorce.

Children can be wonderful, as we can attest, as we have six children between us. The joy children can bring to the lives of parents is reason enough to have them. Having acknowledged the considerable benefits of children, however, we can't help but remind you that children are *very* expensive, as evident in the estimates of the annual cost of child rearing reported nearby. This is especially true when you consider the value of the parents' time applied to rearing the children. The real money and time cost of rearing one child and getting the child through college, measured in today's dollars, can easily exceed a half million dollars (for middle- and higher-income parents). However, in assessing the impact of marriage and family on net worth, there is an even more significant point worth mentioning. Plans to have children can cause parents to delay the bulk of their saving to a later date when they don't have the expense of children. The impact of the delay can be substantial, as should be obvious from the examples of delayed saving in the second chapter (Rule 2), in which a person who delayed saving 10 percent of income from age twenty-two until age fifty could expect a 75 percent or more reduction in net worth at retirement time.

At the same time, children can extend the time horizons of their parents, giving parents a greater incentive for realizing the extended future. Children give parents a reason for living longer, and to do all of those things (like taking care of themselves physically and emotionally) that will enable them to actually live longer. In addition, if parents are interested in their children's welfare, the parents' relevant time horizon can extend beyond their own demise to the time when their children will be on their own and may need financial support. Moreover, having children appears to lower the probability that couples will divorce, which can add to the couple's time horizon and lower their medical care costs.[14]

In spite of the cost of children, a married woman and man tend to accumulate more assets than they would if they simply lived together.[15] The legality of the marriage contract means that if one spouse decided to leave and take the family assets, the other spouse would retain a claim to what is taken; not all would be lost. Anyone merely living with someone else would have a tougher time making property claims stand in court. They have to deal with the prospect that the other partner can leave at any time and at little cost.[16]

Based on these arguments and our own observations, it seems fair to say that marriage can make for more income to be saved and invested *and* a greater incentive on the part of each spouse to invest it. Married people can also expect to have a longer life expectancy and, possibly, a longer time for the power of compounding to work than singles.

Need to Be Choosy

Marriage *can* be a definite plus for any forward-looking frugal person, but you must always be choosy in selecting a spouse—especially if you are frugal. An extravagant spouse can easily neutralize the best of

The Cost of a Child

Many prospective parents have little idea of how much it costs to rear a child—until they've had to pay the bills. We have included below three rough estimates—A, B, and C—for the cost of rearing a child in a family with two children. We give three estimates because the cost of child care varies with income for two reasons. First, families with higher income can and do spend more on their children for clothes and food. Second, a major cost of rearing children is the time cost of the parents. The higher the income, the greater the parental time cost.

You can see in Table 5.1 that the expenditures for various items—food and clothing, for examples—are fairly modest, as estimated by the U.S. Department of Agriculture. However, when conservative estimates of the value of parental times are added in (see the endnotes for details), the cost of child rearing mounts substantially.

TABLE 5.1
ESTIMATED ANNUAL COST OF REARING A CHILD IN A FAMILY WITH TWO CHILDREN, 1995

| | Annual Family Income: | | |
| | A | B | C |
	Less Than $32,800	$32,800–$55,500	More Than $55,500
Food	$1,150	$1,386	$1,768
Transportation	$979	$1,369	$1,642
Clothing	$535	$619	$822
Health care	$415	$512	$608
Child care and education	$350	$595	$1,001
Miscellaneous	$528	$801	$1,406
Housing	$1,794	$2,532	$4,102
TOTAL of above expenditures	$5,751	$7,814	$11,349
Value of parental child care time per child	$16,390 [17]	$22,747 [18]	$32,794 [19]
Total of all expenditures and parental time	$22,139	$30,561	$44,143

Sources: For expenditures per child, U.S. Department of Agriculture, Center for Nutrition Policy and Promotion, Expenditures on Children by Families, 1995 Annual Report; for estimates of the value of parental time, authors' calculations (see notes).

intentions and plans of the most frugal American—and can be the source of ongoing spousal arguments. What the frugal person doesn't spend can easily be spent by the spouse, the net effect of which is exasperation, loss of trust, and little in the way of a retirement nest egg. When we released a pamphlet that outlined many of the themes of this book, we got a flood of letters from readers; one of the more poignant observations came from a woman in the state of Washington: "I'm the saver in my house. My fiancé, on the other hand, isn't. I try to explain to him the overall picture of how much money he would save in a month or year. He lives for today, and I save for the future. It's frustrating but maybe if he reads your study . . . maybe . . . maybe he might try to save, too."

Indeed, this woman does have a problem on her hands. We suggested her problem might be partly remedied with marriage, given that he may now be a spendthrift because, in the absence of vows, he is unsure of what the couple's future will be. At the same time, she needs to worry about her fiancé's profligate spending tendency because for many men (and women) old habits are hard to break—especially by someone else—and because his behavior might affect her incentives to save within the marriage. An extravagant spouse can force a frugal spouse to forgo frugal ways, just as a matter of defense. Even frugal people who set aside savings must cope with the pain (however slight) of denying themselves the pleasures of immediate consumption. They are willing to forgo current consumption, however, because of the expected greater benefits from a higher level of consumption in the future, as we explained under Rule 3. As we noted there, the pain of buying a used rather than a new car today can be more than offset by the round-the-world cruises in the future.

If a husband denies himself the new car today, only to have the wife spend the savings on something else for herself, you can imagine that the frugal husband will begin to think that his actions provide only pain and no gain. Hence, in self-defense, the frugal spouse can be expected to curb his frugality. The extravagant spouse might then follow with spending even more, given that she can begin to think that if they both start spending more freely, the savings will not be around for very long. This reasoning can cause both spouses to think that they had better step up their spending plans before the other does. All savings can evaporate as the husband and wife follow a tit-for-tat, progressively freer-wheeling spending strategy.

Of course, both husband and wife are in a good position to solve their "war of consumption." They can simply agree to be frugal. But very general and vague agreements can easily break down as each tries to test the limits of how the other interprets the agreement and will act to impose limits on the other. As each seeks to test limits, and as each gets by with pushing the limits back a bit, the other spouse can do the same, and they both can end up back where they were, spending more than either would prefer that they spend jointly.

The Logic of Budgets

Setting family budgets may be seen as a waste of time to many people, given that time must be devoted to forming agreements over how much is going to be spent by whom on what, and then time must be spent on tracking how actual expenditures compare with the budgeted amounts. However, there is much to recommend about budgets: They formalize spousal agreements, defining in very clear money terms who can spend how much on what. Spouses then have a means of monitoring each other's spending patterns. Budget agreements (which, of course, can vary in precision from a verbal "understanding" to a written document kept in a computer file) can fortify the incentive of each spouse to remain frugal (or to become more frugal or less extravagant than previously).

To further control extravagant, unnecessary spending, we also recommend that spouses have separate checking accounts (and separate credit cards), especially when one has trouble controlling expenditures and may not always have the interest of the other in mind. Some feel that separate accounts go against the wishes of many couples to share everything. However, there is a problem with shared accounts: When one couple spends something, part of the cost (maybe 50 percent) of the item bought is seen as borne by the other spouse. What one spouse spends, the other can't.

Hence, when spouses do not have the interest of the other fully at heart, which sometimes happens, shared checking accounts lower the calculated costs of buying anything to each of the spouses. If one spouse buys a sweater, say, for $100, the other spouse may figure even subconsciously that he is being forced to pick up a portion of the cost—maybe $30 or $50—by curbing consumption to counter the spent $100. The spouse buying the sweater can reason that the sweater really costs no more than $70 to her personally, since at least $30 of the cost will be borne by the other spouse. Accordingly, at the lower cost, each spouse has to worry that the other will spend more on many things than that person would if the full cost of the purchases were borne personally.

When the spouses have separate checking accounts, the couple can assign part of their joint income to savings and then split the remaining amount to be spent in whatever ways seem to be appropriate (given how the household bills are paid). Then, with separate checking accounts, when one spouse buys anything, the funds come out of the personal checking account. The purchase does not reduce the purchasing power of the other, nor does it create any undue power struggles or permission seeking. With separate checking accounts, the cost of whatever is bought to the spouse doing the buying goes up. In the case of the sweater, the price goes from $70 (or maybe $50) to $100.

There is a fundamental rule in business that if you raise the cost of anything to buyers, less will be bought. That rule applies here. With separate checking accounts, spouses tend to buy less than they would if they had a joint account. This means that they can save and invest more. If the couple is able to save only $500 more a year from curbs in their purchases because of their separate checking accounts from the time they were married at, say, age twenty-five until age sixty-seven and earn 8 percent a year, they will have an additional $164,792 in net worth.

Separate checking accounts (and credit cards) might not make marriage bliss. There will still be a need for a lot of coordination of purchases between the couple. But separate checking accounts can surely cut out major bones of marital contention over who can spend what (as well as "Who's got the checkbook?"). Separate accounts can also increase (albeit slightly) the odds of the marriage enduring long enough for a substantial retirement portfolioto be amassed at retirement time.

Divorce and Wealth Loss

A century ago, when couples said "I do" and affirmed their allegiance to each other "until death do us part," their commitment in one sense was a strong one, given that divorce was costly, shameful, and rare. At the same time, the commitment until death was nowhere near as limiting as it is today. A hundred years ago, life expectancy was less than fifty years, two-thirds of what it is today. Death would often dissolve marriages long before the couples' troubles would build to the point of divorce. Marriages might indeed have a built-in obsolescence, and people's rising life expectancy may be creeping beyond the natural life expectancy of marriage.

Clearly, for whatever reason, divorce is on an upward trend, although there has been a recent downturn in the divorce rate over the last ten years or so. In 1920 (the year of earliest available data) only 8 of 1,000 married females (fifteen years of age and older) in the population divorced. At mid-century 10.3 per 1,000 married females divorced. In 1980 the divorce rate peaked at 22.6 per 1,000 married females, only to fall back to 19.8 in 1995. Still, the 1995 divorce rate was nearly two and a half times what it was three-quarters of a century earlier.

Divorce has many causes, no doubt. Couples are indeed living longer and run into the problem of tiring of each other.[20] But just as surely, divorce has been aggravated by the fact that spouses in today's world don't need each other as much as they once did, say, when American families lived on farms and ranches miles from one another and transportation was costly. Today people can get from the market many of the things spouses once provided each other: Spouses' mutual interdependence is therefore not as great as it once was. Divorce may also be a result of the sexual liberation of men and women and the deteriorating sanctity of marriage.

The liberalization of the divorce laws has also encouraged divorce in two ways. First, it has lowered the cost of divorce (through, for example, "no-fault divorces," which means that the spouses do not have to show cause for a divorce that is sought). Second, the greater ease of getting a divorce has also likely lowered the incentives dating singles have to extend their search for "Mr. Right" or "Ms. Right." When single people knew that divorce was extraordinarily difficult, as was the case a half-century back, you can bet people were more cautious in choosing a mate. A mistake could be very costly, given that marriage was virtually for life. Now, however, when divorce is relatively easy, many people will not worry as much about making mistakes in selecting a mate and will try to save on the cost of finding the most compatible mate, with the understanding that they can move on, through a "quickie divorce," if a mistake becomes evident after the "I do's" have been said.

Either way, the easier divorces get, the greater the number of divorces (all other considerations held constant), a cause-and-effect connection that is evident in the statistics.[21] With the advent of "no-fault divorce" in the United States in the early 1970s, the divorce rate jumped precipitously—by half—during the following decade, from 14.9 divorces per 1,000 married women fifteen years of age and older in 1970s to 22.6 in 1980.[22] Since the passage of the Family Law Act of 1975, which introduced the concept of "no-fault divorce" in Australia, the divorce rate there has quadrupled.[23]

What does the prospect of easier divorces mean for wealth accumulation? The impact is not positive. The breakup itself can be very costly because both spouses will often require the advice of separate lawyers, and each lawyer can be expected to charge $100 to $250 an hour for work in and out of court. And one or more of the lawyers may seek to incite conflict with the admonition, "Demand more than you expect to get from the family assets because your spouse will be trying to do the same," knowing that the advice will increase the legal bills. The legal costs for an amicable divorce can easily be $1,000 or more (and that is cheap in some areas of the country). And a battle royal between the spouses in their lawyers' offices and court can run way up beyond $10,000.

Randy Fraboni—who worked as an electrician in rural Metamora, Illinois, and who was, reportedly, a frugal guy who drove used pickups— understands all too well how legal fees can mount with a contentious divorce. When he was divorced at age thirty-eight, at which time he sought full custody of his two children (then four and seven years old), he was billed by his lawyer for $35,000 (which he was contesting at this writing).[24] The total cost for the divorce was $74,000: $26,000 in fees for Fraboni's former wife's attorney, $7,000 for the attorney representing the children, and $6,000 in court costs in addition to the $35,000 for Randy Fraboni's. That's a big financial loss for any family, and the fees incurred do represent the upper limit for people with modest means. However, the family's loss is far greater when computed in terms of the retirement wealth that evaporated (or was transferred to the lawyers!). If the Frabonis had been able to stay together and had invested the lost legal fees of $74,000 in a stock index fund, at age sixty-seven they would have had over $689,478 in additional retirement wealth, assuming an appreciation rate of 8 percent. As it was, Randy Fraboni argued that the divorce left him broke, emotionally exhausted, and angry.[25]

As great as the costs of divorce can be, the greatest cost of divorce may be incurred by married couples who do not now expect divorce. The mere greater prospect of divorce reduces the incentive spouses have to accumulate mutually held assets. With divorce relatively easier and the statistics rising, spouses have reason to think that divorce is more likely, meaning that a measure of any built-up net worth will be lost in lawyers' fees. Many spouses also figure that there is some chance that the other spouse will get more than a fair share in the divorce. Hence, each spouse may wonder privately, "Why should I give up the good life now if all I'm going to do is pad the pockets of lawyers or my runaway mate sometime down the road?" At the very least, the prospects of divorce may cause couples to delay their saving and investing program until they have years of experience in the marriage and are confident that the marriage will last. As may be evident from our review of the power of compounding in the second chapter (Rule 2), those lost years can cut deeply into couples' retirement net worth.

A partial solution to the impact of divorce on marriages and wealth accumulation might come in the form of two marriage contracts, as tendered in the state legislature in Louisiana. A couple can choose to sign a contract in which divorce is as easy as it is today. The other marriage contract would make divorce nearly impossible, much as it was decades ago.

We suspect that the couples who sign the difficult-to-break contract will accumulate, as a group, more wealth that the couples who sign the easier-to-break contract.

Divorce as a Gateway to Poverty

Divorce is an economic crippler, especially for women. According to studies, divorce on average reduces the family income of divorced women between a fourth and a third,[26] a consequence that is not shared by divorced men, whose standard of living often improves.[27] After five years women have *on average* regained a major portion of their lost economic ground (mainly through remarrying, but also through improved skills and more aggressive job searches).[28]

Nevertheless, the income lost in the interim is likely to scuttle the saving and investment plans of many women for a period of time, a consequence of divorce that can have a substantial impact on the woman's wealth at retirement. To see this point, suppose a married woman who is thirty years old is able to save $5,000 a year from her income while married. Suppose also that when she is divorced at age thirty, she must stop saving altogether for a period of five years. How much does she lose in net worth at a retirement age of sixty-seven, assuming a rate of return of 8 percent? Those five years of lost savings lead to a reduction in her net worth at age sixty-seven of $371,827. If the divorce is postponed until age fifty, then her lost net worth at retirement is much lower, $79,774 (assuming the same drop in savings for five years and the same rate of return[29]).

No doubt, the *average* improvement in women's incomes five years after divorce hides the fate of many women who never recover because they never remarry; have more medical problems of their own because of the stress of divorce; have to deal with children whose medical, emotional, and educational problems escalate because of the divorce; and are unable to pursue careers because of child care costs. Single parents (mothers or fathers) also lose the benefits of specialization in the household, and the parent with the children, most often the mother, is often unable to fully collect the court-ordered child support from the other parent.

All too frequently, the consequence of the confluence of these economic forces is poverty, from which the single parent strapped with children is unable to reemerge. Divorce is a gateway to poverty no matter how you see it. And the divorce itself, because of the resulting poverty, eats relentlessly at the parent's *potential* net worth at retirement, creating a no-win situation.

If you want to make it in this country, understand that divorce is something you want to avoid, especially after having children. Divorce

Cost of Divorce to the Rich

If you plan to be rich and have a family, you should be mindful of the high and rapidly escalating child-support costs the courts have begun to impose on the high-income-earning spouses and parents. While child support payments have been rising for all divorced parents, the payments for rich divorced parents have expanded twenty-fold over the last decade. Michael Karp of Haverford, Pennsylvania, is one such rich divorcé and parent of four children (ages nine to thirteen at the time of his divorce), earning $5 million a year from his real estate and telecommunications investments.

When Mr. Karp was divorced, he had to shell out $23,266 *a month* for the support of his children, even though the children would be with him half the time. His former wife, Amy Karp, successfully argued before the courts that without such high payments, her children would feel like "second-class citizens" when they were with her. At this writing, the courts have ruled in favor of Mrs. Karp, with one court citing another case in which the judges ruled that children of wealthy parents are entitled to "good restaurants, good hotels, good shows and good camps." Mrs. Karp maintained that to make her children feel well-cared-for she needed the following amounts each month[30]:

NEEDED MONTHLY EXPENDITURES FOR FOUR RICH KIDS
IN ONE DIVORCE CASE

Housing	$5,608
Clothing	$958
Food	$1,068
Household help	$2,768
Books/magazines	$120
Vacations	$1,758
Flowers	$88
Furniture	$1,601
Other	$9,297
Total	$23,266

Are such expenditures "justified"? We must sidestep that issue, leaving it to the courts, where it should be settled. We only wish to suggest that such awards might affect the prospective rich parents' incentives to marry, have children, accumulate income-earning assets, and remain together.

can eliminate the benefits of specialization and cooperation that a couple has, it can hike child care costs and ensure that the custodial parent has to work double-time, at work and with the children. With children in tow, single parents—most likely mothers—automatically reduce the range of potential spouses the next time around.[31] Many people simply do not want to support, financially or emotionally, someone else's children. (It's not in their "selfish genes" to do so.) They can see the children as a threat to their own standard of living, both in the immediate future and, through the power of discounting, in their retirement years.

Our analysis of marriage and divorce reveals that you should choose your life partner very carefully, regardless of what the divorce laws are. You may have to search for a long time, delaying your marriage *and* saving plans, but those costs and delays can be seen as a necessary preliminary investment in a durable working partnership. An unbroken relationship, in turn, will allow for greater efficiency in home production, greater outside-the-home earnings, shared child rearing—and greater saving and investment once you do start your retirement planning. If you find a partner you can count on to be there in the years ahead and your partner can count on you, the two of you can also increase your risk taking, which means you can increase your rate of return on your investments (since risk and returns tend to go hand in hand). You can therefore reap the disproportionately greater power of compounding that goes with the higher rate of return.

Of course, all the lessons learned regarding the economic consequences of divorce should be taught to our children early on. Children who have children—married or not, divorced or not—tend to throttle their own chances of ever making it. If they do make it in this country, they must overcome monumental economic, social, and emotional obstacles. Young parents often have to drop out of high school (if not middle school!) to have and care for a child or, if they are able to stay in high school, they are unable to go on to college. Either way, their formal schooling suffers, and that fact alone, as we learned under Rule 4, will curb child parents' ability to build a satisfying early life as well as their ability to start building a significant net worth for retirement.

Having a baby is generally crippling emotionally and developmentally for a teenage girl, but to have a baby without being married (or in a committed relationship) is even worse, mainly because of the added child care work, the lack of long-term financial support, and absence of the division of labor that two parents can provide. Although there has been some improvement in the pregnancy rate for teenage girls in the first two-thirds of the 1990s, the teen pregnancy rate for unmarried girls is as significant today as it was as recently as 1980.[32] Today, one of the country's major newspapers reports that two-thirds of Hispanic and white teenage mothers are unmarried. A disheartening 95 percent of black

Cutting Your Losses in a Divorce

There is a basic rule in dealing with others in all walks of life, and whenever possible in bad circumstances: Cut your losses. This rule is often (but not always, of course) applicable to marriages that have gone bad. The longer an inevitable divorce is delayed, the more damage the divorce can do to both spouses' emotional state, physical health—and chances of building a fortune. The problem with delaying the inevitable is that when a marriage goes sour, many spouses begin to hesitate contributing to their joint assets, figuring that their contributions will be split with the other spouse at the time of the divorce.

As a consequence, the looming prospects of a divorce can retard the growth in the couple's jointly held assets, as they both might be inclined to switch from saving to spending more of their incomes. Their more profligate spending ways can escalate, as they both begin to feud over money and other matters and as they each try to spend progressively more and save progressively less.

If the couple's marriage begins to degenerate when, for example, they are both thirty-five years old and the degeneration process lasts for five years, during which time they reduce their joint saving and investing by $1,000 during each of the five years, then the threat of divorce will reduce their potential combined retirement net worth by $50,612 at age sixty-seven, assuming an appreciation rate of 8 percent. That kind of wealth loss should be a sufficient incentive for the couple to work things out or to call it quits so that each can get back to saving and investing for retirement.

Of course, it is not always possible to *know* when to call it quits in a marriage. Nor do we wish to encourage divorce. All we can do is point out that if the couple in our above example divorces after two years of feuding and impaired savings, instead of five years, and if they each then return to saving half of the lost $1,000, or $500, then they will each have $14,004 (for a total of $28,008) more in net worth than they would have had if they struggled to keep the marriage going for another three years. The loss in net worth to the couple that continues to stay together, with impaired savings, until late in life can be enormous. When they divorce late in life, there is little time for each to repair the damage done.

teen mothers are unmarried. How does this affect the girls financially? A teenager with a baby but no husband is three times more likely to end up on welfare than a teen mother who is married.[33]

Positive Parental Influence

Surely parents have a social and financial reasons for guiding their children through the early years of sexual activity, or inactivity. Parents often get stuck with the cost of care for their young children's children, and they very likely must help their own children-parents for a longer period than would otherwise be expected. Such help cuts into their retirement planning. Parents must recognize that they can alter, albeit in limited ways, the sexual proclivities of their children in a number of ways—for example, through education—that we need not cover here. What we do stress is that parents should alert their children to the costs of parenting that they must inevitably bear, not only in terms of out-of-pocket expenditures, but also in terms of lost income—*and, as we have stressed throughout the book, in terms of lost buildup of their children's net worth at retirement.* A baby can literally cost a lost fortune!

Parents can also influence the chances of their children's marriages lasting. Nonfrugal parents tend to establish lifestyles for their children that their children cannot replicate on their own without cutting into reasonable saving plans. The bride's parents typically pay handsomely for the wedding and might have a higher stake in the marriage lasting, given that the bride is most likely to be saddled with the cost of rearing the children alone, if the marriage dissolves. The bride's parents should, as a result, be concerned about the signals they send when the couple is planning their wedding.

In 1997, the average cost of a wedding in the United States was $19,104,[34] which is very close to the average cost of a wedding in 1990, after adjusting for inflation.[35] A wedding celebration is important, in that it provides an arena in which the bride and groom can make a public declaration of their commitment to each other in front of relatives and friends. And the wedding should be fun, as well as a chance for friends and relatives to gather and enjoy the good fortune and feeling the couple has found together. There are, however, other more long-lasting (albeit less romantic) ways to use a portion of the planned wedding cost, such as the down payment for a house, more education, or the startup costs for a business, all of which would encourage the couple to stay together.

Clearly, the cost of weddings varies greatly, all the way down to $95 for a walk-up ceremony at the Nashville Bridal Path Wedding Chapel to the sky as the limit (with one reporter showing how you can easily spend over $50,000 on a wedding for as few as two hundred guests[36]). And the cost of the wedding can be contained by carefully selecting the time of the wedding (say, midafternoon, when a big reception or meal would not be expected) and the place (one's own church, where punch and cookies are served at the reception).[37] A couple should enjoy their wedding day, but should keep frugality in mind as they start their new life together.

Let's not forget about the considerable expense to the bride's parents, if they pay for the wedding. Assuming the wedding occurs when the bride's parents are, say, forty-eight, the $19,104 wedding cost translates into a reduction in the bride's parents' retirement net worth of close to $82,447 at age sixty-seven (assuming a rate of appreciation of 8 percent). Then, the bride's parents have no guarantee that they will not have to support their daughter and, possibly, her children if the marriage falls apart.

How can the bride's parents improve the chances of the marriage remaining intact? Suppose the parents of the bride finance the wedding but spend half of what they normally would. For example, suppose the parents spent half of the average cost for a wedding, or $9,552. We consider that amount more than reasonable, given that even wedding consultants maintain that they can put on a nice wedding for 100 to 150 guests for $5,000.[38] Then suppose that the parents deposit the other half—$9,552—in an investment account for the bride and groom that appreciates at 8 percent a year in real terms. And say the parents stipulate that the couple only gets access to the account on their thirtieth wedding anniversary. If they divorce (or stop living together as a married couple) before their thirtieth anniversary, the account reverts back to the bride's parents (or to some charity). When a full and expensive wedding celebration is proposed, the bride and groom have limited financial reason to stay together if their troubles mount, especially if the couple is not frugal. With the investment account, the couple that does not stay together can lose the prospect of receiving their last "wedding gift" of just under $96,118 on their thirtieth wedding anniversary.

Contrary to what you might think, we truly appreciate the limited impact of financial incentives in holding marriages together, and our proposed solution is hardly a cure-all for the mounting pressures to separate that can occur within a marriage. However, our proposal might work for those couples who, from time to time, may be on the verge of parting ways but who are not sure that they should. The prospect of getting the thirtieth anniversary wedding gift might just be enough, in some cases, for the couple to patch over their differences.[39]

Marriage can never be total bliss, and no one should be fooled about this fact of life, no matter how powerful the feelings of love before marriage. Marriage won't make up for laziness or lack of patience and frugality. Marriage can even be hell, and a drain on wealth with the wrong spouse—as friends who have been divorced have reminded us. But the potential hellish nature of marriage is all the more reason that couples should be cautious in whom they marry. They should also recognize that above all, marriage requires a lot of work, understanding, and trust. When done right, marriage remains one of those important social institutions that can improve people's chances of doing well in America—in terms of health, happiness, and wealth.

Practical Advice for Achieving the Good Life

Marriage harbors many economies that allow couples to earn and save more and build a retirement fortune with relative ease. Marriage can also help you develop a satisfying life—if it is done right. To do it right, we submit that you should:

- Be very choosy in the selection of your spouse. To choose with care, always keep in mind the emotional, financial, and physical costs of divorce. Understand that all costs of divorce escalate dramatically when you have children. Then realize that you very likely have understated the costs, especially the emotional costs.
- Remember the old adage, "The devil is in the details"—especially in marriage. Most married couples recognize that they have to deal with the larger problems of their married life that have to do with buying a house and having children. Most married people will admit that they easily overlook the "small stuff"—the need for daily expressions of kindness, thoughtfulness, and attention to the other spouse.
- Take time to get to know your potential spouse, which means resist the temptation to get married on the first thoughts of passion and love. Consider the benefits and problems of getting married with as much attention as you might expect to give to the prospects of divorcing your spouse once you are married. This means consider holding off raising the issue for months so that you can get to know your potential spouse. When you become engaged, deliberately set the wedding date months, if not a year, in advance to give you more time to consider how the two of you work together.
- Resist having children before you complete your education. Remember that your house will not likely be your family's most costly purchase, as real estate agents are inclined to think. Children are typically far more costly than houses.
- If you or your child are in your teens and sexually active, use birth control. Remember that the cost of rearing a child through college equals the cost of a minimum of a quarter million condoms.

- Establish separate bank accounts and credit cards for the reasons given in this chapter: They can increase your frugality and the frugality of your spouse.

- If you and your potential spouse have significantly different incomes and net worth going into the marriage, consider developing a prenuptial agreement—even if you are the one with the lower income and net worth. Such a prenuptial agreement can increase the incentive that both spouses have to contribute as much as they can to the marriage, without fear that the other spouse will appropriate the contributions in a divorce.

- When you are inclined to fret about the problems of your marriage, remember the various costs of divorce. Before going for a divorce, consider a trial separation and counseling. But, just as importantly, acknowledge the importance of the need to cut your losses in a bad marriage; and the earlier you do, the better. An early divorce can reduce the assets that must be divided and, accordingly, your attorney's fees. An early divorce can also increase the amount of time you will have to rebuild your lost net worth.

- If you do divorce, try to find ways of shortening the "grieving process" in order to get on with your life. Consider doing what a growing number of newly single people are doing, holding a "divorce party" to which you can invite friends and relatives who can help you put the marriage behind you. Then, sit down and draw up a plan for the rest of your life.

An Exercise for Achieving the Good Life: Improving Marriages

Good marriages can do wonders for couples, both emotionally and financially. However, almost all marriages suffer from lack of communication and attention to problems that can, over a long period of time, give rise to major problems. In this exercise, we ask married readers to consider jointly the problems that they confront in the hope that the airing of the problems will lead to remedies and a longer lasting marriage (singles can skip this exercise).

1. Identify what you consider the three most prominent benefits from being married, and ask your spouse to do the same independent of you. Compare your list with your spouse's list.

2. Identify what you consider to be the three most prominent nonfinancial problems in your marriage, and ask your spouse to do the same independent of you. Compare your list with your spouse's list. Think of ways the two of you can jointly resolve the identified problems.

3. Identify what you consider the three most prominent financial problems in your marriage, and ask your spouse to do the same independent of you. Again, compare your list with your spouse's list. With your spouse, estimate how much your listed financial problems are draining your savings each year. Indicate the amount here.

4. Determine the potential increase in your net worth at retirement if you can correct the financial problems indicated in question 3, assuming an annual return of 8 percent. Follow these steps on your Texas Instrument BA II or Model 35 hand calculator:

Press [2nd] and then press [MODE].

Enter your estimate of how much more you can save each year by correcting your financial problems indicated in question 3 and press [PMT].

Enter 8 and press [%i].

Enter the number of years until retirement (your target retirement age minus your current age) and press [N].

Calculate the potential increase in your net worth by pressing [CPT] and then [FV].

RULE 6

Take Care of Yourself

One of the most important rules you can follow is: Take good care of yourself. For as long as you can remember you have been reminded of the importance of eating right, exercising regularly, getting enough sleep, and avoiding unhealthy habits. And even if you haven't always followed this advice faithfully (and who has?), you have never really doubted that taking good care of your health can make life more productive and enjoyable. But what does taking good care of yourself have to do with getting rich? Much more than you might think.

For starters, what is the advantage of accumulating lots of wealth if you destroy your health in the process? Health without wealth is far more attractive than wealth without health. An unhealthy life is uninviting, no matter how much money you might have. And taking good care of yourself is an important way to increase your income. Healthy people miss less work, are more productive when they are at work, and so are more likely to get promoted and earn larger salaries. Healthy people also tend to look better, and like it or not, a good physical appearance pays in many ways, including higher incomes.[1] And it should surprise no one that research shows that people's health is one of the strongest and most consistent determinants of "happiness" and a sense of "psychological well-being," which contribute to higher incomes.[2] Of course, higher incomes make it easier to increase savings, and, as we have seen, a modest improvement in savings can lead to a substantial increase in your net worth at retirement time.

Moreover, by taking care of yourself, you can increase the probability of living to a ripe old age. Make no mistake about it, as impressive as the increase in life expectancy has been in America, many Americans are fully capable of extending their longevity even more. Surprisingly, the average life span of Americans in the late 1990s ranked twenty-third in the world, behind that of such countries as Costa Rica and Cuba. One of the reasons people in some low-income countries live longer on average than we do in the United States is that, according to one researcher, people in other countries "don't have the money to be eating steak every night. Also, they don't have the wealth to be driving automobiles, so they have to walk."[3]

We aren't advocating poverty as a way of increasing your health. Far from it. In general wealth and health are mutually reinforcing, with wealth increasing the opportunities you will have for better medical care and a healthy lifestyle, and good health increasing your opportunities for added wealth. But wealth can also increase opportunities for indulgences that are unhealthy. Having the personal resolve to resist the unhealthy temptations that come from living in a wealthy country will pay long-run dividends both financially and, more important, physically.

Choosing to Live Longer

Like getting rich, good health and long life are not completely a matter of choice. Some people are simply born with a genetic endowment that, barring accidents, practically guarantees them a long and healthy life. One of the best things that could happen to you if you want to live a long time is to be born a female. There are slightly more males born than females, but the ranks of the males thin much more rapidly with age. There are only 55.4 men for every one hundred women between the ages of eighty and eighty-four; only 43.7 men for every one hundred women between the ages of eighty-five and eighty-nine; only 33.5 men for every one hundred women between the ages of ninety and ninety-four; and only 26.5 men for every one hundred women ninety-five or older.[4] The only good news here for men is that if you are not popular with women your age now, you will be if you can make it to ninety!

Also, when you are born is important. For example, if you had been born around 1900, your chances of living to one hundred were one in 2,500 if you were female and one in 5,000 if male. Children born today have a much greater chance of making it to one hundred: one in 50 for females and one in 200 for males.[5]

But again, like getting rich, good health and long life are also strongly influenced by the choices we make. You can, to a significant degree, choose a longer and healthier life. And since you can't do anything about when you were born, your genetic endowment, or your sex at birth (there is no evidence that men who have sex change operations acquire the life expectancy of women), it is sensible to concentrate on those things you can do to increase your health and longevity.

There is a long list of things you can do and not do that will add both life to your years and years to your life.[6] For example, according to some estimates you can add an average of about eight years to your life by not smoking. Eating properly and not putting on excessive weight reduces your risk of an early death. Moderate but regular exercise is another way to improve the quality of life and reduce excessive weight, high blood pressure, and other common risk factors that can shorten your life. Moderate drinking (up to the equivalent of two glasses of wine a day) can increase your longevity, but drinking can significantly shorten the lives of those who abuse alcohol.[7] There is no doubt that you can increase your chances for a long and healthy life by making healthy lifestyle choices. The financial advantages of making those choices are the primary topic of this chapter.

Researchers have long known that good personal habits can add years to your life. They've debated, however, whether good personal habits add life to the extra years, or simply extend the number of years of physical disability.

A recently released medical study reveals good news. The study tracked 1,741 men and women who graduated from the University of Pennsylvania in 1939 and 1940 for the next forty-plus years.[8] In 1962, when the alumni had reached the age of forty-two, researchers classified them by their personal habits relating to smoking, diets, and exercise into categories of "low risk," "moderate risk," and "high risk."

They then evaluated their health for seven successive years beginning in 1986, giving each a rating on the researchers' "disabilities index" (which included numerical assessments of each person's ability to engage in eight basic tasks: dressing and grooming, arising, eating, walking, bathing and other hygiene, reaching, gripping, and executing basic chores). They found that at age seventy-four the high-risk alumni had a disabilities score twice the disabilities score of the low-risk alumni. Those low-risk alumni who had died at the time of the last evaluation had experienced shorter periods of disabilities before their deaths than had the high-risk alumni. The alumni in the low-risk category postponed the onset of disabilities by about five years. The researchers concluded that the vitality of life we experience in later life may have as much, or more, to do with the life choices we make as it does with our genes.[9]

But this line of research only seems to settle what is obvious from casual observation of our older friends and relatives. Just as obvious is that there is a strong positive association between good health and income. One way of illustrating that association is to consider how mortality rates decline as income increases. In Table 6.1 mortality rates are

Ways to Live Longer

If you think that you cannot affect how long you live, consider these facts:

- A male who smokes forty or more cigarettes daily will lose eight years of life.[10]
- 90 percent of premature deaths can be attributed to any of the following behaviors that are subject to individual control: smoking cigarettes, overeating, misusing alcohol, failing to control high blood pressure, not exercising, or not wearing seat belts.[11]
- Death in an accident is seventeen times more likely on a motorcycle, motor scooter, and motor bike than in a car.[12]
- 40 percent of traffic accidents result from three behaviors: speeding, failing to yield right of way, or following too closely.[13]
- A drop in a person's blood cholesterol by 20mg/dl reduced deaths due to heart disease by 16 percent.[14]
- An active life and a long life "are practically synonymous. Those who regularly expend energy–either by walking, climbing stairs, or participating in sports and exercise program—can expect to live longer than those who pass their hours lounging."[15]

shown for white males and white females (adjusted for the age of people between twenty-five to sixty-four) for different annual incomes measured in 1991 dollars.

Table 6.1.
Income and Mortality Rates

DEATHS PER 1,000 PEOPLE PER YEAR

Family Income (1991)	White Males	White Females
Under $9,174	13.5	6.7
$9,175–$18,348	10.9	6.2
$18,349–$27,522	9.0	5.5
$27,523–$36,696	7.8	5.3
$36,697–$45,870	8.4	5.1
$45,871 or more	7.6	4.7

Source: Updated from 1980 income figures in Ralph L. Keeney, "Mortality Risks Induced by Economic Expenditures," Risk Analysis 10, no. 1 (1990): 147–59, Table IV.

An association between higher income and lower mortality, such as shown in Table 6.1, does not establish which causes which. The purpose of this chapter is to show that taking good care of yourself (reducing your expected mortality rate) can increase your financial well-being. But it could also be that the cause and effect runs the other way—those who are wealthy are in a better position to spend more on health clubs, good food, and medical care, which reduces their mortality rates. And indeed, there is evidence that wealth does cause an improvement in health.[16] But this evidence also indicates that the cause and effect go both ways, with good health increasing income and wealth. There is nothing surprising about this. Those who are healthy generally have longer and more productive careers, and are therefore capable of earning and saving more.

The Problem of Being Like Gates

In terms of becoming wealthy, there are two important advantages from a longer life expectancy:

1. The longer you live, the longer you can let the power of compound interest increase the value of your savings.

2. The longer you live, the greater the return you can receive on the wealth you have accumulated at retirement.

Let's consider the importance of longevity in accumulating wealth with an extreme, but interesting, example. Bill Gates is the richest man in the world, with $51 billion in net worth when we wrote this. Except to politicians in Washington, D.C., this is a mind-boggling amount of money. For example, consider how long it would take you to accumulate $51 billion with an incredibly generous wage, but without the aid of compound interest. If you got a job paying $10,000 an hour at age twenty and you worked forty hours a week, fifty-two weeks a year, until age seventy, your total earnings before taxes would come to $1.04 billion, barely over 2 percent of what Bill Gates is worth. If, instead of retiring at seventy, you continued working at $10,000 per hour for another 2,452 years (until age 2,522), paid no taxes, and saved every dime (but without investing it) you would then have $51 billion—about what Bill Gates has now.

Obviously, no matter how well you take care of yourself, you are even less likely to live over twenty-five hundred years than you are to start making $10,000 an hour at age twenty. But bear with us. There is a point to our example, as unrealistic as our illustration might seem. Consider now a *slightly more* realistic (but still unrealistic) strategy for becoming as rich as Bill Gates, a strategy that takes advantage of the power of compound interest. Start working at age twenty-two at a job that allows you to save $8.22 each day, or $3,000 a year (which assumes you don't take advantage of the opportunity to save before-tax dollars). Invest that amount every year at an annual return of 8 percent and you will be worth almost $53 billion when you are *only* 205!

Obviously this strategy is not as realistic as we would like. The amount you would have to earn to save $3,000 a year is very realistic, as is the 8 percent rate of return, but your chances of making it to 205 aren't much better than those of living to 2,522 without some startling medical breakthroughs and a really healthy lifestyle.[17] But realistic or not, we will refer back to this example toward the end of the chapter to make a very realistic observation about your return from Social Security. More important, the example illustrates a serious point that is the primary message of this chapter—when taking advantage of compound interest *just a few extra years of life can make a big difference in the amount of wealth you accumulate.* Also, once you achieve a level of wealth that is reasonably within your grasp, the advantages of having a lot more can become rather insignificant. So it shouldn't trouble you that getting as rich as Bill Gates by taking better care of yourself is unlikely. The important thing to keep in mind is that the extra years you can achieve with healthy living can make a big difference in your financial wealth, not to mention maintaining your most precious asset—your health.

A Little Extra Time—A Lot of Extra Money

We now consider some realistic possibilities for increasing your wealth by taking better care of your health, beginning by examining the life expectancies of those who are still relatively young. If you were born in 1980, your life expectancy at birth was 70.0 for males and 77.4 for females. But this doesn't mean that, say, at age twenty-five, males can expect to live only 45.0 more years, and females only 52.4 more years. By virtue of making it to twenty-five you have avoided being one of the early fatalities that brings the life expectancy down for newborns. Twenty-five-year-old males can expect to live 49.2 more years, or until age 74.2, and twenty-five-year-old females can expect to live another 55.0 years, or until age eighty.[18]

But these figures surely understate your life expectancy. Life expectancy has been increasing steadily for a long time, and there is no reason to expect that increase to suddenly stop—indeed it may accelerate.

For example, life expectancy at birth went from 47.6 years in 1900, to 71.7 in 1970, to 76.5 in 1995 (averages of male and female). So as you get older, the life expectancy for those your age will no doubt increase. According to projected mortality rates for early in the twenty-first century, a fifty-five-year-old male can expect to live another 28.02 years (or to age eighty-eight, plus one week).[19] Depending on your age and sex, by the time you reach fifty-five, your life expectancy could easily be another thirty or more years. And keep in mind, by taking good care of yourself you have a good chance of beating these life expectancy figures by a good margin, since they are averages.

And beating the longevity odds can pay big dividends. Assume that at age twenty-two you start investing $3,000 a year at an 8 percent annual return. If you retire at age sixty-seven you will have accumulated $1.26 million. However, if you are healthy at age sixty-seven and believe you have six years more life expectancy than average, you might decide to keep working and continuing your saving and investing program until age seventy-three. If so, you will have $2.01 million at retirement. Those extra six years of working (less than 12 percent of your working years) add more than 60 percent to your wealth. And because you have taken good care of yourself and expect to live six more years than the average, you can anticipate the same number of retirement years during which to enjoy the extra wealth. Furthermore, you can convert the 60 percent extra from retiring later into more than a 60 percent gain in your retirement income if you do live an extra six years.

If you retire at age sixty-seven, you can convert your $1.26 million into an income stream that will continue as long as you live by purchasing a lifetime annuity, which can give you an annual income of $166,000 until you die. This annuity is based on an 8 percent interest rate and the expectation that you will live almost nineteen more years (which is based on projected life expectancies early in the next century, somewhat more than is expected now).[20] If you die the day after you buy a lifetime annuity, you lose and the insurance company that sold the annuity to you wins. On the other hand, you cannot outlive the annuity. If you live to 110, you keep getting the $166,000 every year and you are a big winner.[21] So the longer you wait to retire, and therefore the less time the insurance company expects you to live, the larger the annuity you can buy with a given amount of money. By waiting until seventy-three to retire, you not only have 60 percent more wealth, but you can buy a larger annual income with each dollar of your wealth since now, according to the insurance companies' longevity tables, you are expected to live only another 14.5 years. You can use the $2.01 million you will have if you retire at age seventy-three and buy a lifetime annuity that pays about $294,000 each year, or over 77 percent more than the $166,000 each year you would get if you retire at age sixty-seven.

But the good financial news from taking good care of yourself and living longer isn't over yet. Remember, you waited until age seventy-three to retire because you expect to live six years longer than average. So instead of receiving $294,000 for 14.5 years, you expect to receive it for nineteen years.[22] You not only get 77 percent more income per year by waiting to retire until age seventy-three, but because you have taken care of yourself, you will receive that higher income for about the same number of years as the person of average longevity who retires at age sixty-seven.

Of course, a healthy person may still want to retire at age sixty-seven and use his good health and expected longevity for a longer retirement. But even in this case, the healthy person's good health can pay off financially for the simple reason that, assuming he uses some of the accumulated wealth at retirement to buy a lifetime annuity, he will receive it for more years. Even a few extra years can generate a large financial payoff because it doesn't take many additional years to increase your postretirement life span by a large percentage. For example, if you retire at age sixty-seven and are expected to live another fourteen years (about the current expectation), then adding seven years to your life allows you to receive your annuity 50 percent longer than average.

The Financial Consequences of a Shorter Life Expectancy

On the other side of this coin, a shorter life expectancy, even if only a few years shorter, greatly reduces your retirement returns. This is one reason Social Security is such a poor investment for minorities, particularly poor minorities. The life expectancy for a nonwhite male at birth was 67.9 in 1995, as opposed to 73.4 for a white male at birth. This difference, large as it is, becomes a huge relative difference when seen from age sixty-seven, the age at which one will become eligible for Social Security early in the next century.[23] For example, the average low-income single black male living in an inner city can expect to get back in Social Security payments only 88 cents for every dollar of Social Security taxes he pays into the system.[24] His expected rate of return is negative. The reason: His life expectancy is not long enough to make the system pay for him.

We are not necessarily recommending the purchase of a lifetime annuity at retirement, and certainly not recommending using all your retirement savings to buy one. Most people like knowing that there will be something left after they are gone to give to their family and loved ones, or to a favorite cause. The advantage of discussing a lifetime annuity is that it allows us to point out the tremendous financial gains that are possible from living a few extra years. You don't have to buy a lifetime annuity with your retirement wealth to benefit financially from living longer. Social Security and many of the retirement plans people have through their employers are lifetime annuities, paying out a specified amount as long as the retiree lives.[25] So, the longer you live, the better the return on these retirement plans. Also, the wealth you have accumulated from saving and investing can be put into a safe fixed-income investment and provide you with a steady income stream as long as you live, without reducing your principal.[26] Again, the longer you live, the greater the financial benefit you receive. Of course, outliving your financial assets can be a concern—although this is a concern most people would choose to confront if the alternative is dying early. Fortunately, there are ways of striking a compromise between ensuring that you will not outlive your assets, no matter how long you live, and having something left over to leave to your loved ones.

Retiring on the Installment Plan

We have discussed the financial benefits of taking advantage of good health and greater longevity by working longer. This advice may seem to go against the trend toward retiring earlier in life rather than later. For example, the percentage of men sixty to sixty-four years of age who remain in the labor force has been declining in the United States and many other industrial countries since at least the early 1960s. In 1960 some 82 percent of American men in the sixty to sixty-four age category were still working. In the mid-1990s the rate was down to 53 percent.[27] Explanations for this trend include the increased labor force participation of women, which increases family income and makes it possible for men to retire early, and a bias in Social Security in favor of early retirement.[28] Even if this trend continues, staying active in the labor force beyond the traditional retirement ages of sixty-five or even seventy will be a smart move for an increasing number of people. People who are healthy, no matter what their ages, can add satisfaction and fulfillment to their lives, while benefiting financially, by remaining productive. Because of this, we predict that the trend toward early retirement will soon reverse, for several reasons:

1. As long as people are healthy they can realize a lot of satisfaction from the stimulation and feeling of accomplishment working provides. Maybe we all need to acknowledge the wisdom of James Russell Wiggins, who continued to go to his *Washington Post* office every day at the age of ninety-five and who quipped in an interview on why he has lived and worked for so long, "Routine is the salva-

The Money Keeps Coming

You cannot outlive a lifetime annuity no matter how long you live. But with a lifetime annuity, there is nothing left when you die. Other options guarantee you a lifetime income and still leave open the possibility of having something left over. For example, at retirement you can buy a variable annuity that will pay out a specified amount each month, or quarter, for a specified number of years, say twenty. If you die before that time is up, your beneficiaries begin receiving the payment and will continue to do so until the twenty years are up. If you live longer than twenty years, the payments continue to you for as long as you live, but your heirs receive nothing. These annuities pay less than a straight lifetime annuity, since they guarantee a payment for a specified number of years, and they don't guarantee that your heirs will get anything. But they provide some security for heirs for a time, and ensure that you don't outlive your money.

Another option is called stock dividend laddering. This requires that you shift your investments into stocks that provide a good yield in dividends, with the dividend date differing so that you receive a steady dividend income. Since this keeps your assets in stocks, there is the risk that the total value of your assets will fluctuate with the stock market, but since dividend payments are not extremely sensitive to fluctuations in the stock price, there is not much risk to your dividend income. But if even that risk makes you uncomfortable in retirement, you can consider "bond laddering," under which you buy high-grade bonds with different interest-payment dates so you receive a steady, and even more secure, income.[29]

Of course the best way to protect against outliving your money is to build up such a sizable sum at retirement that you can, at regular intervals, withdraw sizable amounts from your investments without having to worry about ever depleting your assets unless you live well past your hundredth birthday. There can be tax advantages to this approach, since your withdrawals are taxed as capital gains rather than the higher rate (at least for most people) at which ordinary income from annuities, dividends, and interest are taxed. Tax considerations are important when making decisions on how to take your retirement income, so consult your tax accountant. Also, there are typically significant insurance and money management fees with annuities and stock dividend and bond laddering.

tion for old age."[30] Of course, healthy people value leisure, but leisure can best be enjoyed in relatively small doses. Retiring at age sixty when your life expectancy is another thirty-five years will look like too much leisure to most people. As E. Lee Bryan said, "My wife says I flunked retirement." After coming out of retirement,

Bryan has started an information technology company and taken courses in German and computer science at Duke University.[31] Of course, the satisfaction that comes from working can also be accompanied by work-related stress that can be more difficult for older people to tolerate. So expect people to take their projected years of "retirement" on the "installment plan," that is, through annual vacations or maybe a sabbatical from work every now and then. The vacations, or "work sabbaticals," might somewhat deplete your annual savings, but that doesn't mean that you will actually have less wealth when you really do retire. Vacations or work sabbaticals can enable you to continue to work and save for more years, during which the power of compound interest will be at work, building up your net worth.

2. Work is becoming less physically demanding, so working longer is less of a physical burden. Indeed, more jobs are requiring the type of mental and creative challenges that can make work stimulating, enjoyable—and possible—for older people. Consider the case of Dr. David Sensenig, who worked as a surgeon until age seventy-four. Now seventy-seven, Dr. Sensenig is preparing for the Pennsylvania bar exam, having gone to Temple University Law School. He says, "I'm not looking for an associate's job working 70-hour weeks and hoping to be a partner in 10 years," but he continues, "I think I can be of service in the medical malpractice field."[32]

3. Most people may still retire in their sixties, or earlier, but retiring from one job will mean shifting to another career rather than heading to the porch and an easy chair. Career shifting will become a more common activity for people of all ages, and so it will seem quite natural for future workers as they approach the traditional retirement ages of sixty-five or seventy.[33]

4. Technology is making it easier for people to work at home, and work flexible hours, further increasing their opportunities to remain productive well beyond the age when people now retire. With fax machines, computers, e-mail, and the Internet, people can access data and information from around the world, prepare reports that look professionally done, and keep in touch with the office at any hour of the day and night, and never leave their homes.

5. More and more people are in defined contribution pension plans rather than defined benefit plans. In defined contribution plans,

the employer and employee contribute some specified amount, or percentage, to the employee's account that is invested by the employee (choosing from a menu of investment possibilities), with the amount received at retirement depending on how much the investments have increased in value. In defined benefit plans, the benefits are determined by formulas including years of service and pay, with a rather loose connection between the benefits received and the contributions made, and almost no connection between benefits and returns on investment. And typically you can't start receiving payments from a defined benefit plan until you actually retire and quit drawing your regular salary, so the value of your retirement actually begins to decline at some point if you continue working. This is not the case with a defined contribution plan, since you can start drawing on your accumulated investment while still working, and the amount you don't draw on continues to earn a return. So as more of the workforce is covered by defined contribution pensions, the advantage to working more years will increase. Also, the bias Social Security creates in favor of retiring early will become less important. Social Security will become a smaller proportion of postretirement income for most people, and there will likely be policy changes allowing people to invest at least part of their Social Security "contributions" in stocks and bonds, moving Social Security in the direction of a defined contribution plan.[34]

The Blurring of Careers and Retirement

The prevailing view has been that people travel through three distinct stages in their lives; growing up, during which time they get an education and prepare for an occupation; progressing through their careers along a fairly predictable path; and then, usually sometime in their sixties, leaving the workforce for the full-time leisure of retirement. That view was never completely accurate, but it is becoming less so with every passing day. We discussed in our education chapter (Rule 4) how education is increasingly becoming a lifelong pursuit, not something you complete in your early twenties. People still prepare for occupations, but with the understanding that technology advances are rapidly changing the skills required for any given occupation, and creating new occupations almost as fast. A successful career now requires continuous learning, through on-the-job experience, employer-provided training programs, and school-based degrees. So the demarcation between education and career is being blurred to the point of obliteration.

At the same time, the improving technology and the continuous learning it demands is also blurring the line between career and retirement. People whose careers have been spent acquiring and using a succession of skills, much like a surfer catches and rides a succession of waves, will feel comfortable continuing their working lives in new directions during their post-"retirement" years. And the new technologies will make it easier for them to do so in ways that accommodate the inevitable imperatives of their aging bodies. People will increasingly be retiring gradually, on the installment plan, so to speak, and by doing so they will be taking advantage of opportunities to lead richer lives both financially and, more importantly, in terms of their sense of self-worth and personal satisfaction.

Consider the possibilities facing those in high school or college today, who take good care of themselves. The prospect of working until age eighty and then enjoying a retirement as long as those retiring at sixty-seven today is entirely reasonable. Consider the effect the extra thirteen years of work and saving would have on your wealth at retirement. Again, assuming that you start investing $3,000 a year at 8 percent interest at age twenty-two, you would have accumulated a total of $3.48 million when you retire at eighty (as opposed to $1.26 million at sixty-seven). Assuming a life expectancy of fourteen years at age eighty, and an 8 percent interest rate, that $3.48 million will buy you a lifetime annuity of about $423,000 a year.

Of course, you may want to work until eighty, but at a more relaxed pace after, say, your early seventies. Assume, as before, that you start investing $3,000 a year at 8 percent at age twenty-two, and keep that up until age seventy-three, when you will have over $2.01 million ($2,013,977). At that time you begin working only part-time, and to maintain your spendable income, you quit saving and draw off 8 percent a year of the $2.01 million, or $161,118 a year. So, from seventy-three until eighty your wealth remains the same in real terms (after accounting for inflation). At age eighty, when you retire completely, you will have $2.01 million, which can be converted into a lifetime annuity worth (still assuming a life expectancy of fourteen years and an 8 percent interest rate) close to $244,000 a year.

You can easily adjust these payouts in many different ways. For example, you may want to take out more income from your savings from ages seventy-three to eighty when you can expect to be more active than when you are over eighty (of course, in our example you are still earning an income to supplement the $161,118 a year from seventy-three to eighty).[35] The important point is that the better care you take of your health and the longer your life expectancy, the greater the return you can realize, and the greater the array and attractiveness of your saving and investing options.

Smoking Out Net Worth

The financial advantage of taking good care of your health is clearly evident when you recognize that it is often expensive to do things that harm your health. Avoiding behavior that has a negative effect on your health and longevity can allow you to save more, and also increases the time you have to realize the advantages of compound interest.

Choosing not to smoke is a good example of the financial advantages of avoiding unhealthy behavior. The savings from not smoking can grow into a significant retirement bonus. Consider an eighteen-year-old deciding whether to smoke. If the decision is to smoke, then the decision is when to start smoking. So even if the eighteen-year-old decides to smoke, he could also decide to start one year later and save the price of a pack of cigarettes, about $2.25, each day. At age nineteen he could start smoking and invest the $821.25 he has saved ($2.25 times 365). Even if he never saved another dime, at an 8 percent annual return, the $821.25 investment will be worth $33,023 when he reaches age sixty-seven (or when he would have reached sixty-seven, if he dies). If our now nineteen year-old decides to wait another year before beginning to smoke, then he could invest another $821.25 when he becomes twenty. With this decision he not only increases his chances of making it to sixty-seven, but has another $30,577 when he does, for a total of $63,600. This net worth may not seem huge, but it is almost 13 percent more than the median net worth of all families and a little over 60 percent of the median net worth of retirees in America in 1995, which was $104,100.[36] Not bad for refraining from smoking for *just two years*, and having the patience to let the savings grow.

Of course, the young person who refrains from smoking until he is twenty will likely never begin, having had more time to think through the decision. By continuing to save and invest the $821.25 a year that would have been spent on a daily pack of cigarettes (we make the very conservative assumption that the price of cigarettes does not increase), at age sixty-seven he would have $435,544 in wealth by not smoking. And in arriving at this wealth figure, we have ignored any saving in medical costs the nonsmoker may have realized.

The above example understates the financial gains from not smoking for a reason that we cannot ignore, since the issue of longevity is central to this chapter. Assume that our eighteen-year-old who is considering smoking will have a life expectancy of seventy-five if he smokes (which is higher than the current life expectancy for smokers, but life expectancy will increase for everyone, smokers included, in the years ahead) and eighty-five if he doesn't. In this case, he can continue to work and save until age seventy-seven, if he doesn't smoke, and still enjoy an expected retirement just as long as the smoker who quits working and saving at age sixty-seven. And by saving and investing the cost of smoking a pack a day until seventy-seven, he will have $952,204 more at retirement than the smoker who retired at age sixty-seven, not to mention a longer and healthier life.

Weighing Net Worth

Another way many Americans can improve their physical and financial health is by maintaining their weight. As indicated in the nearby box, over half of all Americans are overweight. In the last two decades, there has been a 33 percent increase in the number of Americans who are considered obese (defined as 20 percent or more overweight). Obesity is viewed by experts as a "major risk" factor in heart attacks, as well as other diseases such as diabetes and high blood pressure.[37] It has been estimated that maintaining an appropriate weight for your sex, height, and age adds an average of 303 days (almost ten months) to your life when compared to those who are 25 percent overweight.[38] So losing weight can improve how you feel and look, and increase your life expectancy.

Along with these advantages, there are also financial gains to be realized from maintaining your weight. Just the cost of the extra food consumed when overweight can add up over time. Those who are overweight commonly snack between meals on junk food, which is not only high in calories and fats, but is also very expensive for the nourishment you get. Also, those who don't maintain their weight often have to spend more on clothing as their weight fluctuates. And, of course, the harmful health effects of overweight eventually mean greater expense for doctor visits and medicines. Although maintaining the proper weight will not increase your longevity by as much as not smoking, it can result in comparable saving. And the extra longevity you do realize by maintaining a healthy weight can add to the time you have to build your wealth and enjoy it.

Reconsider our example in which you save $3,000 a year at 8 percent until age sixty-seven, at which point you will have a net worth of $1.26 million. If you were to take the added ten months of life and extend your career and saving by that amount, you would save an additional $2,500 in your sixty-eighth year, and you would continue to allow your net worth to appreciate for the ten months, which would add $86,685 to your net worth. The total potential gains in your net worth from keeping to a reasonable weight: $86,185.

American Scales Go Higher!

The percentage of Americans who are "overweight," or risk health problems from the extra pounds they carry, rose from 24.4 percent in 1960 to 33 percent in 1988 to 55 percent in 1998. From Table 6.2 below, you can assess whether you should trim a few pounds, if you don't already know that you should:

TABLE 6.2.
HEALTHY WEIGHT RANGES FOR ADULTS

Height*	Weight** (in pounds)
4'10"	91–119
5'	97–128
5'1"	101–132
5'2"	104–137
5'3"	107–141
5'4"	111–146
5'5"	114–150
5'6"	118–155
5'7"	121–160
5'8"	125–164
5'9"	129–169
5'10"	132–174
5'11"	136–179
6'	140–184
6'1"	144–189
6'2"	148–195
6'3"	152–200
6'4"	156–205
6'5"	160–211
6'6"	164–216

*Without shoes
**Without clothes
The higher weights in each range apply to those with more muscle and bone, generally men.
Source: Report of the Dietary Guidelines Advisory Committee on the Dietary Guidelines for Americans, 1995.

Drug Addiction as Wealth Destruction

One of the most harmful things you can do to your health is to become addicted to drugs. This is well known. But in addition to destroying your health, drugs can also destroy your wealth. Indeed, drugs are one of the more certain ways Americans can end their lives in dire poverty. The problem is not just the high price of drugs, although that is an important consideration. The biggest problem is that drug addiction destroys a person's ability to live the type of life that makes the creation and accumulation of wealth possible. Drug addicts are not likely to have the steady habits or the patience and foresight to be productive, to see the long-run opportunities available to Americans, to save and invest, to maintain a marriage, and to take care of their health. As a person's drug addiction progresses, the required expenditures to alleviate the craving go up, which means more and more of the addict's time and money being devoted to obtaining the desired drugs. This means the addict has less ability and time for earning a living and saving and investing.

The whole process is one of self-perpetuating degeneration, a collapse of the addict's sense of a meaningful future, and progressively less reason to save and invest for the future. No wonder many addicts contemplate suicide as their addiction gains such control of their degenerating lives that the future becomes a meaningless abstraction. There is no reason to plan for retirement because, in the grip of such an addiction, there is little prospect of making it to retirement age.

Aside from describing the health risks, which are substantial, one way of discouraging young people from ever taking that first fix is to remind them of the full costs of taking it. (Because kids have a tendency to feel immortal, pointing to the wealth risk in dollars and cents may do more to drive the point home). It's not just the price of the fix, but all that is given up because of it. The cost is clearly substantial, surely far greater than most young Americans imagine.

Consider the fate of Standford Cooley, who was a full-blown heroin and cocaine "druggy" at age thirty-three. He had to raise $50 to $75 a day in cash just to feed his addiction, which he obtained by becoming an accomplished shoplifter.[39] Regardless of how he raised the required funds, Cooley's habit was very expensive. If he spent an average of $62.50 a day on heroin and cocaine, he had to fork over to his suppliers $22,813 a year. That's bad enough, but just think of his *total* cost over a long stretch of time. And the loss was even greater than the cost of the drugs. His income-earning ability was surely curbed by an addiction that limited his preparation for productive work, and undermined the steady perseverance required to do such work even if he had the training. Conservatively, the total annual cost of Cooley's drug habit—drug expenditures plus lost after-tax income and associated medical bills—was $40,000 a year. It is clear that if Cooley had remained free from drugs, he could have lived a life with far more dignity, creature comforts, and personal satisfaction on

$20,000 a year, while saving the other $20,000. As a measure of the financial cost of Cooley's addiction, let's assume that his habit took hold at age twenty-five and lasted until age forty-five, when we optimistically assume that Cooley kicks his habit, begins earning a steady income, and lives a normal life. If he had saved the $20,000 each year from age twenty-five to forty-five, and let it continue to earn 8 percent, he would have $5,482,525 when he turned sixty-seven. Again, we don't expect anyone to accumulate this much on $40,000 a year; rather, such calculations offer a measure of the exorbitant cost of getting hooked on drugs. No matter how you measure it, the cost of drug addiction is enormous.

Young Americans must be warned of the physical dangers of drugs and made aware of the tremendous financial costs as well. Those who are not deterred from using drugs by the health risk may be deterred by the financial risks. They need to be shown these figures, which can easily be altered with different assumptions. Still, no matter what the assumptions, the cost of drugs is truly astounding.

Increasing Your Life Expectancy

Although the amount of additional wealth possible in not abusing your health is impressive, it is not surprising. Cutting back on the things that cost money and shorten your life can increase the amount of wealth you can accumulate—you can save more and invest more for a longer period of time. But what about things that can increase your life expectancy, such as exercise programs, physical exams, healthier food, and safety devices (for example smoke detectors and fire extinguishers for the home), but that cost money that could otherwise be invested? The answer depends on how many years you will actually add to your life. As we are about to see, it doesn't take much of an increase in life expectancy to more than make up for expenditures that can improve your health.

Consider, beginning at age twenty-two, saving and investing $3,000 a year at 8 percent interest. Assuming you continue this saving/investment routine until age sixty-seven, you will accumulate $1.26 million. Next assume that instead of investing the entire $3,000 each year, you devote $600 a year (or $50 a month) to help ensure a healthier retirement by increasing your spending on health-related products and activities—say, by buying a membership in a health club—leaving $2,400 to invest at 8 percent each year. Although this is a 20 percent reduction in the amount invested each year, it takes less than three years of extra life expectancy to come out ahead financially if the extra years are spent working (about 6 percent more work). If you retire at age seventy your $2,400 a year investment will have accumulated to $1.27 million. Furthermore, at age seventy you can obtain a much higher annual income by spending your net worth of $1.27 million on a lifetime annuity than you can get with the same net worth at age sixty-seven (not only do you have a little more net worth at age seventy, but the older you are the larger the yearly income each dollar will buy). And if you live three years longer than expected because of what you spent on your healthy lifestyle, your retirement will be just as long as the average person who retires at sixty-seven, so you will receive your higher annual retirement income for just as long.

More realistically, some portion of the $600 a year in health-related expenditures will probably come out of other expenditures, so that saving may be reduced by, say, only $300 a year (or to $2,700 a year). In this case it only takes slightly more than one additional year of life expectancy to come out ahead financially. At 8 percent, $2,700 a year beginning at age twenty-two will accumulate to $1.22 million at age sixty-eight and to $1.32 million at age sixty-nine. So spending money on healthy living is not only a good investment in your physical well-being, it can also be a good investment financially, even when the expenditures increase your longevity only slightly.

Having regular physical exams, including dental and eye examinations, are also good ideas even if they don't increase your longevity. If you catch a problem early, the chances are increased that it can be taken care of more cheaply and with less suffering and inconvenience. Also, quite apart from any saving or improved health that results, regular medical exams provide a peace of mind that has an immediate value. So don't shortchange your health in an attempt to save more money. It may actually cost you money in the long run.

A Quick Look at Social Security

Even without the type of saving and investment we are discussing in this book, you will benefit financially by living longer. Most people, for example, have an "investment" (as it is wrongly called) in Social Security. This is not really an investment, since no one has a Social Security account in which individual payments are invested. Rather, the money you pay into Social Security taxes is immediately paid out to existing Social Security recipients. Any payments you eventually receive will depend on whatever changes the Congress has made in Social Security legislation when you become eligible, and the taxes being paid by those working during your retirement.

Nevertheless, when you do retire, you will have a claim against the system as long as you live—and the longer you live, the more you will receive and the larger the return from your Social Security "investment." But looking carefully at the return you can expect from Social Security is an excellent way to see the advantage of relying on your own initiative to take care of your financial future, rather than relying on government programs. Given realistic assumptions about what a relatively young person can expect to pay into Social Security, and the amount that person can expect to receive at retirement, the only hope for even a very modest return is a life expectancy that is unrealistic in the near future. Consider someone in mid-career who, because of a low income, is favored by Social Security. Someone born in 1960, making only $10,000 a year in 1998, and expecting an income increase of 1 percent a year (in real terms) will realize about a 3 percent return on Social Security "contributions" if she lives to be 88. But someone born the same year (1960) with an annual income of $50,000, which also increases at 1 percent a year in real terms, will contribute more to the Social Security system and will get less back proportionately in benefits. For this person to realize a 3 percent return he would have to live to the ripe old age of 143.[40] Those who were born in the 1970s, or later, or who are in mid-career but earn substantially more than $50,000 a year, can forget about ever realizing even a modest return from Social Security. They would not get a 3 percent return even if they lived *forever*, and collected their Social Security checks the whole time.[41] For young people, it is quite literally true that it is easier to get as rich as Bill Gates (recall, that requires living to *only* 205) than to get even a modest return from Social Security.

We have all heard people who refuse to quit smoking or reduce their excessive eating and drinking with the rationale, "We are all going to die anyway"—that is, what happens is beyond your control, so what's the point of exercising any control? Indeed, there are lots of things beyond our control, and certain death is definitely one of them. But how we lead the life we have been given and what we achieve during that life financially and otherwise is up to us, and depends on the choices we make. By concentrating on those things you can do to improve your life, and acting as if they are the only things that really matter, you expand the control you have over your circumstances and diminish the control that your circumstances have over you. That message of personal empowerment is fundamental to getting rich in America: Taking charge of your life can lead to great financial success but is a pleasant byproduct of a life lived with a sense of responsibility.

The connection between maintaining good health and achieving financial success is a good example of how important the choices you make are. By far the most important payoff from choosing a healthy lifestyle is the increased probability of good health and greater longevity. But it is also nice to know that taking good care of your health can be financially rewarding as well. Healthier people are generally more productive, and therefore can expect to earn more. But more importantly, healthier people generally live longer and are therefore able to work, save, and invest a few extra years without reducing the length of their retirement. And it takes only a few extra years of investing to make a very big difference in how wealthy you become. As important as good health is, for many people it is not enough motivation to consistently make healthy choices. Becoming wealthy may not be the most important reason for taking care of yourself, but it is another rather compelling reason for doing so.

Finally, a note to those young people reading this book—or to those who will hear its message from you—who have the most to gain, both physically and financially, from taking good care of themselves. Young people are tempted to believe they don't need to worry much about their health because modern medicine will find cures for what'll ail them in old age. Indeed, there is some basis for this hope. Heart bypass surgery; heart, liver and lung transplant; advances in chemotherapy and the discovery of new cancer-fighting approaches; more effective blood pressure medication, and improved diagnostic equipment are just a few of the ways medical science has, in the past half century, prolonged the lives of people whose lifestyles would have condemned them to an early grave not many decades ago. And there is every reason to believe that the ability of medical science to offset the harmful effects of unhealthy behavior will continue to improve.

But having said that, it's important to recognize that there will always be limits to what medical treatment can do to reverse the damage we inflict on our bodies. A healthy lifestyle will always pay rich dividends physically, and it will always pay rich dividends financially. Those who live the longest are the ones who will be able to invest the longest without reducing the length of their retirement, who will do far better on their pension plans, who will receive the largest payout on their lifetime annuities, and who will lose the least on their Social Security "contributions."

Of course, no matter how long you live, the growth in your savings will be significantly affected by the return you get on your investments. A low return makes it impossible to accumulate much wealth over any conceivable lifetime. On the other hand, a high return can result in an impressive increase in wealth over a relatively short period of time. Unfortunately, there are limits to the return you can realistically hope to achieve on your savings, and attempts to get extremely high returns can easily result in your getting no return at all, or even a negative return. Realizing a solid rate of return is possible with a little knowledge about the connection between risk and return, and a lot of patience and discipline. Investing wisely is another good example of the importance of the choices you make, as we shall see in the next chapter.

Practical Advice for the Good Life

Good health can add substantially to your physical and financial well-being, mainly because of the power of compounding that can continue to work on your net worth as you continue to work, save, and invest. Here are some tips that can improve your health and longevity and help you take full advantage of the power of compounding:

- Try to get some exercise every day. Exercise is a lot like saving; a little bit done regularly will pay big dividends over the long run. Twenty to thirty minutes of brisk walking at least four or five days a week helps control weight, improves your ratio of high- to low-density cholesterol, improves your lung function, helps maintain bone mass, and makes you feel better. Take opportunities to walk an extra block or two. If your office is only a few floors over the ground level, take the stairs rather than the elevator. If your office is too far up to walk, get off the elevator a few floors below your office and walk the stairs the rest of the way.

- Make exercise fun. Schedule regular walks with friends. Listen to music or books on tape while walking. Keep a rough tally of how many miles you have walked, or jogged, or bicycled, and make a game out of "collecting" those miles. The best exercise requires continuous movement for twenty minutes or more and elevating your heart rate to a moderate amount (the appropriate rate depends on your age and condition). Weight training can also be good for maintaining muscle tone and improving how you look and how you feel. But any exercise that gets you moving is good. The best exercises are those you enjoy enough to keep doing on a regular basis.

- Control your weight. Gaining weight is something most people do slowly by consuming just a few more calories than they expend each day. The easiest way to control your weight is by consuming slightly fewer calories each day, and burning up a few more. Instead of eating that snack from the vending machine when you get hungry late in the afternoon, take a ten-minute walk. The walk will take the edge off your appetite by increasing your blood sugar.

- Eat healthy foods—lots of fruits and vegetables. We are not recommending being a vegetarian, although a vegetarian diet can be healthy if you are careful about consuming the right combinations of vegetables to get adequate amounts of protein. The most important rule is, get the most out of the calories you consume by eating good food and avoiding junk.

- Don't smoke. If you do smoke, quit. It can be difficult, but millions of Americans have done it, and so can you. Not smoking is one of the best things you can do for your health.

- If you drink, do so moderately. A drink or two every day can be good for your health, but above that, alcoholic beverages quickly become a health hazard.

- Don't do drugs. They are not only bad for your health, they also destroy the discipline and future orientation that is essential in following the rules for building a fortune and a satisfying life.

- Get enough sleep. If you are dragging in the afternoon, you are probably not getting the sleep you need. Sleep deprivation is not only bad for your health over the long run, it increases the chances of accidents that can do a lot of damage to your health in the short run.

- Be careful. The biggest health risk that young people face is accidents, particularly car accidents. Drive defensively by being alert, paying constant attention to what other drivers are doing, or might do. Avoid dangerous situations by not driving at excessive speeds, tailgating, or weaving in and out of traffic. Don't let other drivers make you mad. A mad driver is a driver at risk. Be an extremely defensive pedestrian. You may have the right of way as a pedestrian, but don't challenge anyone in a car no matter how right you are. There's no advantage in being dead right.

- Do some volunteer work occasionally by helping the sick. You will be performing a useful service and you will feel good about yourself. It will also make you aware of the blessing of good health and the importance of taking care of it.

- Stay mentally active as well as physically active. Be alert to things that you enjoy learning, and that can improve your performance on your current job or prepare you for other jobs. Think about what you can do to stay productive and earn money in your "retirement" years.

Exercise for Achieving the Good Life:
Finding Ways of Taking Better Care of Yourself

Most Americans have at least a few bad habits. Many of us smoke, drink, and eat more than we should. This exercise will help you estimate the improvement in your net worth, assuming you correct just a few of your bad habits.

1. On a sheet of blank paper, make three columns. In the first column A list three things you do that are bad for your physical and emotional well-being. In the second column B indicate how much you spend each month on the items in column A. In the third column C indicate how much you can reasonably lower the expenditures in column B.

2. Now, total column C and multiply by twelve (feel free to extend your list beyond three items) and indicate the total here.

3. Determine the potential increase in your net worth if you make the changes in your behaviors each year indicated in item 2, assuming an annual return of 8 percent. Follow these steps on your financial hand calculator (one similar to a Texas Instrument BA II or Model 35):
    Press [2nd] and then press [MODE].
    Enter the total from question 2 and press [PMT].
    Enter 8 and press [%i].
    Enter the number of years until retirement (your target retirement age that
        you have used in other exercises in earlier chapters minus your current
        age) and press [N].
    Calculate the potential increase in your net worth at retirement by pressing
        [CPT] and then [FV].

4. Now make a rough guess as to how much longer you will be able to live and work if your made the corrections in your behaviors indicated in item 1.

5. Rerun the calculation made in item 3. Only this time add the number of years (or fraction thereof) in item 4 to the number of years until retirement and then press [N].

RULE 7

Take Prudent Risks

Earning a good income, saving regularly, and letting the power of compound interest work for as long as possible are critical in the journey to prosperity. But that's not enough. You have to invest your savings wisely, which means getting as high a return as possible without taking unnecessary risks.

This does not mean that you should try to avoid risks when deciding how to invest. Any activity with the potential to yield a return carries some risks. Indeed the riskiest thing you can do in terms of creating and accumulating wealth is to concentrate too much on avoiding risks. When considering an investment program, being willing to accept some avoidable risks can increase the return you get on your investment by enough to add hundreds of thousands of dollars to your accumulated retirement wealth. The secret to successful investing is to take prudent risks—meaning only those risks that have the real potential to increase your return. This may sound obvious, but a very common mistake among investors, even some rather sophisticated investors, is taking risks that do not add to their return.

You may be thinking, "If even sophisticated investors are unable to get the best return for the risks they take, then how can I?" Saving money may be difficult, but at least everyone knows how to do it; you simply spend less than you earn. But doesn't investing wisely require a level of specialized knowledge, skill, and sophistication that few people have? So how can we expect you, who has to devote full-time to your job and family, to become an expert on investing? We don't. And the reason we don't is that people can be very successful investors without having a lot of specialized knowledge, skill, or sophistication.

Indeed, there are good reasons for believing that not knowing much about investing can be helpful in getting the best return for the risks you take. The first thing to recognize is that the investment information anyone can have, including the experts, is extremely limited. And nowhere does the old saying, "A little knowledge can be a dangerous thing" apply more than it does to investing. A little knowledge is exactly what the investment experts have—a very little knowledge. Sure, experts know a lot more than most about how the economy is doing. They know about the mechanics of buying and selling stocks, what the prices of stocks are now, and what they have been in the past (the appendix at the end of the book discusses the basics of stocks and bonds).[1] But when it comes to the questions every investor wants answered—Which stock prices are going up and which are going down? When will they do so? And by how much?—no one can answer them with confidence, no matter how sophisticated an expert they are. And those frugal Americans who think they know enough to answer those questions are unlikely to do as well investing as those who recognize that they can't.

We are not arguing against using experts to help you with your personal finances, including your investments. There are many issues requiring expert advice that need to be considered when making investment decisions. For example:

- Information on taxation can save you lots of money by deferring or avoiding taxes, but it is a full-time job keeping up with the changes the U.S. Congress constantly makes in the tax code. Good tax accountants can be very valuable to your financial health because they can cut your taxes.
- Insurance on your life and property is an important supplement to an investment program, but few people have the time or interest to become well informed on the insurance type and coverage best suited to their situations, which means they must rely on the advice of experts.
- Wills and trust agreements are also important considerations in developing, protecting, and directing one's net worth, and advice on what to do, and help in doing it, requires specialized professionals, namely lawyers.

But when it comes to knowing which stocks are going to increase the most in value, and when, it should not be surprising that not even the experts have much, if any, advantage. There are simply too many things that cannot be known or anticipated that can affect the prospects of a company for anyone to know about. And even if you knew what all these things were, predicting how they are going to change and how those chances affect the prices of particular stocks is beyond anyone's ability. Given all there is to know about companies and their finances, and all the things that can affect their prospects, no one can know more than a smidgen of all there is to know to determine the best stocks to buy, or sell.

But if you cannot rely on experts to help you with your investment choices, whom can you rely on? There is only so much time in the day and week to spend on investment strategy, and those who work hard to save for their investments simply do not have the time to know all they need to know to investigate different stock options.

The good news is that you don't have to know very much to be a successful investor. Indeed, we are going to suggest a simple investment approach that, for most people, will give you a better rate of return, while you take less risk, than you can get by relying on experts to help you choose stocks. Our approach is simple in that it doesn't take any special knowledge to implement it. But it does require patience and the ability to resist the temptation of get-rich-quick schemes that can sound so enticing. Afterward, we will discuss in more detail the reasons why this rule will let you beat the experts, and then suggest some modifications you may want to consider as you approach retirement.

Buy the Market

Investing in the stock market is one of the easiest investments you can make, and offers the greatest long-run return, with the possible exception of starting your own business.[2] And there are compelling reasons for believing that the best approach to investing in the stock market is to put most of your money in a mutual fund whose investment portfolio mirrors a broad-based market index, such as the Standard & Poor's Index (which are referred to as "index funds") and leave it there. The S&P is not the only index on which index funds are based, but it is the most common, and historically it has provided an impressive yield for the risk involved. By investing in a broad-based mutual fund, you will almost surely do better over the long run than by investing in individual stocks (either chosen by you or recommended by your broker), or by investing in a managed mutual fund, one in which the managers adjust the mix of stocks, and move in and out of the market, in an attempt to generate the highest yield, to beat the market.

Index Funds for the Long Haul

There are five substantial advantages of investing in a broad-based index mutual fund and leaving the money there:

1. Investing in index funds is easy to do, requiring no special knowledge or insight.

2. Such funds provide a high degree of diversification that eliminates almost all the risks that you are not getting paid for.

3. The risks that remain with investing in index funds are not very troubling, especially for young investors.

4. The long-run return from index funds is higher than you can expect from almost any other investment.

5. Management fees associated with index funds won't eat up much of your return because an index fund requires very little managing.

Over the seventy-two-year period from January 1, 1926, through the end of 1997 the compounded annual rate of return (or annual "yield," including price increases and dividends) on the S&P Index was 11.0 percent. This seventy-two-year period covers decades of higher growth rates (16.2 percent during the 1950s) and lower growth rates (1.8 percent in the Depression decade of the 1930s). There is obviously no guarantee that the Standard & Poor's Index will continue to have an annual yield rate of 11.0 percent, but

Index Mutual Funds: S&P 500, Wilshire 5,000, and Russell 2,000

The best-known stock market index is the Dow Jones Industrial Average, or the "Dow." It was created in May 1896 and reflected the weighted average price of the stock of twelve major companies. It now consists of thirty stocks, and so, despite its common use as a barometer of the stock market, the Dow cannot be considered a broad measure of the market.

There are a number of broad indexes of the stock market, with the most popular being the Standard & Poor's Composite Index of five hundred companies. The Standard & Poor's Index is made up of five hundred of the largest U.S. companies, representing about 75 percent of the U.S. stock values. Although not the most inclusive index, the S&P serves as a good proxy for all U.S. stock markets, and most of the money in index mutual funds is in funds indexed to the S&P 500.

The most inclusive index is the Wilshire 5000, which was created in 1974 and currently includes the stocks of about 7,600 firms. Even the Wilshire is not a completely inclusive index. The Russell 2,000 is a broad-based index, but only of stocks of relatively small firms, commonly called small capitalization (or small cap) stocks.

As we will see, over the long run investments in a broad index of small cap stocks have done better than those in the S&P 500. But the risks associated with the performance of the small cap stocks have been much greater.

this is a reasonable prediction of future returns over the long run, given its long history of averaging 11.0 over widely varying economic conditions.[3]

The S&P hasn't provided the highest return from a broad-based index. You would have a compounded annual rate of return of 12.7 percent from the beginning of 1926 though 1997 by investing in a broad-based index of small company stocks, such as the Russell 2,000. So by basing the rate of return in our examples throughout this book on the S&P Index (see below), we are being conservative.[4] But compared to most investments, the 11.0 percent return on the S&P Index has been just a little short of spectacular.[5]

For example, from 1926 through 1997, the average annual return was 3.8 percent on U.S. Treasury Bills, 5.3 percent on intermediate-term government bonds, 5.2 percent on long-term government bonds, and 5.7 percent on long-term corporate bonds. The difference between these returns on the growth of your investment and the return provided by the S&P is truly dramatic over time. (We explain the differences between stocks and bonds in the appendix to this book.)

For example, as shown in Table 7.1, if one dollar had been invested in the Standard & Poor's Index at the beginning of 1926, at the end of 1997 it would have grown to $1,828.33. If the dollar had been invested in U.S. Treasury Bills at the beginning of 1926, at the end of 1997 it would be worth a meager $14.25. If invested in intermediate-term government bonds, it would be worth only a little more, $39.86. If the dollar had been invested in long-term government bonds, it would be worth only $39.07. And if invested in long-term corporate bonds in 1926, the one dollar would have grown to $55.38 at the end of 1997. If you invested the dollar in 1926 in an S&P Index fund, your net worth would have been twenty-eight times larger at the end of 1997 than if invested in the next best alternative investment mentioned above. We think that is impressive, especially when you think in terms of investing not a single dollar, but thousands of dollars.

Table 7.1.
S&P vs. the Alternatives from 1926 Through 1997

	January 1, 1926	December 31, 1997
Standard & Poor's	$1.00	$1,828.88
U.S Treasury Bills	$1.00	$14.25
Intermediate Government Bonds	$1.00	$39.86
Long-term Government Bonds	$1.00	$39.07
Long-term Corporate Bonds	$1.00	$55.38

Source: Stocks, Bond, Bills and Inflation: 1998 Yearbook, Chicago: Ibbotson and Associates, 1998.

In recent years the return on the S&P 500 has been even more impressive. For example, over the five-year interval 1991–95 the compounded annual growth rate on the S&P was 16.57 percent; 15.20 percent over the interval 1992–96; and 20.24 percent over the interval 1993–97. These returns are obviously unusually high and should not be counted on to continue indefinitely. But history suggests that over the long run investing in a broad-based mutual fund can be counted on to outperform alternative investments. (You can be more aggressive in your investments by buying shares of "Spyders" and "Diamonds," covered in the box on page 153.)

The Risk of Risk-Free Investments

United States bonds are often referred to as risk-free investments because the federal government guarantees the return. Certainly Uncle Sam expounds on the safety of buying federal bonds. For example, you will pay slightly more than $281 for a government savings bond that yields 5.2 percent annual interest and which will be worth $1,000 in twenty-five years. If you buy this bond you are guaranteed the $1,000 at the end of twenty-five years and the 5.2 percent return. The only threat to this guarantee is the possibility that the federal government loses its power to tax, and no one lies awake at night worrying about that possibility. But you will end up paying dearly for the safety of government bonds. For example, if you had put the $281.00 into a Standard & Poor's 500 mutual fund at 11 percent, in twenty-five years you could expect to have, if history is the guide, $3,818 instead of $1,000. Over the long haul, the real guarantee you get from investing in anything guaranteed by the government is that you will end up with thousands of dollars less than you could have had. But the problem isn't just the government guarantee. Any financial instrument that promises a fixed return with little risk of default, whether government bonds or the safest corporate bonds, will pay a much lower return over the long run than will stocks whose return fluctuates.

A good rule, especially for young people, is never invest in anything that provides a guaranteed yield—it's simply too risky.[6] Why did we qualify this statement by saying "especially for young people?" Young people (who, let us say, are in their twenties) have a lot of years ahead of them before they retire. They can be sure that the market will go through some down swings, just as it has in the past, and provide very low, even negative, returns over some intervals of time. However, young people have enough time to wait for the market to recover and continue on its long-run upward trek. On the other hand, older people (those approaching retire-

"Spyders" and "Diamonds"

If you prefer to buy and sell shares in the market, rather than putting your savings in a mutual index fund, you can buy "Spyders" and "Diamonds."

Spyders (or SPDRs, for Standard & Poor's Depository Receipts) are securities representing ownership in something called the SPDR Trust, which effectively buys the stocks in the S&P Index. Spyders are traded on the American Stock exchange under the symbol SPY. The price of a Spyder is about one-tenth the S&P Index. That is to say, if the S&P Index is 1,000, the price of a Spyder will be $100, which means 100 shares of Spyders will cost about $10,000, plus commission.

Diamonds are a security representing ownership in the Diamonds Trust that buys shares of the thirty stocks that are in the Dow Jones Industrial Average. Diamonds are also traded on American exchange under the symbol DIA. The price of a Diamond share will be approximately one/one-hundredth of the Dow index. When the Dow is at 9,000, a Diamond will sell for about $90, which means those hundred shares of Diamonds will run $9,000.

There are several notable advantages of buying Spyders and Diamonds:

- Spyders and Diamonds provide automatic diversification.
- You can deduce what has happened to your investments by simply observing what has happened to the Dow and S&P indexes, which are widely reported.
- Spyders and Diamonds can be bought on "margin," which means you can borrow funds from your broker (or bank) to increase your investments (and as long as your share prices rise faster than the interest you are charged, your net worth will rise).
- Investors receive dividends.
- The trust expenses are very low (even lower than major index mutual funds).
- You can trade shares of Spyders and Diamonds just like you can trade shares of any company, and you can make the trades from hour to hour.
- And if you are so inclined, you can complement your trades of shares of Spyders and Diamonds with trades in options, or puts and calls (a topic we can't consider here, but which you might want to investigate).

If interested in more information, check with a stockbroker. Not all brokers know about Spyders and Diamonds, but they can generally direct you to those who do.

ment age) have to run the risk that the market will fall just before they retire and need their investment for generating an income. To reduce this risk, it is a good idea for people of all ages to have some cash reserves to take care of those expected and unexpected financial drains that we all face from time to time. Furthermore, we would expect that as people age, they might want to gradually shift progressively more of their assets from stocks to more secure, fixed-income assets, such as government and corporate bonds.[7]

There is another important risk involved in buying U.S. government bonds: inflation. The government provides no guarantee that your investment will not be eaten up by inflation. Of course, inflation reduces the real purchasing power of the return on any investment. But the expected return on a mutual fund investment becomes even more attractive relative to the return on a government bond, once inflation is taken into account. For example, before inflation is considered, the 11.0 percent return from the Standard & Poor's is 2.89 times greater than the 3.8 percent return on U.S. Treasury Bills. But once we reduce these returns by 3.1 percent, which, as we noted early in the book, was the average inflation rate from 1926 through the end of 1996, we get a real return of 7.9 percent (11.0 percent minus 3.1 percent) for the Standard & Poor's Index, which is over eleven times greater than the real return of 0.7 percent (3.8 percent minus 3.1 percent) on U.S. Treasury Bills. So inflation increases the relative return on investments in broad-based mutual funds.

Also, in judging how to invest your savings, you must realize that mutual funds charge management fees, which reduce your net annual yield from investment. The more time the fund managers spend managing their clients' savings, the greater their costs (there are commissions to be paid when buying and selling stocks), and the higher their management fees. The management fees for mutual funds tied to the Standard & Poor's Index are often around 0.25 percent (that's one-quarter of 1 percent), which is very low in comparison with actively managed funds that average about 1.25 percent (but can be as high as 2 percent).[8]

But if the average inflation rate of 3.1 percent, plus a management fee of 0.25 percent, is subtracted from the 11.0 percent average return on the Standard & Poor's Index, we get a return of only 7.65 percent, not the 8.0 percent rate of return we have used in examples in our earlier chapters. But, as we noted in the first chapter, there are good reasons for believing that the official inflation rate overstates the increase in the cost of living because it doesn't adequately take quality improvements in goods and services into consideration. We don't need to go into a detailed discussion of how the most widely used cost of living (or inflation) index—the Consumer Price Index (CPI)—is constructed, or why it probably exaggerates the inflation rate.[9] But a presidential commission, headed by Stanford University economist Michael Boskin, reported in late 1996 that, at least for the previous couple of decades, the CPI overstated inflation by an estimated 1.1 percent per year.[10] So if inflation is reduced by something between 0.5 and 1.1 percent, we end up with a S&P real rate of return (after inflation and after management fees) of between 8.15 and 8.75 percent, both of which are larger than the real rate of 8 percent we have been assuming. Of course, our use of 8 percent may be pretty close to the real return received when we account for the fact that people will not have all their savings in stocks until the day they retire. As older investors approach their retirement year, they will likely shift a growing portion of their investments to more secure long- and short-term bonds.

Beating the Market

You are likely asking, "But why accept the market rate of return as measured by the Standard & Poor's Index? The S&P Index contains lots of companies whose stocks perform poorly and many others whose stocks perform much better than average. Why not obtain advice from the experts on exactly which stocks are expected to yield above-average returns and invest in a portfolio containing just those stocks?"

Such counsel is readily available. For example, we read from a mutual fund advertisement in a recent issue of *Newsweek*, "We search for bargains today to offer you growth potential tomorrow. [We] excel at uncovering bargains that others have missed . . . by seeking out securities that are *undervalued*" (emphasis added).[11] And toward the end of every year magazines such as *Money* or *Fortune* feature cover stories on the "Hot Stock Picks" for the upcoming year. So with all this advice out there, why settle for the S&P "average"? Why not get a higher real return than the 8 percent or so that the Standard & Poor's has historically provided?

You can in fact do better than an 8 percent real return if you are willing to take lots of risk and put in lots of effort trying to figure out which stocks to buy. People who start their own businesses, put in long hours, and dedicate most of the earnings to expansion often realize very high rates of return. Indeed, a high percentage of those who become millionaires through their own efforts do so by starting and running a business.[12] Such entrepreneurial risk taking lies at the heart of wealth creation and a vibrant growing economy. But if you are employed in a salaried job and are relying on stock market investments to obtain the best return possible, given a reasonable level of risk, there are compelling reasons for being skeptical about "opportunities" to secure rates of return in excess of those generated by the market as a whole, as measured, for example, by the Standard & Poor's 500 Index.

The first problem with relying on the experts to identify the best companies to invest in is that the overwhelming majority of experts simply don't know enough to consistently beat the market. As noted earlier, compared to the information that determines the price of any particular stock, the most knowledgeable expert can lay claim to only the smallest amount. The price of a company's stock is determined by the various, and often conflicting, expectations of large numbers of investors, by technological advances, and by the impact of global events that no one can foresee. For example, an idea in the head of some currently unknown computer enthusiast could lead to a dramatic drop in the stock price of Microsoft. Or the religious passions of some Middle Eastern terrorist group could lead to an armed conflict that increases the value of oil company stocks and lowers the value of airline shares. Examples are endless. There is simply no way any one expert, or group of experts, can gather all the knowledge and anticipate all the events from around the world that would be required to accurately predict those stocks that will outperform the market.

Of course, it is possible for people to obtain information that few others have on the prospects of a particular company. The chief financial officer of a corporation, for example, will know before anyone else if corporate profits are going to be higher than expected. Such information greatly increases one's chances of buying a stock right before it goes up in price. Unfortunately, this is referred to as "insider information," and it is illegal in the United States to buy or sell stock on the basis of this information.

But people who are not insiders can use public information to study the past performance of companies, examine their current financial statements, find out what new projects they are considering, and make informed judgments on their future profitability. Shouldn't this information result in a better-than-average return to those who have it? The answer is probably not. The problem is not that the information is without value. Even though no one can ever get all the information needed to make completely accurate predictions, one can probably secure information that increases, at least marginally, the probability of predicting future stock prices more accurately. The problem is that anyone can go into the business of acquiring information and using it to identify the most profitable stocks. And if that information allows some person to make a return in excess of what can be made with the same effort in other activities, then more people will be attracted into the stock predicting and picking business. This will continue until the prices of those stocks, which are expected to experience the greatest increase in value, are bid up to the point where, on average, they provide no higher return than other stocks.

Obviously, there will always remain enough uncertainty that some people will do better than average on the basis of luck. And it is also possible that some people have a special talent at judging which companies are more likely to prosper and can realize a better-than-average return because of this talent. A few people do seem to be able to consistently beat the market, but even in those cases it should be recognized that when a large number of people are trying to beat the market, a few will do very well on the basis of nothing but luck. But assuming that a few investment advisers do have a special talent at choosing the right stocks, they are unlikely to do you any good for very long as expert advisers. If some people really do know how to make extraordinary returns choosing stocks, what motivation do they have to share their knowledge with others? Those with such special knowledge can do much better exercising that knowledge on their own behalf than on behalf of others. A prospector who discovers the mother lode tries to keep the location a secret, not tell everyone where it is.

Of course, those who are widely believed to have superior insight into choosing stocks can charge for their services by starting a mutual fund with a high management fee, and we would expect that any gains to be had by investing in any mutual fund would be largely, if not entirely, offset by the fund's management fee. If not, the fund managers could make more money by not starting the mutual fund and using their information to trade on their own account.[13] The problem is distinguishing early on the good mutual fund managers from the bad ones, but that is not an easy task given that there are over 8,000 mutual funds in existence at this writing, which is more than the number of stocks in the most broad-based mutual funds. And every one of these funds will try to convince you that it is the "best." Remember that you can make mistakes in selecting mutual funds just as you can make mistakes in picking stocks.

And even if an expert stock picker were willing to share valuable information on which stocks to pick, it still won't do you much good unless you are one of the first people informed. Otherwise, by the time you get the information, the purchases of other people will have driven the prices of the favored stocks up to the point where they no longer provide superior returns.

Beating the Experts

Few things are sillier than getting excited over stocks proclaimed as profitable picks in magazine articles. If the recommended stocks really were great profit opportunities, the information would have been so widely known before you read it in a magazine article that the profit opportunities might have been competed away.

This doesn't mean you can never make an above average return on a stock you read about in a magazine, or in a managed mutual fund. There are so many unforeseen events affecting stock prices that there are always companies like Intel, Microsoft, and Coca-Cola that will do much better than the general market for a long period of time. The question is can you, or the experts you are relying on, consistently pick enough of these winners, compared to the losers that also inevitably get picked, to outperform the market over the long run? Unless you are extraordinarily lucky, the evidence seems to be no.

Even in the short run most of the managed funds don't do as well on average as the Standard & Poor's 500 Index. According to a 1997 article, "Since 1993, index funds that mirror the Standard & Poor's 500 have posted higher returns than 80 percent of all actively managed mutual funds."[14] A more recent article in the *Wall Street Journal* stated, "Active fund managers are struggling to beat the indexes. As of Friday, just 26 percent of actively managed U.S. stock mutual funds were beating the S&P 500 so far this year [1998], according to Morningstar Inc."[15] During the first quarter of 1998, stock mutual funds had an impressive growth rate of nearly 12 percent. However, the S&P did even more remarkably, rising by nearly 14 percent in that quarter! And, again, the S&P beat nearly four fifths of the mutual funds.[16]

Over longer periods of time, the managed funds do even worse. Numerous scholarly studies support this statement. For example, one study shows that the Standard & Poor's Index has significantly outperformed the average actively managed mutual fund over the period 1971–91.[17] Another study has shown that those managed funds that do beat the market in one year are no more likely than other managed funds to beat it the next year, indicating that beating the market over short periods is more a matter of luck than skill.[18] Over the past decade, only 14 percent of actively managed stock funds beat the S&P Index.[19] Nevertheless, 74 percent of the investors interviewed by the *Wall Street Journal* were confident that their mutual funds would consistently beat the market.[20]

Even if you picked an actively managed mutual fund that did outperform the S&P, that does not mean that you would be better off than if you had invested in an indexed fund. The reason is that actively managed mutual funds charge higher management fees and incur greater transactions costs than indexed funds in which the managers perform a rather mechanical function and don't move in and out of different stocks. So with an actively managed fund you often start with a 2 percent deficit—the managers of your fund would have to consistently outperform the market by 2 percent for you to do as well as someone who invested in a Standard & Poor's Index fund. You are highly unlikely to find a mutual fund that consistently outperforms the market by 2 percent. Far more likely if you go with an actively managed fund is that your fund managers will provide you a return less than the market, and charge you extra for the favor.

The reduction in your annual return because of the management fee might be small, but even a small percent reduction in your return attributable to management fees can make a tremendous difference in how much wealth you accumulate over your career. For example, if you saved $3,000 a year beginning at age twenty-two and invested it in an S&P Index fund at 8 percent, you will have accumulated $1,255,278 by the time you reach age sixty-seven. Next, assume optimistically that you go with a managed fund that grows one half percent faster than the S&P 500 (8.5 percent), but yields 6.5 percent because the fund charges a management fee that is 2 percentage points higher than your index fund. In this case your $3,000 a year saving and investing plan from age twenty-two would be worth only $790,007 at age sixty-seven. That "small" difference of 1.5 percent in return would reduce your net worth by $465,271 when you are ready to retire. Even if your mutual fund managers beat the market by 1 percent per year (a highly unlikely possibility) and your return, after fees, was only 1 percent less than the S&P Index, your accumulation at age sixty-seven would be $920,255, still $335,023 less than if you had invested in an S&P indexed fund.

Much more likely than a higher rate, your 2 percent extra in management fees will buy you a lower-than-market return. And your loss will be much higher than in these examples.

Another cost to trying to beat the market can be extra taxes. By holding a broad-based index of the market you not only avoid most of the buying and selling costs of trying to pick winners and discard losers, but you also avoid the taxes that are imposed on the short-term capital gains realized with selling stocks held for less than a year and a half. Instead, most of the tax burden from holding the market is on long-term capital gains, which are taxed at a smaller rate, and which can often be deferred until after retirement. This lighter tax treatment makes a big difference in the amount of money you can accumulate over time.

So our advice to most people who invest in the stock market is not to try to beat the market. The easiest, and, in the long run, the most profitable thing to do, is to simply buy the market through a broad-based mutual fund and beat the experts.

Timing the Market

A common way mutual fund managers claim to beat the market is by moving the funds assets into stocks when the market is expected to go up and out of stocks and into cash and bonds when the market is expected to fall. The big problem with such claims is that the managers are not very good at picking the turning points. Of course, with many fund managers trying, some will appear to have special powers of predicting the future for a while, but anything they make for their clients when successful, they soon lose for them with their failures.

Joseph Granville became a timing guru in the late 1970s as a result of some impressive predictions, and his buy-and-sell recommendations could move the market. But he repeatedly warned against buying stock in the early 1980s, predicting a major crash, and his followers were left behind.[21]

A new guru, Robert Prechter, who accurately predicted the run-up in stocks, followed Granville. But after the crash of October 1987, Prechter recommended selling stock and moving into bonds with the prediction that the Dow Jones average would fall below 400. Of course, stocks rapidly recovered and continued upward, costing Prechter's followers a bundle in sacrificed returns.

The October crash had created another guru, however. Elaine Garzarelli predicted in mid-October a decline in the Dow of over 500 points, and within a week her prediction came true. Her success attracted a host of loyal followers. Unfortunately for them, Garzarelli continued to predict big drops in the market, and they missed out on the impressive rebound in stocks.

Not only do the timing gurus seldom manage to do a good job timing the market, but even if they did, the result would not necessarily be very profitable. For example, if you had invested a given amount in the market each year from 1988 to 1997 on the days when the Dow was at its highest, you would have realized a return of 18.2 percent. If you had invested the same amount in each of those years on the days when stock prices were at their lowest, your return would have been 20.2 percent.[22] An extra 2 percent can make a big difference over the long run, of course, but how likely are you to pick stocks at their very lowest each year? Don't try to time the market, and don't believe anyone who claims to be able to make you money by timing the market. Even with a few lucky guesses, after the higher brokerage fees for buying and selling, and higher taxes, timing will reduce your return.

The Beardstown Ladies' Mistake

Of course, you don't have to pay experts to recommend particular stocks or manage your mutual fund. There are plenty of books available that supposedly tell you the general approach successful investors use to beat the stock market. Unfortunately, even if an approach did beat the market in the past, by the time it is available for the $24.95 price of a book (less in paperback), its wide use will have rendered it unlikely to move you ahead of the investing pack. Also, you can never be sure the authors of the book have been as successful as their book jackets claim. They may have a short-run lucky streak, or their returns may not be nearly as good as indicated.

One of the best-selling investment books of the 1990s was *The Beardstown Ladies Common-Sense Investment Guide: How We Beat the Stock Market and How You Can Too.* The Beardstown Ladies, a group of several charming middle-aged (and older) women from Beardstown, Illinois, formed an investment club in 1983 and were heralded by their publicists as among the "great investment minds of our generation," given they supposedly posted a spectacular 23.4 percent average annual return from 1984 to 1993. That would have been an impressive return indeed, far outpacing the 14.9 percent annual return from mutual funds tied to the Standard & Poor's Index over the same period of time.

Unfortunately, the 23.4 percent return was the result of an accounting error, which was not discovered until early 1998. Once the error was corrected, it turned out that the Beardstown Ladies' return was actually 9.1 percent for the 1984–93 period—not bad, but significantly less than the 14.9 percent anyone would have received from a Standard & Poor's Index fund.[23]

To see how much of a difference the Beardstown Ladies' advice (pick your stocks carefully) and our advice (buy the "market") makes, suppose you decided to save $2,000 a year between 1983 and 1993 and bought exactly what the Beardstown Ladies bought during that period, getting the same compounded rate of return of 9.1 percent. Your portfolio in 1993 would have been worth $35,310. Had you invested in shares of an S&P Index fund and gotten its compounded rate of return, 14.9 percent, your portfolio would have been worth $48,431, a difference of over $13,000, or 37 percent more. If you continued investing $2,000 a year by picking stocks and continued to achieve a 9.1 percent annual rate of return for twenty-five years, your portfolio would mount to $189,581. Had you stayed with the S&P Index fund that continued to achieve 14.9 percent, your portfolio would have been worth $483,358, a difference of $293,777, or 155 percent more.

We understand and acknowledge that the S&P will not likely continue to rise by nearly 15 percent a year for twenty-five years. But our point remains firm: You can still expect to beat the Beardstown Ladies, or most other investment experts, by a good margin no matter what the rise in the S&P. Even a small increase in the rate you get from buying the market can amount to a sizable difference in your portfolio over the long run.

Applauding Those Who Try to Beat the Market

So why pay good money for what will almost surely be bad advice? This is not entirely a rhetorical question. Most investors do pay good money for what typically turns out to be bad advice by relying on and paying experts to help them choose which stocks to buy and sell, and when to buy and sell them. Why? A very interesting question, indeed.

Despite the strong case for putting your money in an indexed fund that mirrors the market rather than trying to beat the market, either by yourself or with the help of experts, this is not what most investors do. The amount of money in index mutual funds has grown rapidly in the 1990s, but it remained at only around 6 to 6.5 percent of all stock market investment.[24] Part of the explanation for the relatively large percentage of investors who are paying for "expert" advice on stock picks is that many people are invested in the market through company or government retirement plans, and don't have any real say in how their investments are chosen.

Also, of those who make stock market investments over which they do have control, many are not aware of the case against trying to outperform the market and are persuaded by the claims that those who specialize in giving investment advice can beat the market. There are plenty of people, however, who do know the arguments for tying their investments to a broad index of the market, but who still pick individual stocks or actively managed funds in an attempt to do better than the market. While many will succeed over short periods of time, and a very few will succeed over long periods of time, the overwhelming majority will end up doing worse than the market. So why do they keep trying?

The most obvious answer is that over time the people who are trying to beat the market are constantly changing. Many young investors think they can beat the market, and some do, but most eventually give up as they age. But other young investors come along and make the same effort. Another obvious answer is that they do not believe arguments against doing so. They really do believe that they can, by studying the companies and checking with the experts, not only outperform the market, but also do so by enough to more than cover the cost of their effort. Our response to these people is, more power to you. We applaud those who try to beat the market for at least three reasons:

- They are exhibiting the type of confident and take-charge attitude that we see as vital for those who want to become financially successful.
- The arguments we made against trying to beat the market in the previous section depend critically on people trying to beat the market. If everyone followed our advice and simply bought an index mutual fund without attempting to respond to information on the relative prospects of different companies, then you could do very well as the only one taking advantage of such information. So passive investing in an index fund is the most profitable strategy for most people because so many other people are actively pursuing what they hope is a more profitable strategy, and, by doing so, keeping the prices of stocks tending toward the values justified by the best information available.
- We would never criticize those who are trying to beat the market because for many people the best, maybe the only, way to keep the investment game interesting enough to keep them playing is by yielding to their competitive urges to beat the market. And more crucial to the long-run success of an investment strategy than a little higher rate of return (as big a difference as that can make over the long run) is to keep saving and investing year after year. It is better to try to do better than the S&P 500, even if that means actually getting a lower return, than to lose interest with a lockstep approach and discontinue your investment program.

So we also don't want to suggest that *no one* should ever try to beat the market. One reason for recommending index funds is that the overwhelming majority of our readers are in the full-time business of working for a living; they simply don't have much time to pick stocks. And improving your percentages at picking the *right* stocks takes a tremendous amount of time to collect and evaluate vast volumes of information.

We have a very good friend who does extraordinarily well at picking stocks and other investment vehicles. But our friend is so successful because he spends most of his waking days at his office working very hard determining economic trends in the country and world and deciding which stocks he should buy. It is because of the hard work and success of our friend, and others like him that our advice to buy index funds makes sense for most people. The people who work hard and long at picking stocks actually help keep stock prices properly aligned, reflecting the various companies underlying market and financial successes and failures. In the jargon of financial experts, they ensure that the nation's stock market remains tolerably "efficient," which means that you can invest in index funds with reasonable confidence that stock prices reflect the companies relative and absolute values (at least over reasonable periods of time).

Diversification and Prudent Risk

Whether or not you try to outperform the market, one consideration is critical, and that is that you need *diversification* in your investment portfolio. Indeed, diversification is the primary advantage of mutual funds, whether actively managed or tied to a market index. (With an S&P Index fund you get a share in five hundred companies.) Even if you are better than average at picking stocks, there is still a good chance that any one pick you make will be a loser. But if you pick a large number of stocks, the probability increases that your return will reflect your superior ability to pick high-growth stocks.

To draw a simple analogy, if you have a weighted coin that comes up heads 55 percent of the time (the probability that you pick a winning stock on any one choice), you would be foolish to bet everything you own on one toss (one stock). But if you bet, say, $10 on each toss (stock), then the probability that you will come out $100 ahead on every hundred tosses (stocks)—fifty-five wins and forty-five losses—approaches 100 percent as the number of tosses (stocks) increases.

Another way of considering the advantages of diversification is given in Figure 7.1, which shows the return over time of two hypothetical stocks, both of which yield 8 percent on average. The bold line shows the return of one of the stocks and the light line shows the return of the other. If you held just one of the stocks you would face a significant amount of risk because of the variation in the return over time. By holding both stocks however, when the return of one is down, the return to the other is up, with the return to both holding steady at 8 percent—the risk has been neutralized.

Of course, this is a simple, and unrealistic, example. Diversification reduces risks, but can never eliminate them totally. Even with a large number of stocks in your portfolio, you cannot expect the variations in individual stock returns to be perfectly offsetting. And you can never diversify away from fluctuation in the entire market. No matter how diversified your stock portfolio, the value of that portfolio will be significantly affected by the ups and downs of the stock market. This is a risk

Figure 7.1.

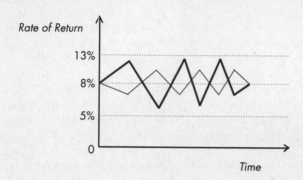

that cannot be avoided when investing in stocks, and, because it cannot be avoided, it is the risk that you get paid for taking. Diversification turns the risk inherent in the stock market into a prudent risk by eliminating the risk associated with individual stocks that, because it can be avoided, does not translate into higher returns.

The fact that investing in stocks is always somewhat risky explains why the return from investing in the market is, over the long run, so much higher than from government bonds that guarantee a stated amount at a specified time (remember our earlier advice: Unless you are close to retirement and in need of your savings, don't invest in anything with a guaranteed yield). You get paid for taking the bumpy ride inherent in the stock market, for taking the risks of unpredictable fluctuations (sometimes strongly negative fluctuations) in the value of your investments, and not knowing how much your investment will be worth at any future time.

Patience and Greed

The risk that remains with a diversified portfolio of stocks is a prudent risk, both because it increases your return, and because it is not a very costly risk for most investors, especially young investors. There will be

Diversification and Real Estate

One good reason to invest in real estate is that you have to live somewhere, and owning your own home has several tax advantages:

- The two largest costs of owning a home, mortgage interest and property taxes, are deductible from your taxable income; rent is not.
- Any capital gain realized from selling your home, up to $500,000 for a married couple, is not subject to federal tax.
- You have to send in your mortgage payment every month, some of which goes against what you owe, so you are forced to save. If you can afford it, and don't think you are going to be moving within the next few years, buying a home is probably a good investment.

The main problem with a home as an investment is that its value is highly dependent on local economic conditions. For example, the closing of a military base or an industrial plant in an area can significantly reduce local property values. Obviously it is difficult to diversify around this risk by investing in lots of houses in different parts of the country. On the other hand, real estate investment can allow you to increase the diversification of your investment portfolio. For example, you can invest in commercial property through Real Estate Investment Trusts (REITs), which are shares of actively managed commercial properties. One REIT will probably not offer you much geographical diversity, but that can be accomplished with real estate mutual funds that hold a diversified portfolio of REITs. This not only diversifies your real estate investment, but it can also diversify your overall investment portfolio.

For example, real estate provided very attractive returns during the inflationary 1970s, a time when the performance of the stock market lagged. The history on the returns to REITs doesn't go back as far as with stocks, but over the period beginning around 1970 through the mid-1990s the return was about the same as that yielded by the general stock market.

downturns in the stock, and some will be steep and last for quite a while (and the market was in a minor tailspin as this book was being finalized in early October 1998, with both the Dow and S&P indexes standing around 17 percent below their historic highs in the middle of the previous July). But people who have invested for retirement, and still have ten years or more until retirement, can ride these downturns out with confidence that they will be reversed, and that they will receive a good long-run return for taking what amounts to a sequence of short-run risks. The secret is to be patient, and not to panic when others do.

Jeremy Siegel begins his book, *Stocks for the Long Run,* with an interesting story that illustrates the advantages of staying with your stock investment program in the face of stock market downturns. In 1929 John Raskob, a financial executive with General Motors, was interviewed for an article in the *Ladies' Home Journal.* Raskob recommended buying stocks on a regular basis as the best way for growing rich, claiming that by doing so the investor would realize a return of 24 percent a year over the next twenty years. As a classic example of bad timing, the article featuring Raskob's advice was published just a few weeks before the stock market crash in October 1929, the beginning of the worst stock market decline in United States history—within three years the value of stocks had declined by 89 percent. The interesting part of the story is that, despite being widely ridiculed, Raskob's advice was actually sound, if a little overly enthusiastic. The investor who invested the same amount each month (Raskob suggested $15—worth a lot more in 1929 than today) in the stock market, beginning when Raskob's advice was published, would have done better within four years than the person who had invested the same amount in U.S. Treasury bills. In twenty years, the stock market investor would have had $9,000 in wealth (far better than the Treasury bill investor) and in thirty years he would have had over $60,000, which would have represented a 13 percent return. This is less than the 24 percent Raskob predicted, but still a return far greater than received by those who avoided the stock market crash by getting out and staying out of the stock market.[25]

The story of Raskob's advice illustrates four important rules for successful investing in the stock market:

1. Add to your investments consistently.

2. Don't worry about the day-to-day and month-to-month (and even year-to-year) fluctuations—don't panic when the market turns down.

3. Be patient.

4. Don't get greedy for unrealistic returns.

You will certainly hear from stockbrokers, friends, and others who stand ready to offer advice on how you can do much better than an index mutual fund. When this advice is given, don't let greed for unrealistic gains get the best of you. As the old saying goes, "When it sounds too good to be true, it probably is." And don't panic when the stock market drops, which it will. Keep your eye on the long run, hang in there, and keep investing. Remember, the surest way to get rich in the stock market is slowly—which paradoxically is (unless you are unusually lucky) also the fastest way.

We obviously believe that for most people the best stock market strategy is a simple one—add regularly to an index mutual fund and hold. You can do very well investing in the stock market without being an expert, or having to pay for expert advice. There is no reason to be discouraged from starting a saving program because you don't think you know enough to invest wisely. Recognizing that you don't know enough to beat the market can be your biggest advantage over those who believe that they do.

Starting and Investing in Your Own Business

We have devoted most of this chapter to investing in the stock market. This may seem strange since, as noted earlier in this book, most millionaires in America own their own businesses—they got rich by investing most of their money in their businesses, not in the stock market. There can be no denying that one of the key paths to truly high rates of return is starting a successful business and reinvesting most of your profits back in that business.

The major reason that we will not devote much space to business ownership is that we know that most people will not start and run their own business, but will spend their careers working in businesses owned primarily by others. While you will never accumulate enough to rival the wealth of Bill Gates working for a salary, we think it is important for ordinary workers to know that they can become millionaires without being entrepreneurs. And for those who do not have a business to invest in, the stock market offers an attractive alternative.

Becoming a successful business owner requires inspiration, entrepreneurial spirit, an intuitive sense of what appeals to customers, and, maybe most important, a willingness to put in long hours of hard work. If you have those attributes and want to start your own business, our advice is do it.

There are a few things about running your own business that tie into our message of taking prudent risks to those who want to get rich:

1. The potential for high profit from business ownership is partly explained as a return to the considerable risk involved. There is a high probability that you will incur heavy losses from starting and run-

ning your own business. Starting and running a business is much riskier than investing some of your salary in an index mutual fund. You will not lose everything you invest in such a fund, even in the event of a major downturn in the market, and all you have to do to recoup the short-run losses you do experience occasionally is wait. Losing almost everything is a real possibility when starting a business, and the greater that possibility, the larger the potential return will be.

2. One reason researchers have found that most millionaires are business owners is that they are reporting on the owners who actually "made it" in business. If you start a business with the prospect of a high rate of return and *if* you actually make it in the business, then it stands to reason that you will likely end up with a lot of wealth. However, the researchers often ignore all those would-be successful business owners who tried but failed, and many people who start their own businesses fall into that category.

3. Not all the potential return from business ownership is explained by risk. Much of the return is a payoff for the long hours business owners devote to their businesses. Much of the calculated return on the investment is really income for working the extra long hours. The income is similar to that earned by someone who takes a second job, and instead of starting a business, you might consider taking a second job and investing the added income. As discussed under Rule 2, by investing a portion of the earnings from working longer hours, say on a second job, you can accumulate a tremendous amount of extra wealth.

4. Business owners often do well because they save a much higher percentage of their income than most people do. Many business owners take a small salary out of their profits and save the rest by reinvesting their earnings back into the business, especially in the early years. A growing business demands saving at a rate that, if practiced by most salaried employees, would greatly increase the amount of wealth they accumulated. And because the business owner's savings are invested back in the business, it is not as diversified as the investments that other savers can easily make. This, of course, takes us back to the increased risk of business ownership and the higher potential rate of return to that ownership.

5. Those who start and run their own businesses typically ignore the adage in support of diversification: "Don't put all your eggs in one

basket." But they can do quite well by following another adage: "Put all your eggs in one basket, and then take really good care of that basket." Many business people do well because with a lot of work and attention to details, they do take very good care of their investments. When investing in the stock market, putting most of your savings into one stock would be taking an unnecessary, and imprudent, risk. There is typically not a lot you can do through long hours of hard work to increase the prospects of the one company in which you have stock. In your own business, your long hours and hard work can make a difference, and can make the risk of business ownership, though high, a prudent risk.

Successful entrepreneurs not only make themselves wealthy, they increase the wealth of countless others by providing more productive employment opportunities and better products at lower prices. If you are one of those people with an entrepreneurial impulse, follow your heart. But it's important to note that you don't have to start your own business to become quite wealthy. Whether you are an entrepreneur or a salaried employee, the key to financial success is the same: Work hard, earn a reasonable income, save as much as possible, invest it wisely by taking prudent risks, and be patient. And if you don't have a business to invest in, don't let your lack of knowledge about the stock market discourage you from investing in stocks. It takes no special knowledge to invest in an index mutual fund, and you will probably do better in such an investment than those who, because of their supposedly "superior" knowledge, attempt to beat the market.

Getting On with It

Most Americans have always understood that they can do better in life if they work hard. More and more Americans are beginning to realize the advantages of ownership in companies, mainly through holding shares of stocks. In 1998 over 40 percent of Americans owned stock either through brokerage accounts or through their mutual funds and pension plans. That's twice the percentage of Americans who held stock in the early 1980s. And, as markets have moved upward in recent years, Americans' wealth has also increased. In 1998 the market value of the stock holdings of Americans was $5 trillion more than it was four years earlier, which amounts to an increase in wealth for each and every American of almost $19,000 (or over $75,000 for a family of four).

As we were in the process of writing this chapter, the stock market had been hitting record highs, then dropping sharply, rebounding to new highs, and then dropping again. Many people think stocks are overvalued and expect a major correction—read large decline—in the stock market before long. They may be right. Of course, no one knows with any confidence what the market will do, or when, but it is almost a sure thing that it will suffer large drops in the future. But the risk of not knowing exactly what the value of your stock market investment will be worth at any particular time in the future is the reason the return from investing in stocks has historically been so high. The risk of investing in the stock market is a prudent risk because it is a risk that you are paid extremely well for taking, and a risk that is not very threatening over the long run.

Those who aren't inclined to start their own businesses, but who have the discipline and patience to save consistently and invest for the long run, and are not easily panicked when others are racing for the exits or tempted by promises of unrealistic returns and quick riches, have what it takes to take advantage of the superior long-run returns from investing in the stock market. The time to get started is now.

Practical Advice for Achieving the Good Life: Investing Wisely

Getting a good return on your investment is an important step in building a financial fortune. Fortunately it doesn't take a lot of highly sophisticated and specialized knowledge to take this step. More important than financial knowledge is the ability to keep your focus on the long run, the ability to resist the temptation of get-rich-quick schemes, and the stability to avoid panicking over short-run setbacks. These are characteristics that will serve you well in all aspects of living the good life, but they are particularly important to carrying out a successful investment program. The most important thing to know for achieving a good return on your investment at reasonable risk is that stocks have consistently outperformed other financial instruments over the long run, and that it is very difficult to consistently beat the market. Here are some tips for getting a good return by taking prudent risks.

- Keep investing in the market regardless of whether it is up, down, or just moving along sideways. Instead of worrying about downturns in the market, consider them opportunities to obtain more stock for the money being invested. In fact, early in your investment program, you should welcome market declines since the amount of stock you are buying is big relative to what you have already bought.

- But don't wait for the market to drop before starting to invest. As discussed in the box on timing, trying to time the market is a loser's game. The time to start investing in the market is as soon as possible.

- Think of yourself as an investor, not a speculator. There is a big difference between investing and speculating in terms of the time horizon that guides you. Investors are interested in the long-run growth of the assets, whereas speculators are interested in short-run profits. The problem with speculation is that for most people, attempting to seize short-run profits from fluctuations in stock prices will result in a lower return, and less wealth accumulation over the long run.

- Try to avoid the urge to check how the market, and your mutual funds or portfolio of stocks, are doing every day. Make every effort to keep in mind that the long run is what counts, with what happens on any given day, week, month, or even longer periods, not making much difference. Of course, if you enjoy checking the averages—if it makes investing more interesting for you—go ahead. But make it a point now and then to ignore the financial pages of your paper.

- Don't try to beat the market unless it makes investing a lot more fun. The time you spend examining analyses of different companies and their future prospects could be spent playing golf, going on a picnic with the family, or reading a novel, probably to just about as much advantage financially. But some people enjoy reading company financial reports, so if you do, go for it.

- If you aren't trying to beat the market, go with a discount broker, and check out their on-line Web sites. Here are the web addresses for three of the more prominent on-line brokerage firms: E*Trade (http://www.etrade.com); SureTrade.com (http://www.suretrade.com); and Charles Schwab (http://www.charlesschwab.com). By using a discount broker, you won't be paying extra commission to cover the cost of large research operations that you don't need if you are just buying the market. In fact, if you are buying mutual funds you don't need a broker at all. Most mutual funds have an 800 number you can call for information, and you can invest in them with the addressed envelopes and investment forms they will make available. They will send out regular statements, usually quarterly, and generally you can find out your current balance by dialing an 800 number and following the instructions.

- In any major bookstore you can find books on mutual funds containing information on the types of funds they offer, their past performance, their 800 numbers, and their fees. The fees differ significantly, so unless you want to go with a fund that tries to beat the market, invest in an index fund with low fees.

- Keep in mind that the more risk you take, the greater the expected gain, if the risk is prudent. A prudent risk is one that you can expect to get paid for, like the risk inherent in the ups and downs of the stock market. The risk you take because you have not diversified is likely to be a risk you don't get paid for, and can be imprudent. On the other hand, if you have more information than most on the prospects of a company, or are in a position to influence how well an investment does (such as your own business) then a nondiversified risk can be a prudent one.

If you insist on buying stocks in particular companies:

- Join an investment club. This can be an enjoyable way to learn more about investing. Such a club can also provides a social setting within which meeting your financial goals takes on an extra importance. The National Association of Investors Corporation is a not-for-profit organization that helps people set up investment clubs, and provides useful information on the mechanics of investing in the stock market, different mutual funds, and investment approaches. The NSIC can be reached at: telephone 248-583-6242; fax 248–583–4880; e-mail 76703.4372@compuserve.com; and Web site http://www.better-investing.com.
- Consider running a one- to three-year test: Put a portion of your funds in an S&P Index fund and the rest in stocks you pick. After the test period, check to see which portion of your investments did better.
- Keep abreast of broad business and economic trends. If you are not already reading the business pages of your local newspapers, start. Then begin reading major national business publications (we recommend the *Wall Street Journal*, *Investor's Business Daily*, and *Business Week*). The information obtained probably won't help you do a much better job picking stocks, but it is interesting information, will make your attempts to beat the market more fun, and may help a little bit.
- Develop a list of favorite Web sites where you can find information (preferably free) on companies and can track stocks that interest you. We frequently use BigCharts (http://www.bigcharts.com), which provides up-to-the-last-fifteen minutes information on what is happening in the country's major stock markets, allow you to track up to fifteen companies free of charge, and gives you links to company data; and Daily Stocks (http://www.dailystocks.com), which offers everything BigCharts does, plus an array of market news articles and commentaries, plus links to a host of other financial Web sites.
- Look for local companies that have good products and managers but have yet to gain a national reputation.

An Exercise for Achieving the Good Life:
What a Difference a Percentage Point Makes

When investing in stocks many people don't pay much attention to the commission for buying and selling, or the mutual fund management fees since they seem quite small, just a very few percent. For example, if you buy a round lot (one hundred shares) or more from a full-service broker, the commission will generally range from 1.5 to 3 percent of the value of the transaction (typically the higher the price of the stock the lower the percentage). And mutual fund management fees can run around 2 to 2.5 percent for an actively managed fund. While these fees and commissions may seem small, they can make a big difference over the long run. And they can be reduced by trading less frequently, shifting to a discount broker, or buying an index mutual fund rather than an actively managed one. This exercise allows you to determine how large the payoff can be from reducing these fees and commissions by just 1 percent.

1. Come up with some yearly amount that you plan on saving and investing each year.

2. Determine the payoff from reducing the brokerage fees and commissions by following these steps on a financial hand calculator (we use a Texas Instrument BA II, or Model 35).

       Press [2nd] and then press [MODE].
       Enter the amount in 1 and then press [PMT].
       Enter 8 and then press [%i].
       Enter the number of years before retirement and then press [N].
       Press [CPT] and then [FV].

3. Record the amount computed in 2. This is the amount you will have at retirement if you save the amount in 1 every year at 8 percent from now until you retire.

4. Repeat steps you followed in 2, only enter 7 in the second step (in place of 8) and press [%i].

5. Record the computed amount in 4. This is the amount you will have at retirement if you save the amount in question 1 every year from now until you retire, but, because of higher fees and commissions, get 7 percent instead of 8 percent.

6. Subtract the amount computed in 5 from the amount computed in 3. This difference is how much less net worth you will have at retirement because of the 1 percent higher brokerage fees. (It is also how much greater your net worth will be if you are able to lower your brokerage fees by 1 percent.)

7. Next, determine how much the potential gain in net worth at retirement from the 1 percent lower fees is worth in terms of extra annual income at retirement.

Press [2nd] and then press [MODE].

Enter the amount computed in 6 and then press [PV].

Enter 7 and then press [%i].

Enter the number of years you estimate you will live after retirement and press [N].

Press [CMP] and then [PMT]. The amount computed is the annual income you could buy in a lifetime annuity with the extra wealth you would have if you lowered your management fees and brokerage commissions by 1 percent a year.

RULE 8

Strive for Balance

This book has been about building a fortune in this country with greater ease than you might have imagined—if you want to do so and if you are willing to allow your day-to-day decisions to be guided by a few simple rules. *All you have to do* is recognize the opportunities that abound around you and work to seize a share of those opportunities; develop a long-term perspective; work and study hard; be reasonably frugal and judicious in your purchases; get married and stay married; take care of yourself; accept prudent risks and invest wisely—but above all, be patient.

Fortunes are seldom built overnight. Most Americans who have made it have had to pay their dues. That will not change.

We stress "all you have to do" because we've apparently outlined a fairly tall, or taller, order than it may sound, given that most Americans have so little net worth when they end their careers. But our point has never been that all Americans *will* make it. A number will not be able to follow our rules, regrettably, because of misfortunes they confront. A far greater number will simply not acknowledge the rules we have outlined, or if they do, they won't take them seriously or won't be able to marshal the self-discipline they require, no matter how obvious and important they may be.

Many Americans will continue to think that they have no choice in the matter of how large their fortunes will be; that others owe them a living now and in their retirement years; that they do not have to take responsibility for their futures (given the inheritance that they can expect); that they can scrape by or get by as they refuse to work and study hard, squander their incomes, marry and divorce at will, and impatiently hope to get rich quick. These are the Americans who will never appreciate or take advantage of the fabulous opportunities this country offers.

Some Americans who ignore the need for rules-based behavior, of course, will envy others who have played by the rules we have laid out in this book and have achieved the twin goals of building a fortune and achieving a satisfying life. Our point has always been from the start that the vast majority—though not all—of Americans *can* build a substantial retirement portfolio, if they *choose* to do so and are prepared to acknowledge the inherent sacrifices and inevitable tradeoffs that are required to reap the considerable gains in the distant future.

Nevertheless, many Americans will make it in spite of all the difficulties, in spite of the nay-sayers they confront, in spite of the temptations that are all around us to increase our current consumption. These ever-present temptations come in the form of store shelves that remain stocked with a growing variety of goods and services—including "toys" for young and old alike—and they come in the form of enticing advertisements that are omnipresent on television and radio, billboards, computers, and magazines and newspapers.

But these are the temptations of bounty, and opportunities. Our current generations face enormous temptations today because of the rules-based behavior of generations of successful Americans who came before, and who in the process of building their fortunes created the bounty and opportunities we have all around us. How did they do that? No doubt, most followed the advice laid out in previous chapters, but there was surely more to their success than our first seven rules cover. More than likely, most were principled people with an admirable dose of determination to do what they set out to accomplish.

Being Principled

Being principled means living a life guided by constraints—what we have labeled "rules"—that are limited in number and, more importantly, that have been tested through the ages. All along, we have been suggesting that you be a *principled* person, one who is guided by a vision of a prosperous and satisfying future that transcends current circumstances and temptations and by a commitment to a means of making the vision a reality.

Being principled, admittedly, is a tough assignment. It's one that few, if any, of us will be able to fulfill with perfection. This book has been dedicated to giving you a measure of personal fortitude to deny the power of current conditions in the best way we know how, by laying out in stark terms the substantial future gains that can be yours for the taking. All along, we have been effectively saying that if you can commit yourself, for example, to hard work and a consistent saving program, denying the ever-present lure of current temptations, you will live a more satisfying life, and get rich in the process.

But we would be remiss if we didn't insist that being principled encompasses far more than the type of behaviors we have covered in earlier chapters. Being principled also means conducting yourself in such a way that people understand that you have integrity, that you are responsible for your own actions, that you deal honestly and fairly with others, that your actions are tolerably consistent with one another and with what you say you will do—that you stay the course in spite of fleeting temptations of the moment to do otherwise. We are recommending, in other words, what your grandmother admonished you to do: Constantly strive to be a moral person.

Please don't misunderstand: We do not equate being a "moral person" necessarily with being a "religious person" (someone who follows the dictates, rituals, and readings of a given religion). Religious people can definitely be moral people, as Mother Teresa, Billy Graham, and Pope John Paul II have proven, but "religious" people (or people who harbor the pretenses of being religious) can also be as immoral as anyone else (when they use their religion simply as a guise or substitute for truly moral behavior). By being moral, we mean being true to worthy goals of how you should deal with others in cooperative efforts over a long stretch of time. We mean being what most people think of as a reasonably "good" person. We mean living by rules in our dealings with others.

The payoff from being principled comes in ways other than financial gain. Following rules consistently has its own considerable internal rewards, which we never want to ignore or discount. Being principled can contribute mightily to your feeling good about yourself and to your psychological well-being; we all know the personal, mental, and emotional strain of our actions not matching our core beliefs. Being principled makes the match between what we believe and what we do. We can't imagine anyone's life being very satisfying without beliefs and actions matching with reasonable consistency. Life takes on greater meaning when we stand for something beyond the quickly assessed gains and pains of moment-to-moment decisions that we all are asked to make, sometimes in haste.

The financial payoff to being principled comes from a very simple fact. Those who live by principles can be depended on, and when people can be depended on to do what they say they will do, and carry their load, they are more valuable. When we examined the cost of drug addiction under Rule 6, we were in an important way talking about the costs of not being principled. Drug addicts (and alcoholics) have a tough job holding down good jobs (or any jobs at all) because their addiction greatly circumscribes their ability to be principled, to consistently abide by the rules that could make them dependable, responsible, true to their word, and determined to rise above circumstances.

But the great paradox of principled behavior is that you must see the process of being principled as harboring personal value beyond the practical, financial gains that are so easily identified. Being principled must be something that you do because it is right, a point that we stress here in closing because so much of our previous discussion has been on the practical. If you try to be a principled person solely because the assessed benefits of your self-professed principles are greater than their assessed costs, then you will have a problem that is much the same as that the principled behavior is trying to remedy: Others will fear that as the structure of the costs and benefits that are guiding you in the selection of your principles will change, so will your principles.[1] Hence, somewhat paradoxically, there must be some passionate, even moral commitment to how you conduct your life.

The Importance of Attitude

Our thesis that a sizable fortune is a matter of choice for most Americans is validated all the time by this simple observation: Many ordinary Americans *do* build the requisite self-discipline and, hence, the kinds of fortunes we've had in mind. Some who have built fortunes have had advantageous starts in life; they came from good families in the best of neighborhoods with all the economic and social privileges in the richest country in the world at their disposal.

But many Americans who make it were not born with silver spoons in their mouths. Indeed, many who are now fortunate Americans have had to overcome substantial handicaps in the form of disadvantaged family and community circumstances. Patrick Kelly (mentioned in the first chapter) made it in grand style, given that he grew up in an orphanage and became a CEO of a major medical supply firm that he built, as did Oseola McCarty (in the second chapter) who worked all her life in menial jobs and never earned very much during her career. John Johnson, whose achievements and outlook on life are highlighted in a box later in the chapter, may be even more amazing, given that he literally started life in a tin-roof shack only to become a billionaire, included on *Forbes* magazine's list of the country's four hundred richest people. Similarly, Owen and Erma Smith (whose lives we also highlight in the box on page 181) did very well in a business that you might not associate with an obvious path to a sizable fortune. But that's part of our point; opportunities are not always obvious. You've got to find opportunities, if not create them.

The Good Life in Practice

Owen and Erma Smith grew up during the era of the Great Depression. As was true for so many Americans who can remember the 1930s, the hardship of the Depression forged for them a life course of hard work, savvy investing, and modest living. They learned from experience the value of money and the need for persistent saving. Owen Smith also probably learned a thing or two about survival and perseverance, given that he was an enlisted man in the navy stationed in Pearl Harbor on December 7, 1941. Today, now in their seventies, they have a substantial fortune. And they earned it.

The Smiths got a head start in building their fortune by doing what only a small fraction of their high school cohorts did in the 1940s; they got college degrees. Erma Smith was a high school teacher for many years in Hayward, California. She also worked in the family business that Owen Smith founded, a firm organized initially around selling, constructing, and maintaining swimming pools. They eventually expanded that business in the 1970s to include service to the growing ski industry in northern California. They sold Cascade Pools in the 1980s, only to start a new business in a totally different industry in the 1990s, Nutek, a firm that sterilizes medical waste for hospitals and medical clinics.

Their education and their willingness to take prudent business risks, and to put in the long hard hours that are required to make any business succeed, have paid off. However, they also take pride in what they *didn't* do and *didn't* spend. They describe their early years together this way: "Our home was small and inexpensively furnished. There were no boats, RVs, or country clubs. Dining out was rare and entertainment expenses were minimal. Instead of Disneyland or Hawaii for vacation, there were long weekends in the mountains or visits with family. Giving up smoking was a savings and not using credit cards eliminated interest charges. Many clothes were homemade. Designer clothes, coffee lattes and everything gourmet were not an option." They also recognize that they were "very fortunate to never have a devastating family disaster."

For years now, it's been give-back time for the Smiths, who have made donations to a multitude of causes. Given their interest in education, especially as it relates to teaching young people about the benefits of a market-based economy, they take great pride in having founded and endowed the Smith Center for Private Enterprise Studies at California State University at Hayward. They've also made substantial contributions to other causes, not the least of which are their county's programs for disadvantaged youth. What often goes underappreciated is the extent to which charitable contributions today are the consequence of Americans who, like the Smiths, resisted temptations to spend and spend decades ago and then worked hard to make their savings pay off.

We have related these stories of personal triumphs and have "run the numbers" of how this or that form of saving or this or that change in behavior will convert in time to a fairly sizable addition to your net worth for a good reason: Such stories and the numbers are our best hope of breaking the back of the defeatist claims so often heard in explicit and subtle ways: "It can't be done." Our numbers speak to what can be done and what needs to be done to build a fortune, and our success stories are bound to inspire you to do it.

Talk to any number of people who have done well in life—and whom you admire—and what you are likely to realize very quickly is that they all tell much the same story that John Johnson and Owen and Erma Smith have. Of course, the details of people's lives—exactly how they "did it," when, where, and by what methods—vary, but what is amazing is how underlying themes are much the same. Their story details seem, invariably, to point to much the same truths.

Jesse Owens, one of the greatest Olympians of all times, captured a common theme of success when he recalled that an important key to his success were the words of his coach: "You must have a dream and a ladder to that dream:
1st rung is DETERMINATION
2nd rung is DEDICATION
3rd rung is DISCIPLINE
4th rung is ATTITUDE
The first three rungs are important, but the fourth rung is vital."

One of our intents has been to explore the first three rungs of building a fortune. Those rungs are intrinsic to our rules. But we have also been intent on insisting that Owens's coach was right, the fourth rung—attitude—is vital. Our stories, we hope, have reminded you of the importance of "attitude," which those who have achieved riches and have remained satisfied with their lives have carried with them. In so many unstated ways, this book has always been as much about perspective and attitude—or, more broadly, lifestyle—as it has been about financial wealth.

One of Richard McKenzie's best friends harbors the perspective and attitude—and lifestyle—that we have in mind. He grew up literally "on the other side of the tracks," a not-so-good neighborhood in the east part of the Los Angeles basin. Even in the 1950s—a decade so often described as times of some innocence in this country—this friend had to go to school with people who frequently used and sold drugs. The gun culture was a part of his formative years. He went on to get a Ph.D. with the idea of teaching at the university level for the rest of his life. After deciding that he preferred to live better later in life than he might have to live if he continued to teach, he went into business, taking enormous risks in the process. At one point, he was so highly leveraged in his business ventures that 80 percent of his highly erratic monthly cash flow (or income) was going to interest on his debts.

Nevertheless, he weathered the inevitable financial strains of making a new business successful. When the time was right, he sold his old business and started a new one in a totally new industry (because he felt he would learn a lot while taking the new opportunity), where he was once again successful by working hard and taking risks. He's made it in noble style and lives very comfortably in a section of southern California that he could not imagine living in as a boy.

When we pressed him for practical tips and advice for success to pass on in this book, he told us: "In life there is a season for everything, and there has got to be a season for a lot of hard work. That means getting up at 4 in the morning and staying at the office until 11 at night, but that season makes later seasons of easier living possible. Be 'opportunity ready.' Opportunities can't always be devised or anticipated; they sometimes happen—surprise! The people I've known who have made it have conducted their lives in ways that made them ready to take advantage of opportunities when opportunities came their way. There must also be a time to give back. It's a duty."

Ben Franklin was right (to draw on the epigraph that begins this book): "The way to wealth is as plain as the way to market." We can add that it is as plain as the titles to our chapters:

1. *Think of America as the land of choices.*

2. *Take the power of compound interest seriously—and then save.*

3. *Resist temptation.*

4. *Get a good education.*

5. *Get married and stay married.*

6. *Take care of yourself.*

7. *Take prudent risks.*

8. *Strive for balance.*

From a Tin-Roof Shack to Forbes Magazine's
Four Hundred Richest Americans

Now in his eighties, John Johnson is a billionaire, having founded *Ebony* and *Jet* magazines, as well as more than one line of cosmetics for African Americans. But he remembers all too well the importance of an attitude he embraced as a young black man trying to start a business in face of substantial obstacles. When in 1942 he sought a loan for $500 (which is the equivalent of $5,000 in today's dollars) from a Chicago bank to start *Negro Digest*, his first magazine, he was dismissed with regrettable but memorable words, "Boy, we don't make any loans to colored people."[2]

You can bet he got mad—at first. But then he had a better thought, something he remembered from one of the self-improvement books he had read repeatedly: "Don't get mad. Get smart."

He asked the bank loan officer who in town did make loans to blacks. When the loan officer pointed him to a small finance company, Johnson asked the stunned loan officer to be his reference. He got the loan he needed from the finance company, but only after his mother put up the family furniture as collateral. Johnson has since built an economic empire. *Ebony* and *Jet* now have paid circulations of 2 million and 1 million, respectively. That first loan was, no doubt, very important, but even more important had to be his attitude, built partly on gratitude. "Because my mother made such great sacrifices for me," he wrote in his autobiography, "I didn't just want to succeed for myself. I wanted to succeed for her." He recalls the impact Dale Carnegie's *How to Win Friends and Influence People* had on him: "What Dale Carnegie says is that you shouldn't be preoccupied with unpleasant things. You ought to always try to look on the brighter side of things, to do the things you can do, and not worry about the things you cannot do." Moreover, he mused, "When I go in to see people—and I sell an occasional ad now—I never say, 'Help me because I am black' or 'Help me because I'm a minority.' I always talk about what we can do for them," which means his sales pitch is often, "Sir, I want to talk to you about how you can improve your bottom line, how I can increase your sales among black consumers." Finally, Johnson reasons that there are opportunities virtually everywhere, even where you might least expect them: "There are some advantages to disadvantages." His impoverished beginnings, he writes, "have made me run scared. It made me vow never to go back to welfare, never to go back to poverty. It drives me even today. Some days when I don't feel like getting up, all I have to think about is welfare and humiliation, and I get up early and rush to work."[3]

In summarizing his "creed and faith" for the fiftieth anniversary of the founding of Johnson Publishing Company, Johnson captures important themes of this book: "I still believe in the silent power of the possible. I still believe that there is no defense against excellence that meets a public need and that nothing—neither racism nor sexism nor ignorance—can permanently deny a Mae Jemison, or a Bill Cosby, or a Colin Powell who performs a better experiment or creates a better TV show or a better army. . . . I believe today, as I believed in the beginning, that it is better to light a candle than to curse the night."[4]

None of these chapter titles, or the admonitions that they repeat, should be new thoughts to you. You have heard much of the advice all of your life. We have simply collected the admonitions in one place and validated each, one at a time. As a package, our eight rules are a certain recipe for the type of good life that has been at the heart of this book. Just consider the list again. If you do everything on the list, building a fortune as well as a satisfying life is virtually assured. How could you miss?

If, on the other hand, you followed none of the admonitions, you *might* be able to get by, but it is hard to see how you could do well financially, or have a very satisfying life. Your life would likely be fraught with considerable self-imposed difficulties as you ignored or downplayed your opportunities by letting whims of the moment take precedence over the enormous possibilities of the future. How could people be expected to do well in life if they ignore the opportunities available to them, save little, don't study while in school and drop out of school early, constantly yield to temptation, treat marriage casually, don't take care of themselves (or, worse yet, become addicted to drugs or alcohol), take few prudent risks, and refuse to let principles be their guides? The mere listing of the obverse of our rules speaks to their validity.

Life as an Exploration in Values

Granted, few Americans are going to get all the rules right all the time, and we don't expect you (or others) to follow them religiously every step of your life. Following all eight rules carefully all the time is exceedingly difficult, if not impossible, as we can attest. We have both fallen down on several of the rules from time to time, but there is hope in the fact that success does not require perfection. We need rules that can work with the way life is, not with how we might like it to be. And life is not, and cannot be, an exercise in perfect living. Life is necessarily replete with imperfections in all meaningful dimensions, and rules and our allegiance to them are subject to that dictum.

All that we have really been advocating in this volume is that you do a reasonable job of following most of the rules much of the time, and if you do, you will have a good chance of doing well. We've pointed out how much wealth you *could* have, but the truth is, you could still have a substantial fortune at retirement time without saving as much as many of our examples assume. What do we mean? Simply put, there is a lot of wiggle room in the rules. Suppose you stop your formal education after college, begin your first job at $20,000 a year with your real income rising gradually until age sixty-seven, at which time you still earn only three-quarters of the median family income in the country, and you save only 3 percent of your income from the day you graduate from college, which means you are never an aggressive saver. You can still have a net worth at retirement that is close to three times the median net worth of retired Americans, $382,989.

Do as well on income as might be expected of the typical college graduate, and your hitting our standard for being rich is virtually certain with a reasonable level of saving. Don't do as well on income, but be more prudent in your spending, and you can still reach the million-dollar mark. Get divorced close to age forty (as we did), start over, and be assured that you can recover by your late fifties, if you hustle and understand the demands that the lost time makes on you.

We point out these real-world combinations of behaviors because we actually discourage you from looking on our eight relatively simple rules as absolute truths that must be followed religiously. As in all things, life is about striking a reasonable balance in what we do. That goes for what we eat, how we take care of ourselves, and how we work or save or invest or maintain our core principles—how we follow the rules. At bottom, life is an exploration in values—what we want, what works, and what tradeoffs we can and must make. Life is not laid out before us as an already set maze in which our only task is to turn a series of corners in the right ways to find the opening at the other end. Life is created as we live it, and we must stand ready to adjust to what we discover and what we and others create in the process of marking our time. Rules must be able to flex with the process of life.

Doing Something Important

Our focus throughout on building a financial fortune might leave us open to the criticism from less-than-careful readers that all we care about is money. Not true at all! Indeed, that criticism misses our most basic point altogether (not to mention that money and wealth are not the same thing). We do believe that evidence abounds that wealth (as measured in money) can and does contribute to one's happiness and sense of psychological well-being, at least modestly, and wealth can do this, if in no other way, a friend has reminded us, than by making "misery comfortable."[5] It can also contribute to higher standards of education and health and to less marital discord, as we have also noted, all of which can enhance how we feel about ourselves and how we see the world.

But we see living a satisfying life as far more than "pleasure" or "happiness." And "things" don't always count for much either, given the number of conspicuously rich who flaunt all the "stuff" they have in their closets, garages, and boat docks but who also seem to seek escape with drugs or support from counselors. Living a satisfying life must include more than *consuming*. External riches in themselves are vacuous. Living a truly satisfying life must be as much about internal riches as external ones, for Oscar Wilde reminds us, "Ordinary riches can be stolen from a man. Real riches cannot. In the treasury house of your soul, there are infinitely precious things that may not be taken from you."

Living a satisfying life must also include *doing* something—*doing* anything appears to be better than nothing. But we all know that doing what we each individually consider important is grand, and doing what we really think is important all too often requires a lot of work and personal sacrifices. Indeed, striving to do what we consider important appears to be far more important than having done it, and the struggle to accomplish often seems to be of greater value than what is accomplished.

Then, a satisfying life appears to us to be wrapped up in being wired in with others whom we can count among our friends and on whom we can rely for emotional support in those trying times of life, which we all have. No wonder researchers have found that those people who had five or more people with whom they discussed important matters were 55 percent more likely to feel "very happy" than those respondents who had no friends they could count on.[6] All this is to say that building a fortune for a fortune's sake seems to us a meaningless life goal, and we would never recommend it.

We have focused on building wealth (or net worth) at retirement time not because of the money involved, but rather because of what the *process* of fortune building will allow you to do. Surely that process, if you are successful, will allow you to live very comfortably in your old age, but there must come a point when our old-age comforts are of diminishing value. Just as surely, the same *process* will also allow you to do things in life that are far more important, and far more satisfying, than collecting so many stocks in a portfolio. The person who is capable of organizing life to build a fortune, and doing it in the principled way we have in mind, is also someone who can give back—and give back more than otherwise. If you never structure your life so that you *could* have a fortune, there will never be a potential fortune that you could give up for higher, more satisfying life goals.

If you want to do something important in life, there is no better way than to make something—a good or service—that is of value to others, and, at the same time, adds to the value of your portfolio. But we also hasten to add that if you want to do other things—save the world or whales or trees or distressed children—the *process* of building a fortune is also a process by which you can take on those noble ventures. You will be able early in life to concede some of the fortune you could have had in the dedication of your time to favored causes, or you can give away some of your fortune later in life so that others can help you in the pursuit of your causes.

We chose the words of our subtitle carefully, including the word "building," which is intended to connote the concept of the *process* that is at the heart of everything we have written. The *process* we have in mind is a means to many ends, but the importance of the *process* itself can't be underrated. Such a process that has fairly well-defined ends has to be guided by some relatively fixed set of reasonable rules that will guide your day-to-day and year-to-year decisions. Otherwise, ever-present temptations of the moment will overwhelm the process and cause your efforts to be scattered and undirected. The rules we have in mind can give structure and operational meaning to the future you have imagined for yourself, and can help to make your imagined future a reality.

Rules aren't everything in life, but they can be far more important than many people recognize or, if they recognize it, than they acknowledge and use. This is the case because the rules provide constraints that, paradoxically, are liberating. We hold up our eight rules for your consideration as you continue to plot your life's course for one overriding reason: They have worked for others. They have worked for us. They can work for you as well.

Practical Advice for Achieving the Good Life: Seeking Guiding Principles

This chapter has reminded you that living a principled life encompasses more than our few rules. Pick out people whom you admire for what they have accomplished in life, in financial and nonfinancial ways. Try to determine on your own what you believe were their guiding principles in life. Then take some time and ask them for their own short list of principles. Compare your notes with what they told you. Finally, make your own list of things you need to do to live a more principled life, to be more like the people you admire.

An Exercise for Achieving the Good Life: Summing Up

Your road to a sizable fortune at retirement may be less demanding than you might think, mainly because your effective wealth may be greater than you now realize. To assess where you are at this moment:

1. Take another inventory of your assets (bank account balance, current market value of your financial assets—stocks, bonds, mutual funds, IRAs, savings accounts, etc.—equity in your home, equity in your business, and approximate market value of any other assets of consequence). Total your assets.

2. Take another inventory of your debts (credit cards, car debt, home mortgage, student loans, etc.). Total your debts.

3. Compute your net worth by subtracting the amount in item 2 from the amount in item 1.

4. You might reasonably add to your estimate of your net worth by determining how much you would receive each year from your pension plan if you were to retire today. To obtain a rough estimate of the net worth equivalent of your annual pension income, simply divide your expected annual pension income by 4 percent (or by .04).

5. This book has been about building a fortune and a satisfying life. At the end of most chapters, you have been asked to indicate changes in your behaviors that will help you achieve those twin goals. Here, we ask you to review your answers at the end of each chapter and make a composite list of the changes you proposed to make in your behaviors. We also ask you to estimate how much more net worth you can have at your retirement if you make all the changes you indicated.

A Primer on Stocks and Bonds

Most Americans beyond the teenage years understand the meaning of and need for savings to invest in a house or a car. Bonds and stocks, however, can appear to be foreign, highly sophisticated investment instruments that require specialized courses to understand. That is really not the case Here, we explain bonds and the two major categories of stocks—preferred stock and common stock—so that our discussion will not throw you.

Bonds (and Bills)

A **bond** is a long-term debt obligation of a government or corporation that can generally be traded on the open market. When a company (or government) sells a bond, it is actually borrowing money. The company secures funds for the development of its business, either to purchase plant and equipment or to pay wages and rent. It commits itself to repay the money to the bondholder after a specific number of years (generally more than five and less than thirty) and to make periodic (usually quarterly) interest payments on the debt. A **bill** is a short-term bond (with a maturity of a year or less) issued by the federal Treasury and commonly referred to as a T-bill.

The interest payment that bondholders will receive from the corporation is usually stated on the face of the bond, either in dollars or as a percentage of the par value (face value) of the bond. If a bond is resold, the bond market (that is, the buyers and sellers of bonds) sets a price for the bond based on a comparison of the stated interest rate with the going rate at the time of the sale (in the case of bills the price varies little if any with changes in the interest rate because the duration of the return is so short). If the market interest rate has risen since the bond was issued, the price of the bond will be lowered to compensate. If the rate has fallen, the price will be raised. After the price adjustment, the new bondholder receives an effective interest rate similar to the market rate.

$$\text{effective interest rate } = \frac{\text{stated interest payment}}{\text{market price of the bond}}$$

For example, a bond that pays interest of \$10 annually (called its coupon rate) and sells for \$98 carries an effective interest rate of 10.2 percent.

$$\text{effective rate} = \frac{\$10}{\$98} = 10.2 \text{ percent}$$

Because the market interest rate and the price of a bond are inversely related, investors who sell lose part of their financial wealth during periods of rising interest rates. The new higher rates push down the price bondholders can get for their bonds, for no one wants to hold bonds that bear low interest rates when other financial assets of equal value offer higher interest rates. To attract buyers under such conditions, bondholders may have to sell at a loss. Conversely, a fall in the market interest rate will accompany a rise in the prices of existing bonds. The investor's goal is always to buy securities when prices are low and sell them when prices are high. To do so, however, the investor must predict future interest rates accurately, which is not an easy task.

Because bonds guarantee the investor a fixed interest rate and repayment by a certain date, they are considered a relatively safe investment. The security they offer enables firms to obtain the financial capital they need at lower interest rates—a major advantage of bonds from the firm's point of view. At the same time, bonds permit the owners of the corporation to retain their claim to residual profits. No matter how profitable the firm becomes, bondholders never receive more than the stated interest and repayment of principal.

Preferred Stock

Companies (here the discussion does not apply to governments) can also raise capital by selling stock, or ownership rights to their businesses. Two kinds of stock, preferred and common, are generally offered. **Preferred stock** is a set of ownership rights in a corporation that entitles the investor to a fixed share of profits after taxes. To a certain extent, people who buy preferred stock are buying security. Preferred stockholders are guaranteed their fixed payment from after-tax profits, called fixed dividends, in dollars, as long as the corporation makes a profit. Of course, that security comes at a price. If the corporation does well and profits soar, preferred stockholders continue to receive their fixed payments—nothing more. Preferred stockholders sometimes have the right to elect members of the boards of directors, who oversee the management of the corporation.

Stockholders who buy cumulative preferred stock receive the right to deferred dividends in unprofitable years. Dividends missed because the company made no profit accumulate and must be paid up later when the company becomes profitable again. Convertible preferred stock gives owners the right to exchange (convert) their preferred stock for common stock. As we will see, holders of common stock stand to gain most if a company does well. Convertible preferred stock gives stockholders the security of a fixed dividend payment when a company is new and unstable in its earnings, and the profitability of common stock later, when the company is more successful.

Although preferred stock certificates may bear a nominal price, called the par value, they can be traded at whatever price they will command in the stock market. That price will depend on the stated dividend payment; the current interest rate on bonds (an alternative investment); the buyers' confidence in the firm's ability to meet its fixed dividends; and various rights, such as convertibility, that may go with the stock.

Unlike a bond, preferred stock does not entitle owners to repayment of funds invested in the corporation. Dividends are paid to stockholders only after the interest on the corporation's bonds has been paid to bondholders—as must be done even when the corporation is losing money. For this reason preferred stocks tend to be a riskier investment than bonds, and the dividends they bear are typically higher, as a percentage of funds invested, than the interest paid on bonds. Preferred stock is safer than common stock, however.

Common Stock

Common stock is a set of ownership rights in a corporation that entitles the investor to share any profits remaining after all other obligations have been met. Common stockholders have what is called a residual claim to ownership. They are not entitled to any dividends until all expenses, including taxes, interest on bonds, and dividends on preferred stock, have been paid. Common stock dividends are not fixed. They can vary from nothing to a modest or a very high return, depending on the corporation's profitability and its plans for reinvestment of its profits. Although common stockholders assume the greatest risk of all stockholders and bondholders, they also stand to gain the most. Their dividends, being unfixed, can rise with the company's profits. Like preferred stock, common stock certificates may bear a par value, but their price is determined by people's willingness to buy and sell them. Reinvestment of after-tax earnings often (but not always) improves a corporation's profitability.

Common stockholders can exercise control over the corporation through their right to elect all or most of the company's directors, who approve management policies, fix dividends, and set investment policies. Most stockholders do not exercise their voting power, however. If they are unhappy about the way the company is being run, they can sell their stock and invest in something else. In general, common stock appeals to investors who are willing to assume some risk in hopes of a high payoff but do not want to be involved in managing a company.

Notes

1. Think of America as the Land of Choices

1. As quoted in W. Michael Cox and Richard Alm, "By Our Own Bootstraps: Economic Opportunity and Dynamics of Income Distribution," *Annual Report* (Dallas: Federal Reserve Bank of Dallas, 1995), p. 9.

2. How the Othmers "did it" has been chronicled in a front-page story in the *New York Times.* Karen W. Arenson, "Staggering Bequests by Unassuming Couple," *New York Times,* July 13, 1998, p. A1.

3. We take up investments in stocks and bonds under Rule 7, and because we understand that many readers of this book will be new to such financial investments, we offer in an appendix a primer on what bonds and stocks (preferred stocks and common stocks) are. In that chapter, we do not offer advice on which stocks to buy. Indeed, we point out why you should be very cautious in taking such advice from others.

4. See Tait Trussle, "The Florida Lottery: A Critical Examination," *Journal of the James Madison Institute* (July/August 1998): 5–9; and Charles T. Clotfelter and Philip Cook, *Selling Hope: State Lotteries in America* (Cambridge, Mass.: Harvard University Press, 1989).

5. When we make claims about our twin goals of building a fortune and achieving a satisfying life, we are, in fact, relying on an array of studies conducted over the years that suggest that the two goals tend to go together, especially that there is a connection between a group's "socio-economic status" and its level of life "satisfaction" (as measured by survey respondents' own assessments of their feelings of psychological and social well-being). See J. P. Alston and C. Dudley, "Age, Occupation, and Life Satisfaction," *The Gerontologist* 13 (Spring 1973): 58–61; and D. Phillips, "Social Participation and Happiness," *American Journal of Sociology* 72 (March 1967): 479–88. However, while available measures of "satisfactions" and "happiness" tend to rise with the respondents and

their income levels, the statistical relationships are not always strong and sometimes are mixed in the studies. However, it seems to us that the weight of the evidence does point to the fact that, after adjusting for other factors that can affect satisfaction and happiness, life satisfaction and happiness does rise moderately with income within countries and socioeconomic groups. See Ed Diener, et. al., "The Relationship Between Income and Subjective Well-Being: Relative or Absolute?" *Social Indicators Research* 3 (March 1993): 195–223); Frank Clemente and William J. Sauer, "Life Satisfaction in the United States," *Social Forces* 54 (March 1976): 621–31. Income may not be strongly related to satisfaction and happiness because they are relative concepts, useful for assessing people's satisfaction and happiness within educational and income groups, but poor measures when used across educational and income groups. Studies have found that subjective well-being and income do rise and fall together within countries, but the relationship varies across countries. Diener, et al., "The Relationship Between Income and Subjective Well-Being." It also may be that the "income," per se, as measured in each year may not be what determines people's sense of well-being or happiness. Their well-being and happiness may be affected not so much by transitory year-to-year income levels, but rather what their "permanent income" income level is (meaning how much they expect to earn over a number of years), or their net worth may be the critical determinant, and one study did find that "permanent income" and net worth are better predictors of psychological well-being than "income." Randolph J. Mullis, "Measures of Economic Well-Being as a Predictor of Psychological Well-Being," *Social Indicators Research* 2 (March 1992): 119–35.

6. We have avoided setting our standard for financial success as $1 million in annual income because that appears to be a truly tough, if not unrealistic, standard for the overwhelming majority of Americans. The Internal Revenue Service reports that in 1995 only 87,000 tax returns reported more than $1 million in income out of more than 118 million returns received. That means that fewer that one tenth of 1 percent of American taxpayers had an annual income of more than $1 million in 1995 (as reported by David Wessel, "Again, the Rich Get Richer, but This Time They Pay More in Taxes," *Wall Street Journal*, April 2, 1998, p. A1). However, it appears that the count of those earning $1 million or more in income a year is growing rapidly. In California (national data were not available), the count of taxpayers with $1 million in reported adjusted gross income rose by 66 percent between 1994 and 1996 (as reported by Larry Gordon, "Economy's Rise Pulls the Richest Along with It," *Los Angeles Times*, June 27, 1998, p. A1).

7. The "poverty threshold" varies by how many adults and children are in the family and the ages of the adults (whether the adults are age sixty-five or over). For example, the poverty threshold for a family with two adults and one child was $12,919 in 1997. The threshold for a family of two adults and four children was $21,446. U.S. Bureau of the Census: http://www.census.gov./hhes/poverty/pre97siz.html.

8. From the start of 1926 through the end of 1997, the compounded annual rate of total return on the S&P Index stocks (price appreciation plus dividends) was 11.0 percent, as determined by *Stocks, Bond, Bills and Inflation: 1998 Yearbook* (Chicago: Ibbotson and Associates, 1998). The compounded rate of increase in the Consumer Price Index was 3.1 percent, leaving a real rate of increase in the S&P Index stocks of 7.9 percent (with a management fee for an S&P Index mutual fund of 0.25 percent, the rate of total return drops to 7.65 percent). We use 8 percent because it is a nice rounded figure that keeps analysis as simple as possible, but also because, as we will explain later (see note 16 in this chapter), there are good reasons to believe that the annual rate of inflation, as determined by the Consumer Price Index, is overstated by at least 0.5 percent and maybe as much as 1.1 percent, which implies an annual real compounded total rate of increase in the S&P Index stocks, net of management fee, of at least 8.15 percent and perhaps as high as 8.75 percent over a number of decades. We grant that the real total rate of return depends on the time period selected, and for other time periods, the computed rate of total return on the S&P may be lower than what we use. However, we still believe that our computations based on an 8 percent return are reasonably conservative. We encourage readers to rerun the numbers, using rates of return that are marginally higher and lower than 8 percent. Our central point remains in order: Most Americans can build a substantial fortune if they have a persistent saving/investment strategy for a long stretch of time.

9. The actual yield the couple could receive on thirty-year Treasury bonds at this writing is 5.63 percent. The difference between that yield and the rate at which they draw interest income, 4 percent, is approximately equal to the interest rate on thirty-year Treasuries minus the rate of inflation at this writing. The 1.63 percentage point difference (5.63 percent minus 4 percent) can be reinvested in additional Treasury bonds, thus ensuring that the real value of their bond portfolio remains constant during the couple's retirement years.

10. We have used 8 percent to appreciate the portfolio in real terms. That might be too high for some Americans—but it is also likely to be too low for others. Indeed, in the second chapter (Rule 2), we will run the investment numbers using different rates of appreciation. We happen to

believe that these numbers are reasonably conservative for readers of
this book, because we suspect that the typical reader will possess an
above-average drive to build a fortune and, hence, will find ways of doing
better than 8 percent. That doesn't mean that readers will be able to
obtain the levels of annual stock market gains of 20 or more percent that
have been realized by Americans over the past four years. Recent market
increases have been much higher than the long-run upward trend in
market prices, which have increased about 8 percent a year (after adjusting for inflation) for the past seven decades.

11. Thomas J. Stanley and William D. Danko, *The Millionaire Next Door: The
Surprising Secrets of America's Wealthy* (Atlanta: Longstreet Press, 1996), p. 1.

12. Louis Uchitelle and N. R. Kleinfield, "On the Battlefield of Business,
Millions of Casualties," *New York Times*, p. 14. For a review of the gloomy
claims of many public policy analysts, see Richard B. McKenzie, *The
Paradox of Progress: Can Americans Regain Their Confidence in a Prosperous
Future?* (New York: Oxford University Press, 1997).

13. Stanley and Danko.

14. To consider what has happened that is positive in the American economy over the past two decades, see McKenzie, *The Paradox of Progress*. The
claim that the real incomes of most Americans have risen (when appropriate corrections have been made in the Consumer Price Index) is documented in Richard B. McKenzie, R_x *for Economic Pessimism: The CPI and
the Underestimation of Income Growth* (St. Louis: Center for the Study of
American Business, Washington University, February 1997).

15. Indeed, as this book was being finalized (in early October 1998), the
market was in the middle of a minor tailspin with both the Dow Jones
Industrial Average and the Standard & Poor's 500 Index about 17 percent below their highs six weeks earlier.

16. Garrison Keillor, "Lighten Up, Graduates," *New York Times*, May 27, 1994,
p. A15.

17. One of the authors has discussed the economic progress over the last several decades. Richard B. McKenzie, *What Went Right in the 1980s* (San
Francisco: Pacific Research Institute, 1994); and McKenzie, *The Paradox
of Progress*.

18. Critics charge that American family incomes have stagnated for some
time. Indeed, real median family income (family income halfway up the
income distribution), adjusted for inflation by the standard CPI, was the
same in 1995 as it was in 1977. However, when adjusted with the revised
CPI, the real median family income rose by 31 percent.

19. See W. Michael Cox and Richard Alm, "Time Well Spent: The Declining
Real Cost of Living in America," *1997 Annual Report* (Dallas: Federal
Reserve Bank of Dallas, 1998).

20. As discussed at length by W. Michael Cox and Richard Alm, *The Myth of Rich and Poor* (New York: Basic Books, 1998), chapter 9.

21. George Gilder, *Microcosm: The Quantum Revolution in Economics and Technology* (New York: Simon and Schuster, 1989), p. 63.

22. In 1997 Americans had $6.8 trillion in income, but saved only $121 billion, or 2.1 percent of income. "Perspective: Taxing Savings," *Investor's Business Daily*, August 5, 1998, p. A5.

23. McKenzie, *The Paradox of Progress*, chapter 8.

24. Cox and Alm, "By Our Own Bootstraps," p. 7.

25. Joseph A. Schumpeter, *Capitalism, Socialism, and Democracy*, 3rd ed. (New York: Harper & Row, 1962), p. xi.

2. Take the Power of Compound Interest Seriously— and Then Save

1. Tyce Palmaffy, "El Millonario Next Door: The Untold Story of Hispanic Entrepreneurship," *Policy Review*, July-August 1998, pp. 30–35.

2. Ibid.

3. The annual payment also assumes, very conservatively, that you only get 4 percent interest on the principal.

4. Indeed, we might expect older people to shift their financial holdings gradually from stocks to bonds as they approach their target retirement year, causing their annual rate of return to gradually fall.

5. Eighty-six percent of American families earned more than $15,000 a year in the mid–1990s.

6. See Richard B. McKenzie, "Orphanage Alumni: How They Have Done and How They Evaluate Their Experience," *Child and Youth Care Forum* 26 (April 1997): 87–111.

7. For more details of orphanage life, see Richard McKenzie, *The Home: A Memoir of Growing Up in an Orphanage* (Basic Books, 1996).

8. As reported in "The Economic Perspective: More Work, More Money," *Investor's Business Daily*, May 26, 1998, p. A8.

9. For an overview of Buchanan's life and thinking, which explains why we admire him greatly, we highly recommend James M. Buchanan, *Better Than Plowing and Other Personal Essays* (Chicago: University of Chicago Press, 1992).

10. We suspect that you are surprised at our estimates of retirement net worth at various rates of return, but you are probably concerned that our assumptions are not realistic. We agree, but, we insist again, only because we view our assumptions as conservative. Here are our reasons for thinking our calculations of what is possible are conservative.

   First, we've used a very modest starting income, $30,000. Most people reading this book might reasonably expect to start their first job *after college* at more than $30,000.

Second, we assumed that the person receives only a 1 percent annual raise. Again, we suspect that most readers of this book will get bigger raises than that over the course of their careers.

Third, we recognize that a 15 percent real rate of return (annual yield, which includes both the stock price appreciation and dividends) on investments may be high for most investors. However, in most of this book we focus on a much more modest real rate of increase in the value of investments, and there are very good reasons for believing that most investors can reasonably expect at least an 8 percent annual real rate of return (after adjusting for the true rate of inflation). We noted in the first chapter that from the start of 1926 through the end of 1997, the compounded annual rate of total return on the S&P Index stocks (price appreciation plus dividends) was 11 percent (as determined by *Stocks, Bond, Bills and Inflation: 1998 Yearbook.*) With the compounded rate of increase in the Consumer Price Index at 3.1 percent for the period, the real rate of total return on S&P Index stocks was 7.9 percent (with a management fee for an S&P Index mutual fund of 0.25 percent, the rate of total return drops to 7.65 percent). We focus our calculations on 8 percent for two reasons: (1) it is a nice rounded figure that keeps analysis as simple as possible, and (2) there are good reasons to believe that the annual rate of inflation, as determined by the Consumer Price Index, is overstated by at least 0.5 percent and maybe as much as 1.1 percent (see note 26 in the first chapter), which implies an annual real compounded total rate of increase in the S&P Index stocks, net of management fee, of at least 8.15 percent and perhaps as high as 8.75 percent over a number of decades. We grant that the real total rate of return depends on the time period selected, and for other time periods (for example, the 1960–97 period), the computed rate of total return on the S&P may be lower than what we use. However, we still believe that our calculations based on an 8 percent return are reasonable, given that we seek only to illustrate the impact of achieving a growth in net worth that is approximately equal to the growth in the market, as represented by a stock index.

Fourth, we have assumed that the saving is done once a year, whereas in fact the saving can be spread out over the year—and spreading the saving over the year can significantly raise net worth because interest can be earned on the savings made during the year. For example, we estimated that the person who saves $2,000 once a year from age twenty-two until retirement will have a net worth of $713,899 at age sixty-five and $1.06 million at age seventy, assuming a rate of appreciation of 8 percent. When the calculations are repeated, assuming the $2,000 is saved in twelve equal monthly installments, the person's net worth rises to $809,923 at age sixty-five and to $1.22 million at age seventy. This means that by saving regularly each month ($166.67 a month as opposed to saving $2,000 a year), the person will have $96,024 (or 13.5 percent) more net worth at age sixty-five and $158,247 (or 17 percent) more net worth at age seventy than he would have had, assuming that the same total annual saving occurs only at the end of the each year.

Perhaps the only less-than-conservative assumption we make in our calculations is the one relating to the constancy in the expected real rate of return as the investors age. Early in life, investors are able to take more risk than they are as they approach retirement. This is the case because in their early years investors can accept significant downturns in the market, recognizing that the market will eventually recover and return to its long-term upward trend. Later in life, however, investors must prepare to use their financial wealth for retirement income, which means that they are less able to accept the risk of significant market downturns. (As this book was being finalized in early October 1998, the stock market turned decidedly bearish. Both the Standard & Poor's Index and the Dow Jones Industrial Average hit lows that were 17 percent below their all-time highs in the middle of the previous July.) Hence, as they approach retirement, they will likely shift their investment portfolios from high risk/high rates of return investments (mainly stocks) to low risk/low rates of return investments (mainly bonds). This means that investors' expected rates of return should decline as they approach retirement. We stay with a constant rate of return, 8 percent, because it makes the calculations simpler and because this rate of return could reasonably be investors' average rate of return over the course of their careers, with their getting higher than 8 percent rates of return early in their careers and less than 8 percent rates of return late in their careers.

11. As estimated by Cecil E. Bohanon and T. Norman Van Colt, "Roberto and Fidel: Two Shared Visions of 'Share the Wealth,'" *The Freeman*, April 1998, pp. 200–01.

12. For data on charitable giving among income classes, see *Giving USA: The Annual Report on Philanthropy* (New York: AAFRC Trust for Philanthropy, 1998). The percent of income given to charities by all households in the country has historically been 3 percent or slightly less. The percent of income given by people making $100,000 or more in annual income has historically been 2 percent or slightly less. Although the "rich" give far more to charities in terms of dollars than do the "poor," the poor tend to give away a slightly higher percentage of their income.

3. Resist Temptation

1. See Mario Seiglie, "Is Intelligence the Most Important Factor for Success?" *The Good News* (May 1996).

2. This information comes from the December 1997 table, "Cost of Food at Home Estimated for Food Plans at Four Cost Levels," issued monthly by the United States Department of Agriculture: Center for Nutrition Policy and Promotion. This table is available at http://www.usda.gov/fcs/cnpp.htm. The figure in the table amounts to $1,420 a year, but we assume that the male is living alone, and this requires adding 20 percent (see note 3 in the table). So a family of four would require quite a bit less than four times $1,704.

3. See U.S. Bureau of the Census, *Statistical Abstract of the United States: 1997*, 117th ed. (Washington, D.C.: U.S. Government Printing Office, 1997), Table 714, p. 463.

4. Economists argue that the urgency to consume now, as opposed to later, explains why people don't save any more than they do. In the jargon of economists, people heavily *discount* future benefits and costs (or future gains and pains), which means that future benefits are not valued highly when compared with current benefits and costs. Put another way, people don't save very much mainly because the *discount rate* people use is much greater than the rate of return they could hope to get on any investments they might make. If someone can get only 8 percent on an investment over the years, but the person discounts the benefits from the investment by, say, 18 percent, the value of the benefits is going down faster than the investment is appreciating.

5. As taken from Robert H. Frank, *Passions Within Reason* (New York: W. W. Norton, 1988), pp. 76–80.

6. The information for this example comes from the Kelly Blue Book Web site, http://www.kbb.com.

7. The information on the Camry comes from Ann Perry, "More Buyers Finding Bargains Among Used Cars," *San Diego Union-Tribune*, August 18, 1996, p. I–1. While the maintenance cost is generally somewhat higher with a used car, the insurance cost can be less. For example, as the value of the used car depreciates, the cost of collision insurance goes down, and there is less reason to carry collision insurance at all.

8. See Stanley and Danko, *The Millionaire Next Door*, p. 113.

9. A saving of $1.50 a day is a very conservative estimate when the cost of smoking is considered. The financial gain from not smoking is discussed in detail in Chapter 6.

10. See Clotfelter and Cook, *Selling Hope*, p. 100.

11. For a discussion of some of these studies, see Charles Murray, *In Pursuit*

of Happiness and Good Government (New York: Simon and Schuster, 1988), pp. 124-29.

4. Get a Good Education

1. Our assumptions about the growth in the income difference between a ninth grade dropout and a high school graduate should be viewed as conservative, mainly because the actual difference in the median after-tax annual incomes of the two groups at retirement is likely to be far greater than $16,593.
2. See p. 38 of Monci Jo Williams, "How the Wealthy Get That Way," *Fortune*, April 13, 1987, pp. 32–38.
3. The median before-tax income for high school graduates in the age group twenty-five to thirty-four was $22,428 in 1997, according to the U.S. Bureau of the Census, Current Population Reports. So the average high school graduate will, for the first few years, surely make little if any more than $18,000 a year after taxes.
4. The student who goes to an elite private college without financial help will pay more than this in tuition alone (or his or her parents will). But tuition is still quite low ($2,000 to $3,000, or less) at most state universities. Recall, unless room and board at college is more than you would pay elsewhere, it is not a cost of going to college since it has to be paid regardless.
5. For a discussion of some of these studies see George J. Borjas, *Labor Economics* (New York: McGraw-Hill, 1996), chapter 7.
6. For example, it is very difficult to separate the impact of added years of schooling from the impact of the "qualities" possessed by the people getting the additional education. Moreover, it is not always easy to say how much more "education" a person gets when in school, especially since not all high schools and universities are equal in the level and type of education they provide their students. See Borjas, *Labor Economics*.
7. Ibid.
8. Recall that people with Ph.D.'s make less on average than those with professional degrees. This may seem to suggest that the financial return to the additional years of education required for a Ph.D. is negative. But we have to be careful here. A professor with a Ph.D. may earn less than a lawyer with fewer years of education. But given that a person has decided that he wants to be a professor, the financial return to the additional years required for a Ph.D. are surely positive.
9. In fact, since the education of most students is subsidized to some degree, we would expect people to continue their education beyond the point where the return to the entire cost of the additional year is less than alternative investments.

10. Survey undertaken by Best Buy, as reported by Dawn C. Chmielewski, "Gearing Up for School," *Orange County Register*, August 30, 1998, p. business 5.

11. This information comes from Frazis, H. et al., "Results from the 1995 Survey of Employer-Provided Training," *Monthly Labor Review* (June 1998): 3–13.

12. That employers are less likely to provide training to those workers who are most likely to leave the firm is reflected in the fact that young workers, who tend to change jobs frequently, are less likely to be provided training than older workers with longer tenure with the firm. See Frazis, H. et al., "Results from the 1995 Survey of Employer-Provided Training."

13. See David A. Jaeger and Marianne E. Page, "Degrees Matter: New Evidence on Sheepskin Effects in the Return to Education," *Review of Economics and Statistics* (November 1996): 733–40.

14. This advertisement appeared in *The Economist* (June 13–19, 1998) immediately after p. 16. Economists have attempted to measure the importance of this peer group effect and find that going to school with good students does have a positive impact on how well you do. See Vernon Henderson, Peter Mieszkowski, and Yvon Sauvageau, "Peer Group Effects in Educational Production Functions," *Journal of Public Finance* (1978): 97–106; and Anita A. Summers and Barbara L. Wolfe, "Do Schools Make a Difference?" *American Economic Review* (1977): 639–52.

15. See Stephen V. Cameron and James J. Heckman, "The Nonequivalence of High School Equivalents," *Journal of Labor Economics* (January 1993, part 1): 1–47. Also, those students who complete high school demonstrate that they are capable of staying with their education. Those students in GED programs were once dropouts.

16. See Dennis Berman, "Late Blooming Scholars," *Business Week*, July 20, 1998, p. 106.

17. See Michael F. Russell, "Next Finishing High School a Year Early to Get a Jump on College, Career," *Cleveland Plain Dealer*, November 12, 1997, p. 2E.

18. See June Kronholz, "Professional Students Are Getting the Boot at State Universities," *Wall Street Journal*, March 10, 1998, p. A1.

5. Get Married and Stay Married

1. As reported by Hara Estroff Marano, "Debunking the Marriage Myth: It Works for Women, Too," *New York Times*, August 4, 1998, p. B8.

2. Ibid.

3. The income gap between black and white families is also explained, to a significant degree, by where the families live, how many workers there

are within the families, the education and skill levels of the workers within the families, and the ages of the family members. Some researchers have found that when the income data are adjusted by statistical means for this list of explanatory variables, blacks' wages can be as high as 99 percent of whites' wages at the same age, within the same regions of the country, and with equal education, skills, and family structures, as reported by John Berlau, "Still Big Race Gap in Incomes?" *Investor's Business Daily*, March 30, 1998, p. A1.

4. Marano, "Debunking the Marriage Myth," p. B8.
5. As reported by Clemente and Sauer, "Life Satisfaction in the United States." Married people appear to be happier than singles and divorcees in spite of the fact that the presence of children can impose stress on the married parents, which can lower their level of happiness. Joan Aldous, "Family Change and Personal Happiness: Marital Status, Marital Duration, and Presence of Children as Factors," paper presented to the American Sociological Association, Miami Beach, August 1993; and Chloe E. Bird, "Gender Differences in the Social and Economic Burdens of Parenting and Psychological Distress," *Journal of Marriage & the Family* (November 1997): 809.
6. U.S. Bureau of the Census, "Marital Status and Living Arrangements: March 1997 (Update)," *Current Population Reports*, P20 Series, as reported on the Census Bureau's Web site.
7. We understand that traditional divisions of labor in the home, whatever they happen to be, can reflect the relative power structure of men and women in history, as some propose, but, more to our point, they can also mirror the comparative productive advantages of men and women at different tasks and the efficiency benefits of labor specialization. The assignment of jobs, whatever the arrangement is (and we see a multitude of arrangements in place in American households), can lead to more being done around the home—and to a reduction in the amount of time that the spouses must spend around the home to provide any given level of "home production" (however the couple defines that). We suggest that you should consider "traditional roles" in marriage only because they seem to have worked, having been handed down through the generations because couples who used those role assignments seem to have been successful. This doesn't mean that you should necessarily accept the rigid roles of women as "homemakers" and men as "providers," if such a division is called for because of children, for example. But neither should you dismiss those assignments out of hand, given that there might be benefits in using them. If roles are assigned, the benefits of some specialization can mean that either or both spouses can spend more time outside the home earning an income that can be saved and invested.

8. These research findings are summarized by Bryce J. Christensen, "The Costly Retreat from Marriage," *Public Interest* 9 (Spring 1988): 59–66.

9. Marano "Debunking the Marriage Myth," p. B8.

10. Ibid.

11. As reported in Jonathan Rauch, "What's Wrong with 'Marriage Lite,'" *Wall Street Journal,* June 2, 1997, p. A22.

12. Ibid., p. 60.

13. For an extended discussion of this perspective, see Richard Dawkins, *The Selfish Gene.* (New York: Oxford University Press, 1976).

14. H. Elizabeth Peters, "The Importance of Financial Considerations in Divorce Decisions," *Economic Inquiry* 31 (January 1993): 71–86.

15. Rauch, "What's Wrong with 'Marriage Lite,'" p. A22.

16. One of the benefits gays and lesbians would realize in a legal marriage appears to be more economic than moral: The advent of a legally enforceable marriage contract for gays and lesbians would tend to increase their likely mutual investments in the relationship and their family assets.

17. The value of parental time was computed on the assumption that the two parents have a combined income of $32,800 a year, or a wage for each parent of $7.88 an hour. The calculation for the value of parental time also assumes that both parents spend a total of sixty hours a week caring for their two children and that the parents spend a total of fifty-six hours a week asleep, and the sleep time is one-tenth the hourly wage rate.

18. The value of parental time was computed on the assumption that the two parents have a combined income of $55,500 a year, or a wage for each parent of $13.34 an hour. The calculation for the value of parental time also assumes that both parents spend a total of sixty hours a week caring for their two children and that the parents spend a total of fifty-six hours a week asleep, and the value of the sleep time is one-tenth the hourly wage rate.

19. The value of parental time was computed on the assumption that the two parents have a combined income of $80,000 a year, or a wage for each parent of $19.23 an hour. The calculation for the value of parental time also assumes that both parents spend a total of sixty hours a week caring for their two children and that the parents spend a total of fifty-six hours a week asleep, and the value of the sleep time is one-tenth the hourly wage rate.

20. Maybe marriages were never meant to last more than a few decades without major maintenance costs being incurred, which many couples resist incurring, which implies that growing longevity might be contributing to the country's high divorce rate.

21. For an economic analysis of the likely consequences of "no-fault divorce," see Gary S. Becker, "Why Every Married Couple Should Sign a Contract," *Business Week*, December 29, 1997, p. 30.

22. Since 1980 the divorce rate has gradually fallen somewhat, by 12 percent from its 1980 high, to 19.8 divorces per 1,000 married women fifteen years of age and older in 1995. U.S. Department of Commerce, *Statistical Abstract of the United States: 1997*, Table 145.

23. Of course, the increase in the divorce rate everywhere has been affected by factors other than legal ones. Nevertheless, few doubt that the changes in the law have had a significant impact. Rob Johnson, "Single Minded," *Sun Herald* (New South Wales, Australia), September 21, 1997, p. 8.

24. Kristen McQueary, "Legal Battleground: a $35,000 Attorney Bill Has Sent a Rural Metamora Man Back to Court in Hopes of Salvaging His Financial Future," *Peoria (Ill.) Journal Star*, February 1, 1998, p. A1.

25. Ibid.

26. See Greg J. Duncan and Saul F. D. Hoffman, "A Reconsideration of the Economic Consequences of Marital Dissolution," *Demography* (November 1985): 485–97; Gelbert J. Nestel and Louis B. Shaw, "Economic Consequences of Midlife Change in Marital Status," in *Unplanned Careers: The Working Lives of Middle Aged Women*, edited by Louis B. Shaw (Lexington, Mass.: Lexington Books, 1983), pp. 109–25; Frank B. Mott and Sylvia L. Mott, "Marital Transitions and Employment," in *The Employment Revolution*, edited by Frank L. Mott (Cambridge, Mass.: MIT Press, 1982), pp. 120–45; Saul D. Hoffman and Greg J. Duncan, "What Are the Economic Consequences of Divorce?" *Demography* 25, no. 4 (November 1988): 641–645.

27. Apparently a major reason women bear a disproportionate economic cost in divorce is that during marriage, they provide a disproportionate share of the parenting, which often leaves women with less work experience and education. Karen C. Holden and Pamela J. Smock. "The Economic Costs of Marital Dissolution: Why Do Women Bear a Disproportionate Cost?" *Annual Review of Sociology* 17 (1991): 51–78.

28. One researcher reported in the mid–1980s that during the first year after divorce women suffer an income drop of close to three quarters of their predivorce family income. Lenora J. Weitzman, *The Divorce Revolution* (New York: Free Press, 1985). However, other researchers have found much more modest income losses that are serious nonetheless. Holden and Smock, "The Economic Cost of Marital Dissolution"; and Hoffman and Duncan, "What Are the Economic Consequences of Divorce?"

29. Of course, the drop in the divorced person's savings might be expected

to be greater at age fifty because the person's predivorce income could
be expected to be higher at age fifty than at age thirty.

30. As drawn from court records and reported by Margaret A. Jacobs, "For
    the Rich, Child Support Means Living in Style," *Wall Street Journal*, May 1,
    1998, p. B1.

31. In 1994, on average, 15.4 percent of Americans were poor each month,
    and about 22 percent—or 55 million people—were poor for at least two
    months. The most likely to be poor were families headed by single moth-
    ers. In 1994 nearly half of the female-headed households lived in poverty
    for at least two months in a row, more than three times the poverty rate
    of married couples. And female-householder families had a "chronic
    poverty rate" (which means stayed poor for two full years) eight times as
    great as that of married-couple families. As reported by Mary Naifeh,
    *Dynamics of Economic Well-Being, Poverty 1993–1994: Trap Door? Revolving
    Door? Or Both?* (Washington, D.C.: U.S. Census Bureau, August 1998).

32. The birth rate for teenage girls (fifteen to nineteen years old) dropped 8
    percent between 1991 and 1995 and fell another 9 percent between 1995
    and 1996. "Hailing Mothers Who Aren't" (editorial), *Los Angeles Times*,
    May 10, 1998, p. M4.

33. "Teen Moms" (editorial), *Wall Street Journal*, May 8, 1998, p. A14.

34. As reported by Mary Hance, "For Richer or Poorer," *The Tennessean*,
    April 19, 1998, p. 1F.

35. The real or inflation-adjusted average cost of a wedding in 1990 was
    $18,675, or about 2 percent lower than the average cost of a wedding in
    1997.

36. Elizabeth Comte, "The Big Day," *Forbes*, May 24, 1993, pp. 180–81. The
    reporter estimates that the wedding coordinator, which will be practi-
    cally mandatory for such a wedding, will charge a fee of $3,200. The food
    at an expensive hotel will cost $13,000 for the two hundred attendees,
    while the band will run nearly $11,000. The photographer will run
    $3,000 and the cake will cost $650. Many other expenses are involved:
    bar, florist, video recording, rehearsal dinner, church rental, attendants'
    gifts, all the way down to place cards (a mere $25).

37. Ibid.

38. As reported in Hance, "For Richer or Poorer," in which two prominent
    Nashville wedding consultants were interviewed.

39. Also important to note is that the incentive for the couple to stay
    together mounts as the years pass. During the first year of marriage, the
    account appreciates by under $700. During the twentieth year, it appreci-
    ates much more, by nearly $3,000, and during the thirtieth year, it appre-
    ciates by over $6,000.

6. Take Care of Yourself

1. See Daniel S. Hamermesh and Jeff E. Biddle, "Beauty and the Labor Market," *American Economic Review* (December 1994): 1174–94.

2. See Alston and Dudley, "Age, Occupation, and Life Satisfaction"; Phillips, "Social Participation and Happiness"; Diener et al., "The Relationship Between Income and Subjective Well-Being"; Clemente and Sauer, "Life Satisfaction in the United States."

3. As quoted in Leslie A. Young, "Time Bandits," *Rocky Mountain News*, May 3, 1998, p. 8F.

4. This information comes from the U.S. Bureau of the Census and is cited in "Beyond 100, The Secret: Roll with the Punches," *Atlanta Journal and Constitution*, March 1, 1998, Dixie Living Section.

5. Ibid.

6. For a discussion of these and many other factors that promote good health and lower health risks see John Feltman, ed., *Prevention's Giant Book of Health Facts* (Emmaus, Pa.: Rodale Press, 1991).

7. Ibid.

8. Anthony J. Vita et al., "Aging, Health Risks, and Cumulative Disability," *New England Journal of Medicine* 338, no. 15 (April 9, 1998): 1035–41.

9. Ibid.

10. Feltman, ed., *Prevention's Giant Book of Health Facts*, p. 151.

11. Ibid., p. 153.

12. Ibid., p. 7.

13. Ibid., p. 9.

14. Ibid., p. 143.

15. Ibid., p. 209.

16. See Kenneth S. Chapman and Govind Hariharan, "Controlling for Causality in the Link from Income to Mortality," *Journal of Risk and Uncertainty* 8 (January 1994): 85–93.

17. Without being naively optimistic, we should point out that some scientists are seriously considering the possibility of rather amazing increases in life expectancy. See Ben Bova, "What'll We Do When People Live to 200?" *USA Today*, May 4, 1998, p. 13A.

18. These life expectancy figures and the others in this section are found in the *Life Insurance Fact Book* (Washington, D.C.: American Council of Life Insurance, 1997).

19. To keep the discussion as uncluttered as possible, from now on our life expectancy figures will be for men. This will result in an understatement of the gains from saving and investing since at every age the life expectancy of men is less than that of women.

20. This annuity is based on male life expectancy and so is more than a sixty-

seven-year-old female would receive for $1.26 million because of her longer life expectancy.

21. Another reason for using life expectancies that are a little higher than current expectancies is that those who purchase lifetime annuities generally expect to live longer than average, and the insurance companies factor this into consideration.

22. Since you expect to live six years longer than average when you are sixty-seven, at which point your life expectancy is about nineteen years, we add twenty-five years to sixty-seven to get a life expectancy of ninety-two. This is a little less than adding the six years to the average life expectancy at age seventy-three of 14.5 years, which would yield a life expectancy of 93.5 years. Even the ninety-two-year life expectancy seems quite optimistic today. But when people now in their early twenties who take good care of themselves reach seventy-three, they will very likely be expected to live well into their nineties, or higher.

23. Of course, for those who reach sixty-seven the life expectancy is greater, but the relative differences between white and minority life expectancies remain large. Also, the at-birth life expectancy does a better job of capturing the payoff to Social Security by taking into consideration the large number of people who pay into the Social Security System for years but die before they retire and never collect a dime.

24. As computed by William W. Beach and William G. Davis, *Social Security's Rate of Return* (Washington, D.C.: Heritage Foundation, January 15, 1998).

25. Such plans are often referred to as defined benefit plans, where the benefits are well specified and often only rather loosely connected to the contributions made. Also, most of these plans come with survivor benefit features whereby the retiree can ensure that a spouse, for example, will continue to receive a payment upon the retiree's death in return for accepting a lower payment.

26. If your interest payments reflect an inflation premium, the real value of your principal is being reduced. But even a lifetime annuity that is designed to exhaust the principal upon your death is subject to the ravages of inflation since inflation will reduce the value of the annual income you are receiving.

27. See David R. Francis, "Social Security Induces Early Retirement," *NBER Digest* (Cambridge, Mass.: National Bureau for Economic Research, April 1998).

28. Ibid.

29. See Toddi Gutner, "Making the Money Last—and Then Some," *Business Week,* July 20, 1998, pp. 80–84.

30. As quoted in Jerry Harkavy, "95-Year-Old Scoffs at Retirement," Associated Press wire service, May 6, 1998.

31. See Edward C. Baig, "When a Home Near the Fifth Hole Isn't Enough," *Business Week*, July 20, 1998, pp. 98–101.

32. See Meg Lundstrom, "First Steps to a Second Career," *Business Week*, July 20, 1998, p. 108.

33. According to a *Business Week*/Harris poll of relatively affluent Americans at least forty-five years old, 75 percent plan on continuing work after they "retire" in their sixties. Retirement is seen as chance for more flexibility, not unemployment. See "Business Week/Harris Poll: Nothing Retiring About These Retirees," *Business Week*, July 20, 1998, p. 88.

34. For a discussion of proposals to partially "privatize" Social Security (under which Americans would be able to invest a portion or all of their Social Security taxes in stocks and bonds), see Peter J. Ferrara and Michael Tanner, *A New Deal for Social Security* (Washington, D.C.: Cato Institute, 1998).

35. Also, most people will not choose to use all their wealth to buy a lifetime annuity at age eighty, or any other age for that matter. Our purpose in converting wealth into an annual income through a lifetime annuity is, as mentioned earlier, to have a convenient measure of the value that can be accumulated with a reasonable saving and investment plan.

36. See U.S. Bureau of the Census, *Statistical Abstract of the United States: 1997*, Table 747, p. 480.

37. Associated Press, "Group Upgrades Obesity Risk Factor," AP Online, June 1, 1998. According to another report, "Obesity increases the risk of diabetes, cancer, heart disease and other chronic disorders, pushing up the risk of death from all causes by up to 60 percent." Brian Knowlton, "Blame Society for All Those Fatties," *International Herald Tribune*, June 1, 1998, p. 10.

38. This estimate is reported by John Stossels, "Overcoming Junk Science," *Wall Street Journal*, January 9, 1997, p. A12.

39. As reported by Scott Shane, "Cost of Addiction Carries Hidden Tax; City Doubles Spending on Treatment to Cut Price Paid by Public," *Baltimore Sun*, April 30, 1998, p. 1A.

40. We consider a return of only 3 percent because if you assume a more reasonable return no one has a chance of making Social Security pay. The details of our analysis are reported in Richard B. McKenzie and Dwight R. Lee, "Security in Old Age—and We Mean Old Age," *Wall Street Journal*, June 17, 1998, p. A16.

41. Ibid.

7. Take Prudent Risks

1. Most of our discussion centers on investing in stocks. As will become clear, we believe that the best investment for most people over the long

run is stocks. Other investments, such as bonds, real estate, and starting a business, can obviously have their place in a well-balanced investment portfolio, and will be mentioned.

2. We will discuss the return on starting your own business later in the chapter.

3. This return and other returns we are about to discuss, including the inflation rate, come from *Stocks, Bond, Bills and Inflation: 1998 Yearbook.*

4. Also, the higher return on small company stocks has been more volatile than the return on the S&P Index, and is therefore riskier. For example, the high return on small stocks is largely explained by a spectacular performance from 1975 to 1983. If that relatively short interval is eliminated, since 1926 the return on small stocks is less than the S&P 500. See Jeremy J. Siegel, *Stocks for the Long Run* (Chicago: Richard D. Irwin, 1994), pp. 83-84. The volatility of small stock prices was the topic of a recent *Wall Street Journal* article, Aaron Lucchetti, "Small Stock's Price Swings Scaring Off Some Investors," *Wall Street Journal,* August 19, 1998, p. C1.

5. Of course, you can now identify particular companies whose stocks have increased far more than 11 percent a year over a long period, for example, Microsoft, Intel, and Coca-Cola. But that is hindsight. If, fifteen years ago, you had based your investment strategy on a few individual stocks, you would be far more likely to have picked low-performance losers than what we know now are the winners.

6. This includes passbook savings accounts and certificates of deposit that are guaranteed by the United States Federal Deposit Insurance Corporation, which insures bank deposits up to $100,000, and, of course, government and corporate bonds.

7. A commonly heard rule is to subtract your age from one hundred and have that percentage of your retirement wealth in stocks and the rest in fixed income assets. For example, when you are thirty you would have 70 percent in stocks and 30 percent in bonds. But at sixty-five you would have 35 percent in stocks and 65 percent in bonds. This may make sense for some people, but it does lower your expected return as you get older. For those who have a substantial amount saved as they approach retirement, or expect to remain in the labor force beyond the normal retirement age—taking their retirement on the installment plan as discussed in the last chapter—it makes sense to keep a much larger percentage of their investments in stocks since the consequences of a downturn in the market are not a serious threat to an acceptable standard of living.

8. According to Lipper Analytical Services, the average expense ratio (operating costs as a percentage of assets) for front-end load stock funds (those with fees when you make your investments) rose from 1.14 per-

cent in 1988 to 1.25 percent in 1997. The average expense ration for no-load stock funds (those without up-front fees) rose from 1.17 percent in 1988 to 1.21 percent. See Robert McGough, "Robust Fund Industry Isn't Lowering Fees," *Wall Street Journal*, May 14, 1998, p. C1.

9. One of the authors has dealt with the problems of the Consumer Price Index and how it distorts trends in wages and family income. McKenzie, R_x *for Economic Pessimism.*

10. The official citation on this report on the Consumer Price Index is "The Advisory Commission to Study the Consumer Price Index," U.S. Senate, Finance Committee, *Toward a More Accurate Measure of the Cost of Living* (December 4, 1996). Also see Michael J. Boskin, Ellen R. Dulberger, Robert J. Gordon, Zvi Griliches, and Dale W. Jorgenson, "Consumer Prices, the Consumer Price Index, and the Cost of Living," *Journal of Economic Perspectives* (Winter 1998): 3–26.

11. *Newsweek*, February 23, 1998, n.p.

12. Approximately two thirds of American millionaires who are not retired are self-employed. Of the self-employed millionaires, about one fourth are professionals such as accountants, lawyers, or doctors, and about three fourths are more traditional business owners. See Stanley and Danko, *The Millionaire Next Door*, p. 8.

13. Of course, people can do very well by going with superior mutual fund managers before they are widely known to be superior. Those who invested their money with Warren Buffett or John Templeton come to mind. But again, the problem is knowing in advance who is going to be, or continue to be, superior. Many people have developed reputations for being gifted stock pickers on the basis of a spectacular run of success, and then lose lots of money for a stampede of people who entrust their savings to them.

14. See Laura Casteneda, "Hassle-Free Way to Make Money: Investors Flocking to Index Funds, but There Can Be Pitfalls," *San Francisco Chronicle*, February 17, 1997, p. B1.

15. See Greg Ip, "Why Index Funds Aren't as Mighty as Some May Think," *Wall Street Journal*, March 11, 1998, p. C1. The title refers to the fact that a smaller percentage of mutual fund dollars are going into indexed mutual funds than is commonly thought, not to the performance of indexed funds.

16. As reported in Robert McGough, "Mutual-Fund Investors Jam Overtime Bull Market but Trail S&P," *Wall Street Journal*, April 6, 1998, p. R1. *Newsweek* personal finance columnist Jane Bryant Quinn reported in spring 1998 that in the three-year period 1995–97, some 93 percent of the managed funds failed to beat the S&P 500; in the five-year period 1993–97, 90 percent of the managed funds failed to beat the S&P 500. Jane Bryant Quinn, "Index Funds: Still Good," *Newsweek*, April 13, 1998, p. 53.

17. See Burton G. Malkiel, "Returns from Investing in Equity Mutual Funds, 1971–1991," *Journal of Finance* (June 1995): 549–72. Another article examined 1,751 common stock recommendations made from 1968 to 1991 by money managers at *Barron's* Annual Roundtable, chosen by *Barron's* because they were regarded as "Wall Street Superstars," or the best in the business. The authors conclude that "an investor . . . would not profit by investing in the buy recommendations at the Roundtable. Thus, the so-called 'superstars,' on average, do not seem to possess superior skills in recommending stock." See Hemang Desai and Prem C. Jain, "An Analysis of the Recommendations of the Superstar Money Managers at Barron's Annual Roundtable," *Journal of Finance* (September 1995): 1257–73.

18. See Mark M. Carhart, "On Persistence in Mutual Fund Performance," *Journal of Finance* (March 1997): 57–82. However, another recent study suggests that mutual funds that outperform the market in one year tend to do better the following year, though not significantly so. See Darryll Hendricks, Jayendu Patel, and Richard Zeckhauser, "Hot Hands in Mutual Funds: Short-Run Persistence of Relative Performance, 1974–1988," *Journal of Finance* (March 1993): 93–129.

19. As reported by Jonathan Clements, "Getting Going: The Truth Investors Don't Want to Hear," *Wall Street Journal,* May 12, 1998, p. C12.

20. McGough, "Mutual-Fund Investors Jam Overtime Bull Market but Trail S&P," p. R1.

21. The discussion of the timing gurus is based on Burton G. Malkiel, *A Random Walk Down Wall Street* (New York: W.W. Norton, 1996), pp. 155–57.

22. The modest increase in return from successful timing is based on a study by John Hancock Funds and was reported in Adam Shell, "Procrastination Won't Make You Rich," *Investors Business Daily,* July 24, 1998, p. B2.

23. The Ladies have improved their performance since 1993, with an annual return of 15.3 percent from 1984 through 1997, after correcting for the earlier error. But this still lags behind the 17.2 percent return from the Standard & Poor's Index over the same period. See Barnaby J. Feder, "Do Grannies Know Best, Despite a Fiscal Slip Up?" *New York Times,* March 22, 1998, p. 4 of the business section.

24. See Ip, "Why Index Funds Aren't as Mighty as Some May Think," p. C1.

25. See Siegal, *Stocks for the Long Run,* pp. 3-5.

8. Strive for Balance

1. As reported by John Berlau, "Leaders & Success: Ebony's John H. Johnson," *Investor's Business Daily,* March 26, 1998, p. A1.

2. Ibid.

3. John H. Johnson (with Lerone Bennett, Jr.), *Succeeding Against the Odds* (New York : Warner Books, 1989), n.p.

4. For doubters, we can cite one last study that shows that in the limited sense that money (rather, wealth) can reduce "depressive symptoms" later in life, money can buy a form of happiness. Catherine G. West, et al., "Can Money Buy Happiness? Depressive Symptoms in an Affluent Older Population," *Journal of the American Geriatrics Society* 46 (January 1998): 49–57.

5. As reported in Suzanne Chazin, "What You Didn't Know About Money and Happiness," *Reader's Digest*, August 1994, pp. 120–24.

Index

About the Authors

DWIGHT LEE holds a Ph.D. in Economics from the University of California, San Diego, and has had full time tenured faculty appointments at several universities, including the University of Colorado, Virginia Tech University, George Mason University, and the University of Georgia where he has been the Ramsey Professor of Economics and Private Enterprise since 1985. Professor Lee's research, covering a wide variety of areas in economics, has been published in more than one hundred articles in academic journals, and over two hundred articles and commentaries in magazines and newspapers. He has coauthored eight books, including *Quicksiver Capital, Failure and Progress*, and *Managing Through Incentives* (all with Richard McKenzie). He has lectured at universities and conferences throughout the United States as well as in Europe, South America, Asia, and Africa. He can be reached via e-mail at: dlee@cbacc.cba.uga.edu

RICHARD McKENZIE, who received his Ph.D. in Economics from Virginia Tech, has written widely on a variety of economic policy issues for academic and general audiences. He has published more than twenty books and several hundred journal articles, policy papers, and commentaries. His public commentaries have appeared in virtually all of the nation's major regional and national newspapers, including the *Wall Street Journal, Washington Post, New York Times,* and *Los Angeles Times.* He is the Walter B. Gerken Professor of Enterprise and Society in the Graduate School of Management at the University of California, Irvine. He can be reached via e-mail at: mckenzie@uci.edu